ROOTS &
REMEDIES

OF THE DEPENDENCY SYNDROME
IN WORLD MISSIONS

"There are those who propose that more research needs to be done in order to substantiate the claims of local sustainability advocates. They argue that there is not enough evidence to prove the debilitating effects of foreign funding of local Christian movements. With the appearance of Robert Reese's *Roots and Remedies of the Dependency Syndrome in World Missions*, let them now acknowledge the research has been done and the evidence is in hand. It is my hope that this book will help turn the tide from an atmosphere of dependency between the Western and non-Western church to indigenously supported Christianity on a global scale."

— Christopher R. Little, Ph.D.
professor of intercultural studies, Columbia International University, Columbia, South Carolina and author of *Mission in the Way of Paul: Biblical Mission for the Church in the Twenty-First Century* (New York: Peter Lang, 2005)

"Ideas for how best to accomplish the mission task are a dime-a-dozen—and some of them are worth exactly that. Here is a thoughtful, reasoned, and well-researched volume about the very practical question of money and missions. Be prepared to be challenged, to be provoked, and to have your toes stepped on. But most of all, be prepared to be thankful because after reading this book, you will be wiser."

— Doug Priest, Ph.D.
executive director, Christian Missionary Fellowship, Indianapolis, Indiana

"Every part of the body of Christ must participate fully in carrying out Christ's Great Commission. The dependency syndrome is especially harmful because it eliminates from active ministry and evangelism the parts of the Body that perpetually see their only role as accepting help from other parts of the Body. My book, *The Great Omission*, addressed this issue because I saw the damage dependency has done to the Waodani Indians of Ecuador, as well as to many other similar groups around the world. Robert Reese, in his new book, digs deeper into the dependency issue, showing where it came from historically and how to overcome it. Robert's book should prove helpful to missionaries, mission agencies, churches, and indigenous Christians as we all seek to overcome dependency in order to fulfill the Great Commission."

— Steve Saint
missionary, author, and founder of the Indigenous Peoples Technology and Education Center, Dunnellon, Florida

ROBERT REESE

ROOTS & REMEDIES

OF THE DEPENDENCY SYNDROME IN WORLD MISSIONS

WILLIAM CAREY
LIBRARY

All scripture quotations, unless otherwise indicated, are taken from the Holy Bible, New International Version®, NIV®. Copyright ©1973, 1978, 1984 by Biblica, Inc.™ Used by permission of Zondervan. All rights reserved worldwide. www.zondervan.com

Published by William Carey Library
1605 East Elizabeth Street, Pasadena, CA 91104 | www.missionbooks.org

Francesca Gacho, copyeditor
Hugh Pindur, graphic designer
Rose Lee-Norman, indexer

William Carey Library is a ministry of the
U.S. Center for World Mission
Pasadena, CA | www.uscwm.org

Printed in the United States of America.
14 13 12 11 10   5 4 3 2 1 BP1000

Cover photos:
Top: The Wilberforce Oak, Holwood Park, Kent, showing Church Missionary Society clergymen sitting beneath the tree, c.1873. Bishop Samuel Crowther of West Africa is third from left. Wilberforce House Museum: Hull Museums

Bottom from left: A house church leader in Japan; an evangelism ministry teacher in Ecuador; a pastor in Benin. Printed by permission. © IMB Photos

Library of Congress Cataloging-in-Publication Data

Reese, Robert (Robert B.)
Roots and remedies of the dependency syndrome in world missions / by Robert Reese.
  p. cm.
Includes bibliographical references (p.   ) and index.
ISBN 978-0-87808-013-7 (alk. paper)
1. Indigenous church administration. 2. Missions--Finance. 3. Dependency. I. Title.
BV2082.I5R39 2009
266--dc22
           2009027398

Contents

Foreword

——————

D R. REESE HAS DONE A MASTERFUL JOB of turning an academic dissertation into an easily readable textbook for missionaries, church leaders, mission executives, college and seminary students studying missions. Making that transition is not a task to be taken for granted, but Dr. Reese did it admirably.

This is a contribution to a growing list of books, articles, and other media now available for those concerned about unhealthy dependency in the Christian movement. What he has written can only be done by someone with the experience, perspective, and academic training that Dr. Reese has. These three qualifications give credibility to what he says here.

First, Dr. Reese writes out of more than twenty years experience in cross-cultural church planting in Zimbabwe. He and his family lived in Zimbabwe where he conducted his ministry in the local language. Therefore, he writes as a dedicated and accomplished cross-cultural missionary.

Second, he writes from the perspective of one who has the highest regard for the African church in his heart. Unfortunately, some missionaries actually do not want to see the church they planted stand on its own two feet. This is because they fear not being needed. As one reads the case study on Dr. Reese's personal experience (chapter 5), it becomes clear that his personal fulfillment is derived from the African church's fulfillment. For that he is to be commended.

Third, Dr. Reese writes from the foundation of academic research. This text is replete with historical facts showing that he did his homework. The result is that the reader gets a healthy introduction to the historical issues that shaped the Christian movement and the things that produced the dependency he writes about. More than that, Dr. Reese weaves into the story both encouraging strands and realistic shortcomings of such things as the missionary moratorium of the early 1970s. This is good academics—showing both the positive and negative so the reader gets the entire picture.

Over the past several decades I have been learning and speaking about the dependency syndrome far and wide. I have come to two conclusions. First, unhealthy dependency can be avoided from the beginning in cross-cultural church planting. There are many examples to show where this has been done. Second, unhealthy dependency can be overcome where it has already taken root. In other words, it should not be considered a terminal illness that paralyzes churches or makes them handicapped for the rest of their lives. Of course, overcoming the syndrome will require serious prayer, wisdom, determination and plenty of patience, but unhealthy dependency *can* be overcome. There are many examples to show that this is possible.

I welcome Dr. Reese's contribution to the growing field of literature available for those interested in avoiding or overcoming unhealthy dependency in the Christian movement. I look forward to more dissertations turned into textbooks that will help to guide missionaries, church leaders, mission executives, and all who are involved in cross-cultural church planting.

Glenn J. Schwartz
Executive Director
World Mission Associates

Author, *When Charity Destroys Dignity: Overcoming Unhealthy Dependency in the Christian Movement.* Lancaster, PA: World Mission Associates, 2007

Preface

I HAVE BEEN AROUND MISSIONARIES MOST OF my life. My parents and grandparents were missionaries, and I was born in southern Africa. My grandparents moved from Missouri to Zambia in 1929 where they stayed for several decades to work on mission stations and in local churches of the Tonga people. My parents met in Zambia as single missionaries and were married there. I was born in Zimbabwe where my parents later went to run a mission station. Even as a teenager, I did bookkeeping for an American missionary who supervised and funded a team of African evangelists. I grew up with a good idea of how missionaries worked.

It was also the era of colonialism. When I was born, Zimbabwe was still Southern Rhodesia, a colony of Great Britain. Racial segregation was viewed as normal in both housing and education. As a result, I attended all-white schools and lived in all-white housing in the capital city, Salisbury, now called Harare. Africans were normally servants. While I was still in high school, the white Prime Minister, Ian Smith, issued the Unilateral Declaration of Independence (UDI), which I heard on the radio as it was being broadcast in 1965. I remember looking out of our apartment window and wondering what, if anything, had suddenly changed. Although it appeared on the surface that things were the same, I knew deep inside the UDI was bad news for black people. Sure enough, independence from Britain under a white minority government was not the end of colonialism.

Once independence finally came to Zimbabwe in 1980, my wife and I made plans to return to that country for what turned out to be two decades of missionary service. Now at last we could operate using postcolonial mission methods that would treat Zimbabwe's citizens with dignity. Independence brought euphoria. I remember riding a train from Bulawayo to Harare and listening to young Africans debating whether capitalism or socialism was best for the continent and the country. Zimbabweans wanted desperately to be in charge of their own destiny at last.

And they wanted desperately to be in charge of their own churches. This became apparent in the new churches we helped to plant with our mission team. By 1991, it was clear that we missionaries would need to find a graceful way to hand control over to local people. At this point, we met Glenn Schwartz, who had been invited to speak at a conference run by one of our local church leaders,

Matthew Mpofu. Matthew introduced me to Glenn through an article Glenn wrote on indigeneity. He mentioned that what Glenn advocated was what we needed to do in our churches. I read the article and agreed with Matthew that we should talk to Glenn. My thanks go to Matthew for encouraging me to think through these difficult issues for the sake of Zimbabwean churches.

We hosted Glenn and his wife, Verna, in our home during Matthew's conference. But more importantly, we assembled our mission group and conferred with Glenn about key obstacles that seemed to block our way to a smooth handover of control to local people. One was a small farm we had purchased on behalf of Zimbabweans who were strongly committed to operate a home for old people. The old people in question came long before from other nations to find employment in Zimbabwe and now found themselves living on the streets without a social safety net, totally destitute. The home was already running under local management with local funds, but should it be turned over to Zimbabwean churches to own? The Zimbabweans who were running the home feared that handing over ownership of the farm to churches in general might undermine the original vision of providing care for the destitute elderly.

Glenn's experience in dealing with such issues was immediately obvious. He said that churches should be in the business of pastoring and evangelism, and not in the business of running homes for the elderly. He suggested that we place the farm in a charitable trust to ensure that it would always function as intended under the supervision of those called to run it and of those with expertise to operate such homes. Church elders did not need the extra burden of deciding what to do with land purchased by others for other purposes. This advice turned out to be sound. We followed Glenn's suggestion to the letter, and the home never became a point of contention for churches. In fact, it continues to operate independently as originally conceived, with local oversight and funds.

The other question that we had for Glenn was even more personal for us missionaries. What should happen to our mission? Should it be absorbed by local churches, or continue to operate independently? Here, Glenn's advice was harder to swallow. He said that it was time for our mission to die so that local churches could be truly born with all the responsibility that we now had as foreigners. Again we accepted this bitter medicine, and things went well for a while as we handed over leadership to Zimbabweans. As time went on, however, local leaders made decisions that were hard for us missionaries to accept. It seemed impossible in the end for us missionaries to become subordinate to local leadership, and conflicts for control of power and money erupted. The mission had never really died after all!

These experiences raised my personal interest in the work of World Mission Associates, founded by Glenn in 1983. This organization specializes in overcoming unhealthy dependency or avoiding it altogether in churches and institutions founded by missions. It is the only such organization that I know. When our mission work ended in 2002, as the Zimbabwean churches we had helped to plant finally began to take total control of all their own affairs, I decided to investigate the phenomenon of dependency at the doctoral level.

This current volume comes from the fruit of that labor, undertaken at Mid-America Baptist Theological Seminary in Memphis, Tennessee from 2002 to 2005, with Howard Bickers as my mentor. My Ph.D. committee observed that my original title *Roots and Remedies of the Dependency Syndrome in World Missions* would be better for a book title than a dissertation, so the dissertation is entitled "Dependency and Its Impact on Churches Related to the Baptist Convention of Zimbabwe and the Zimbabwe Christian Fellowship." The committee also suggested that if I should ever wish to publish this work, it would need to be more general than just for two groups of churches in Zimbabwe. My sincere thanks go to all members of that committee: Stan May, Daryl Cornett, Steve Wilkes, John Floyd, Steve Miller, and of course Howard Bickers.

In this book, I have tried to follow their suggestions, although—as you will notice—I cannot manage to get away completely from an emphasis on Zimbabwe, where I have lived more than half my life. Zimbabwe is not only the laboratory where this book was born, but it is also where my heart is. Nevertheless, I have added data from other places; I have also expanded on the dissertation by adding information from research I have done since leaving Mid-America on the impact of globalization on world missions. Naturally, during my research for my dissertation, I interviewed Glenn Schwartz about the current state of affairs in the world Christian movement. That material is incorporated in my writing. Glenn also invited me to join World Mission Associates, as a new World Mission Resource Center was about to open in Lancaster, Pennsylvania in 2005. Therefore, from 2005 to 2008, I worked with World Mission Associates, and the support that has come from the leadership there has helped make this book into a reality.

In the preparation and revision of the manuscript, several people went through the book and offered multiple suggestions for improvement. The first such editor was my youngest daughter, Charlotte, who spent many evenings during a volunteer year in Serbia to read everything and suggest changes. Others include Glenn and

Verna Schwartz and Jim Harries, who read the manuscript in Kenya and sent copious handwritten notes via a courier. Credit for the final editing and cover design goes to the staff at William Carey Library who worked hard to complete the publication of this book; my special thanks to Naomi Bradley-McSwain, Francesca Gacho, and Hugh Pindur. Finally, Darrell Whiteman reviewed the entire book at the request of William Carey Library, offering many suggestions for publication. All of them have significantly improved the manuscript, and I am grateful for their interest and encouragement.

Also, without the constant companionship of my wife, Mari-Etta, I could not have begun to write this work. For countless hours we would discuss the issues that are raised here because they are issues that deeply affected our lives and ministry. They were the atmosphere we breathed in Zimbabwe and they continue to be part of who we are. With her, I have lived through all the experiences that went into this work. We lived through both the euphoria and the letdown of political independence, and then through the euphoria and letdown of independence for Zimbabwean churches. Now we continue to see how dependency cripples new churches and Christian institutions around the world.

A common assumption was that the problem of dependency would start to fade after the end of colonialism. In fact, the opposite has happened: dependency has worsened. Traveling on behalf of World Mission Associates, I have had the opportunity since 2005 to address this issue in various parts of the world and to interact by e-mail with people in every part of the globe. Through such interaction, I have realized that the issues I became aware of in Zimbabwe are now global concerns. This book explains why dependency has not faded away and offers suggestions on what to do about it. It is my fervent prayer that we might finally move away from dependency to healthy interdependence in the world Christian movement. If this volume can help this process in any way, then my prayers will begin to be answered. I long for the day when we begin to operate in a healthy postcolonial paradigm in missions.

Robert Reese, Ph.D.
Elizabeth City, North Carolina
September 2010

I

HOW HISTORICAL ISSUES SHAPED DEPENDENCY

WHEN ROLAND ALLEN SURVEYED THE CONSIDERABLE ACCOMPLISHMENTS of the Christian missionary movement in 1912, he applauded the progress but lamented:

> Nevertheless, there are everywhere three very disquieting symptoms: (1) Everywhere Christianity is still an exotic [plant] ... (2) Everywhere our missions are dependent ... (3) Everywhere we see the same types ... So far then as we see our missions exotic, dependent, uniform, we begin to accuse ourselves of failure. (1962a:141-2)

Christian missions had successfully planted churches in many lands, but the predominant model was a form of western Christianity that failed to spark vital local expressions of the faith. The foreignness of Christianity tended to create a long-term dependency of the mission churches on the missionaries who had planted them. Dependency is the unhealthy reliance on foreign resources that accompanies the feeling that churches and institutions are unable to function without outside assistance. Missionaries had unwittingly saddled young churches with forms of Christianity that did not fit them any more than King Saul's armor fit the young David (1 Sam.17:38-39). Rather than remove the armor, as David did in order to move and fight more freely, the mission churches continued to wear the imposed armor and hence to be ineffective as churches.

The "armor" in question consisted of imported methods of worship, organization, and administration. It involved foreign institutions that required foreign funding, such as schools, clinics, hospitals, seminaries, publishing houses, and bookstores. It meant foreign models of what a local church is and how it should operate. Finally, it stood for foreign expectations for training pastoral leaders. The dependency that resulted consisted of an unhealthy long-term reliance on foreign funds, technology, personnel, and even theology. The ultimate tragedy of this dependency was that mission churches could not contribute to fulfilling the Great Commission, but remained recipients of aid long after they should have become donors.

How much has this situation changed today? In many ways, world Christianity has changed dramatically since 1912. The end of colonialism in the twentieth century heralded a new emphasis on indigenization of mission churches. Western missionaries have released many of the churches they planted to find their own way in their local context. In many cases, missionaries have withdrawn, turning over responsibility to local leaders. Christianity in the developing world has grown exponentially, signaling a shift in the center of gravity of global Christianity from north to south (Jenkins 2002:2). For many western denominations, most of their members now reside in the developing world, indicating tremendous success in missions.

In this new situation, we might reasonably expect that the problem of dependency had disappeared with colonialism, yet this is certainly not the case. Although it has been almost a century since Allen made his observations, the problem of dependency in mission churches remains a chronic one especially where missionaries from wealthy regions of the world, such as North America or Europe (the North), have planted churches in developing nations (the South).

With political independence in Africa, mainline churches began to indigenize as foreign personnel withdrew, but evangelical churches viewed political independence as a time to send in new missionaries. In the postcolonial period, evangelical missionaries were not always sensitive to the rising expectations of Africans for greater local control, and thus tended to perpetuate dependency. Despite repeated calls by many missionary researchers and by African leaders for self-supporting indigenous churches, dependency remains endemic.

This study investigates the roots of this stubborn entrenchment of dependency, showing how historical factors have contributed to attitudes that foster dependency. It also addresses recent issues, such as partnership, short-term missions, and globalization, which have often fueled the problem. Finally, it suggests remedies for dependency. Evangelical churches, in particular, need to find ways to put dependency behind them, so that healthy churches, at home in the context of the developing world, may rise to their full potential and contribute their rightful share to world evangelization.

Just where did the dependency syndrome come from? It has deep roots in the historical development of the modern missionary movement—a movement that developed during the colonial period. Dependency is an unintended part of the colonial legacy.

European colonialists were not solely at fault. American Christians have often assumed that blame for the weak expression of Christianity in various parts of the global South falls entirely on the domineering spirit that characterized European colonialism and missions. While Americans see themselves as egalitarian and tolerant, this chapter shows that, historically, American missionary attitudes and policies contributed to the dependency syndrome as much as European attitudes and policies.

Missions to Native Americans

To begin with, American missions to Native Americans preceded the modern European missionary movement by 150 years and inspired men like William Carey, the Englishman known as the father of modern missions (Beaver 1968:114). Puritan John Eliot pioneered missions to Native Americans in New England in the 1640s, and Cotton Mather reported on Eliot's work in these words, originally published in 1702:

> [Eliot] had a double work incumbent on him; he was to make men of them [Native Americans], ere he could hope to see them saints; they must be civilized ere they could be Christianized; he could not, as Gregory once of our nation, see any thing angelical to bespeak his labours for their eternal welfare; all among them was diabolical. (1979:560)

Mather referred to the occasion Pope Gregory (AD 590-604) is said to have seen three English (Angle) slaves being auctioned at a Roman market. Gregory reportedly noted that they looked angelic (as a pun on "Angle") and determined to send missionaries to England (Shelley 1982:187). Mather took this story to mean that his pagan English ancestors were far more appealing in demeanor than the Native Americans. In Mather's view, Eliot accepted a much greater challenge than Gregory in undertaking missions to them.

By 1649, within three years of beginning his mission to the Algonquin Indians, Eliot stated, "I find it absolutely necessary to carry on civility with Religion," meaning that he intended to induce major culture change among them (Vaughan

1965:260). Eliot's goal was to bring the Native Americans up to European standards by teaching them to fence land, farm it, manufacture goods for sale, cut their hair, and wear English clothes (Vaughan 1965:261-2).

To achieve this goal, Eliot pursued the slow and laborious task of separating converts of "praying Indians" into villages to civilize them. In 1651, the first "praying" village was formed at Natick, Massachusetts (Vaughan 1965:263), and by 1674 there were fourteen such villages with eleven hundred converts (Vaughan 1965:293). This experiment came to a tragic end that shattered the Christian Indians, when several hundred Native American converts were exiled to a bleak island in Boston Harbor during King Philip's War (Carden 1990:110). Colonists regarded all Indians as suspect during this war with Indian tribes, so that not even Christian Indians were exempt from exile and deprivation during the harsh winter (Tucker 1983:88). Carden commented, "Eliot's desire to turn all of New England's Indians into pious Englishmen was doomed to failure, probably before he even started" (1990:110).

After Eliot's death, Mather accused the remaining Indian converts of being:

> Poor, mean, ragged, starved, contemptible and miserable; and instead of being able, as your English neighbours do, to support the ordinances of God, you are beholden to them, not only for maintaining of those blessed ordinances among you, but for many other kindnesses. (1979:574)

Mather was describing how Christian Native Americans had become dependent on their white neighbors for just about everything—spiritual and physical. Despite later efforts by such missionaries as the Mayhews, David Brainerd, the Moravians, and the Quakers to evangelize the Native Americans, their converts were never considered equals with the colonists. Historian Robert F. Berkhofer, Jr. noted:

> No matter how pious and exemplary the Indian Christian became, the white population still considered him a savage and an inferior, ... [and] on the other hand, the pagans despised him for his departure from the customs of his forefathers. (1965:123)

To become a Christian Native American was to lose identity and enter a cultural no-man's land. Elias Boudinot, a graduate of the Moravian Cherokee School, discovered this the hard way. Boudinot appeared to be a model of a 'civilized' Indian, but when he sought to marry a white deacon's daughter in

Connecticut, the Puritans of the area shunned him. Boudinot married the young woman privately and wrote a book in a vain attempt to gain some white recognition of Indians, claiming that "there is a possibility that these unhappy children of misfortune may yet be proved to be the descendents of Jacob and the long lost tribes of Israel" (1970:iii).

Eventually, enmity between white and Native Americans led to the proposal that all Indians should be moved west of the Mississippi River. In 1820, missionary Jedidiah Morse undertook an arduous journey as far as Green Bay, Wisconsin to study the Indian tribes, and submitted a detailed report to the Secretary of War. He sought to counter the proposed removal of the Indians with the call for a joint venture between government and missionaries:

> This government, unquestionably, should be in its nature parental—absolute, kind and mild, such as may be created by a wise union of a well-selected military establishment, and an Education Family: the one possessing the power, the other the softening and qualifying influence; both combined would constitute ... the parental or guardian authority. (1970:85)

The "Education Family" was a model missionary family who would demonstrate farming to nomadic Indians, so that "the Indians will see and judge for themselves, and become agriculturalists from conviction and choice" (Morse 1970:93). Morse, therefore, favored a paternalistic approach to the Indians, combining the "carrot" of a farming life with the "stick" of military enforcement. This was a final attempt to make Native Americans acceptable to white people by civilizing them out of their traditional way of life. Morse's idealistic plan was rejected, and President Andrew Jackson ordered the removal of all Indians to the west of the Mississippi (Wallace 1993).

Mission historian Ruth Tucker summarized the early mission effort to Native Americans: "As the nineteenth century progressed, missionary work among the Indians decreased. The emphasis was on exotic foreign lands where the native population could not interfere with the advance of American society" (1983:104). The attempt to evangelize and assimilate Native Americans had failed because white Americans saw no alternative to the combination of civilization with evangelism, and could not regard Indians as equals. Such attitudes caused Native American converts to Christianity to remain largely dependent on missionaries, because following Christ was seen as becoming part of white American culture.

Missions to African Americans

Missionaries showed just as much eagerness to evangelize African American slaves as they did Native Americans, but several factors made the situation different. While Native Americans were being gradually decimated by war, disease, and exile, African Americans were growing in number. Furthermore, slave labor was a key economic factor, making slaves indispensable in ways that Indians never were. Churches took seriously the fact that African pagans were living among them and they believed that it was their responsibility to Christianize them.

The Southern Baptist Domestic Mission Board made the following resolution in 1847:

> RESOLVE, That in consideration of the providential manner in which the colored population of our country has been gathered from a region of idolatrous darkness, into one blessed by Christian privileges; and in view of the facility with which they can be reached, and the gladness with which they receive the gospel, and the intimate relations which subsist between us and them; we regard them as presenting a field for missionary effort, second in importance to none other, and one which should be occupied as speedily as possible. (Rutledge and Tanner 1969:134)

According to Arthur Rutledge and William Tanner, the Southern Baptist Convention already had 100,000 black slave members at its inception in 1845 out of a total membership of 350,000 (1969:133). Thus, evangelism of slaves was far more successful than evangelism of Indians.

The problem with African American evangelism arose when slaves began to be freed. Even Puritans who had hoped in vain to assimilate Native American Christians never entertained such notions for blacks. John Bodo commented:

> With regard to the Negro ... there was a remarkable consensus among the theocrats [theological descendents of the Puritans] from the very beginning. They believed that there was no room for him in American society except as a slave. (1954:112)

The unique solution proposed for freed slaves was to repatriate them to Africa in a colony modeled after the British colony of Sierra Leone, founded for ex-slaves. Archibald Alexander explained the logic of this solution:

Two races of men, nearly equal in numbers, but differing as much as the whites and blacks, cannot form one harmonious society in any other way than by amalgamation; but the whites and blacks, in this country, by no human efforts, could be amalgamated into one homogeneous mass in a thousand years ... Either the whites must remove and give up the country to the colored people, or the colored people must be removed; otherwise the latter must remain in subjection to the former. (1971:17)

The idea of an African colony originated with Samuel Hopkins, who saw this experiment as a great opportunity for missions. He not only hoped to send Christian ex-slaves to Africa, but he trained two black missionaries for that purpose when the Revolutionary War intervened (Bodo 1954:114). After the war, Samuel Mills revived Hopkins's plan, forming the American Colonization Society, which sent its first shipload of ex-slaves to the new colony of Liberia in 1821 (Bodo 1954:120). The harsh West African climate almost decimated the small group, and even took the life of Mills himself, who died on a return voyage from Liberia (Bodo 1954:123).

By 1849, however, Alexander reported that the Liberian colony was flourishing. He explained the advantages of the Liberian solution as:

[S]o much clear gain; gain to those who go, by greatly ameliorating their condition; gain to those who stay, by diminishing their number; gain to the white population who desire to be exempt from this class of people, and prospectively an inconceivable gain to Africa, by kindling on her borders the lights of Christianity, civilization, and useful science. (1971:10-1)

Events, however, outran the idealism of African colonization. By 1831, William Lloyd Garrison had launched the abolitionist paper, *The Liberator*, and the American South had espoused the "positive good theory" on slavery, leaving the advocates of colonization isolated in the middle. Furthermore, Liberia had taken in a mere 3,000 ex-slaves in its first twelve years, making it seem irrelevant as a solution (Bodo 1954:132-3).

Garrison mercilessly ridiculed the colonizers' position, that the black race,

although surrounded by ten millions of people living under the full blaze of the Gospel light, and having every desirable facility to elevate and save it, it can never rise until it be removed at least three thousand miles from their vicinage! (1968:26)

Favoring slavery, Thomas Roderick Dew, President of William and Mary College in Virginia, opposed colonization, maintaining that slaves were unfit for freedom and better off as perpetual slaves. He noted:

[The] powerful effects of slavery, in changing the habits peculiar to the Indian or savage, by converting him into the agriculturalist, and changing his slothfulness and aversion to labor into industry and economy, thereby rendering his labor more productive, his means of subsistence more abundant and regular, and his happiness more secure and constant. (1968:336)

Emancipation came nonetheless. Once free of slavery, African American Christians no longer saw the need to have their problems solved by the whites, and they simply withdrew from white-dominated churches. Historian Rufus Spain noted:

Separation from the white-dominated churches was a natural expression of the Negroes' new freedom ... As long as they remained in the same churches with whites, they would be second-class members, but in their own churches they could participate in all phases of church life, and the most gifted Negroes could rise to positions of leadership. (1961:45)

During slavery and afterwards, African American Christians were kept dependent in white churches of all theological persuasions, because whites either wished to dominate them, or send them to Africa. Even before emancipation, but much more so afterwards, black American Christians gained their independence spiritually by segregating themselves into their own churches and making Christianity their own without reference to white America (Raboteau 1978:209).

Overseas Missions

African American Christianity demonstrated its independence and vitality in sending missionaries overseas before white Christians did. The first American missionaries sent to foreign lands were black. George Liele established the first Baptist church in Kingston, Jamaica in 1784, and his childhood friend, David George, planted Baptist churches in Sierra Leone in 1792, the year William Carey is said to have launched the modern missionary movement (Raboteau 1978:140). Such facts are mostly unknown by American evangelicals. Samuel Mills is credited for launching American Protestant missions overseas with the establishment of the American Board of Commissioners for Foreign Missions and the sending of the first white missionaries to India in 1812 (Bodo 1954:244).

Did early white missionaries perceive themselves as agents of American nationalism or as agents of the Risen Lord? Bodo found that these and other early missionaries were:

unconscious of any mission beyond converting the heathen ... So far as we could ascertain, no missionary in our period [1812-1848] ever expressed the hope that their work abroad might prepare the way for American colonization or even pave the way for American influence. Yet, such was the inevitable by-product of missionary enterprise. (1954:244-5)

R. Pierce Beaver likewise concluded that even up to 1914, evangelism remained the primary motivation for missions, whereas nationalism was always "secondary to spiritual and theological motivation" (1968:139). Beaver's survey included the whole theological spectrum, finding that before 1900 most American missionaries were motivated by the desire to evangelize non-Christians.

Neither missionaries nor the churches that sponsor them can escape the impact of cultural conditioning and social trends. As the nineteenth century progressed, American values evolved from a strong emphasis on democracy, individualism, and local autonomy toward a sense of superiority over other cultures, and even toward a God-given right to dominate heathen lands. This represented mainstream American values as epitomized in the term Manifest Destiny. Such attitudes spawned dependency in converts, who were led to believe the missionaries' culture was part of the gospel message.

Manifest Destiny

Since the days of the Puritans, Americans have harbored a sense of special calling by God to be a city on a hill to bring light to the rest of the world (Carden 1990:220; Stout 1986:13). Puritans likened their colony in New England to the ancient state of Israel, called out and specially chosen by God (McKenna 2007:7; Stout 1986:8). They envisioned a partnership of church and state in which every law had a biblical basis (Carden 1990:164), but this model did not survive beyond the Revolutionary War and American independence.

Ironically, the wave of Christian renewal from 1733 to 1745 (McKenna 2007:53-4), known as the Great Awakening (Shelley 1982:361-70), may have been instrumental in destroying the Puritan model of government, even though the Puritan Jonathan Edwards was a leader of the Awakening (Edwards 1965). This was because the Great Awakening tended to lessen the distinction between the clergy and the laity, as ordinary church members experienced spiritual revival, thus helping to democratize Puritan society (Noll, Marsden, and Hatch 1989:55). Furthermore, the Awakening weakened Puritan Calvinism, as the revival appeared to know no bounds, defying popular notions of predestination and touching even Native Americans. Strong Calvinism and a society based on ranks, where the clergy were prominent, were essential pillars of the Puritan model of government. By the time of the Revolutionary War, Jeffersonian democracy with its distaste for elites had captured American hearts (Hatch 1989:44-46).

Some American church historians have argued that Christianity was at a low ebb during the Revolutionary period, despite the effects of the Great Awakening (Noll, Marsden, and Hatch 1989:54; Phillips 2006:108; Shelley 1982:405). Politicians successfully harnessed the Puritan sense of a divine call to stoke the fires of nationalism without the Puritan theology. For example, the Deist Benjamin Franklin drew on Puritan terminology to declare that America's destiny was not to be about power, but about light (Garrison 2004:62). George McKenna goes so far to state, "American patriotism has its roots in Puritanism" (2007:7).

Although Christianity and the Bible had an impact on the nation's laws, the United States was the modern world's first secular state (Noll, Marsden, and Hatch 1989:137). Jim Garrison makes a case for America's origin as partly motivated by Francis Bacon who "created a vision of a better world, not by changing the human heart but by transforming nature itself for human benefit" (2004:60).

The Revolutionary War itself further eroded the strength of Christianity in the new nation, and it was only with the Second Great Awakening (about 1790 to 1840) that the United States became significantly Christian (Latourette 1970a:192-204; Shelley 1982:404-8). This awakening further weakened Calvinism and democratized the young nation to the extent that Nathan Hatch called it perhaps the greatest religious upheaval since the Reformation (1989:225). The common people now rose to prominence in the churches, disdaining elitism and the professional clergy. This splintered American Christianity into multiple sects with lay leaders at the forefront.

In addition, the Second Great Awakening contributed to American self-understanding. Christianity and patriotism combined to reinterpret the American Revolution as a sign that God's hand was on America in a special way. Christianity mixed with nationalism to provide the glue that helped to keep the American states cemented with a divine purpose. McKenna saw the Second Great Awakening as helping to reinforce "America's foundational myth: America as a Christian nation founded in freedom" (2007:80). The United States as a nation was again seen as having a mission to the world, and the success of both the young nation and the missionary enterprise was equated with God's favor on America and its way of life. Bodo noted that Christian leaders at home

> soon connected their evangelistic obligation with the fulfillment of America's mission to the world. They commenced to see this connection as soon as the work of the missionaries began to affect the economic and social structure of non-Christian societies. (1954:245)

The idea of mixing civilization with evangelism was clear in an 1823 sermon delivered by Francis Wayland to the Boston Baptist Foreign Mission Society:

> Point us to the loveliest village that smiles upon a Scottish or New England landscape, and compare it with the filthiness and brutality of a Caffrarian kraal, and we tell you that our object is to render that Caffrarian kraal as happy and as gladsome as the Scottish or New England village. (1824:17)

Wayland implied with these comments that the British and American civilizations were the result of Christianity and the aim of overseas missions. He elaborated on this close compatibility of Britain and America:

> Point us to those nations of the earth to whom moral and intellectual cultivation, inexhaustible resources, progress in arts, and sagacity in council, have assigned the highest rank in political importance, and you point us to nations whose religious opinions are most closely allied to those we cherish. (1824:33-4)

At a period when Americans might have been expected to harbor ill will toward the British, mission-minded Americans felt a deep affinity with their counterparts in Britain. Bodo found that these Christian leaders consistently opposed wars with Britain, but were more favorable toward wars with Catholic countries like Mexico:

> War with Britain meant the sundering of friendly ties whose strength had just begun to be tested in the nascent foreign missionary movement. War with Mexico, while regrettable, promised an opportunity for missionary expansion into Catholic territory—a most welcome challenge. (1954:221)

British missions operated from a Christendom perspective, with the understanding that Britain had a Christian culture and that missions involved the spread of civilization. Since Britain had become the world's preeminent imperial power, missions often cooperated with imperialism (Stanley 1990:11). This was the British version of American Manifest Destiny.

Journalist John L. O'Sullivan coined the term "Manifest Destiny" in 1839, saying that America had a

> blessed mission to the nations of the world, which are shut out from the life-giving light of truth; ... and her high example shall smite unto death the tyranny of kings, hierarchs, and oligarchs ... Who then can doubt that our country is destined to be the great nation of futurity? (1839:430)

Politicians tapped into Christian nationalism, this time to justify national expansion. Manifest Destiny would be used to support westward expansion of the nation at the expense of Native Americans, because this was taken to be God's will and America's destiny. President Andrew Johnson showed unbounded optimism about what American democracy could achieve in these words:

> I believe man can be elevated; man can become more and more endowed with divinity; and as he does, he becomes more God-like in his character and capable of governing himself. Let us go on elevating our people, perfecting our institutions, until democracy shall reach such a point of perfection that we can acclaim with truth that the voice of the people is the voice of God. (Foster 1866:104)

Such words are clearly a contradiction of the biblical concept of human sinfulness, but they nevertheless entered Christian thinking after the Second Great Awakening. Frontier values combined with Manifest Destiny to affect American Christian understanding of mission to the world. Beaver noted that Christian nationalism "appears as a motive to missionary action immediately following the end of the Revolutionary War. It becomes stronger during the nineteenth century and is clearly a religious expression of the concept of manifest destiny" (1968:133). An unrealistic optimism about the task of world evangelization gripped American Christianity, and that optimism was rooted in the doctrine of postmillennialism.

Postmillennialism

America was born with postmillennial hopes that persisted into the early twentieth century. Postmillennialism is the doctrine that the millennium, an indefinite period of universal peace and justice, will be ushered in through the successful spread of the gospel to all nations prior to Christ's return (Erickson 1985:1206-9). McKenna described early American postmillennialists: "They tended to be optimists. They saw America as a providentially blessed land whose people would collectively experience an organic growth in godliness, finally culminating in Jesus' return. It would be a soft landing" (2007:94). The American experiment was seen as the fruit of God's plan to perfect human society, and this perfection was bound to spread to the entire world. American missions would usher in the millennium. John Eliot phrased it this way in reaction to the conversion of Native Americans:

> I doubt not, but it will be some comfort to your heart, to see the kingdom of Christ rising up in these western parts of the world; and some confirmation it will be, that the Lord's time is come to advance and spread his blessed kingdom, which shall (in his season) fill all the earth. (Cogley 1999:93)

The Great Awakening likewise confirmed to Jonathan Edwards that the millennium was at hand: "We cannot reasonably think otherwise, than that the beginning of the great work of God must be near. And there are many things that make it probable that this work will begin in America" (1974:381).

The mission-minded Samuel Hopkins wrote *A Treatise on the Millennium* in 1793, seeking to prove from Scripture "that the church of Christ is to come to a state of prosperity in this world, which it has never yet enjoyed; in which it will continue at least a thousand years" (1972:9). This was meant to have worldwide implications:

> All the families, kindreds and nations of the earth, should be blessed in Christ, by their becoming believers in him. This has never yet taken place and cannot be fulfilled, unless Christianity and the kingdom of Christ shall take place and prevail in the world to a vastly higher degree, and more extensively and universally than has yet come to pass. (1972:12)

Alexander Campbell, leader of the Disciples of Christ, named his periodical the *Millennial Harbinger*, defining the Millennium as "the consummation of that ultimate amelioration of society proposed in the Christian Scriptures" (1830:1). He saw signs that the founding of the United States pointed to the proximity of that event. Consistent with frontier values, he devalued history in general, while elevating American independence. He claimed:

> The fourth of July, 1776, was a memorable day, a day to be remembered as was the Jewish Passover … The American Revolution is but a precursor of a revolution of infinitely more importance to mankind … This [new] revolution, taken in all its influences, will make men free indeed. (1863b:374-5)

Similarly the Baptist, Hosea Holcombe, was optimistic about what American Christianity would achieve. His postmillennial view asserted that human efforts would bring in the millennium:

> We look forward, dear brethren, to the time when the whole earth shall be filled with the glory of God; and it will be through the instrumentality of men and things that this glorious day will dawn upon the earth … Human agency is therefore necessary to bring about the accomplishments of God's purposes. He requires his people to be workers together with him in the stupendous enterprize [sic] of evangelizing the nations. (1840:361-3)

Such confidence in human achievement with an American face lent itself to a strong belief in national and even racial superiority. H. Richard Niebuhr noted that postmillennialism became detached from faith in God's sovereignty to be attached to human sovereignty: "It was nationalized, being used to support the feeling of national superiority and of manifest destiny" (1937:151). He continued, "Henceforth the kingdom of the Lord was a human possession, not a permanent revolution. It is in particular the kingdom of the Anglo-Saxon race, which is destined to bring light to the Gentiles by means of lamps manufactured in America" (1937:179).

Social Darwinism

As Charles Darwin's theory of evolution began to revolutionize the intellectual and social climate of America in the second half of the nineteenth century, Christianity did not remain unaffected. Ironically, evolutionary ideas began to merge with nationalism and postmillennialism in American Christian thinking. Darwin himself envisioned more than a purely biological application for his theory of evolution, saying, "As natural selection works solely by and for the good of each being, all corporeal and mental endowments will tend to progress towards perfection" (quoted in Hawkins 1997:36). Mike Hawkins asserted that Darwin was one of the "major architects" of Social Darwinism (1997:35), adding:

> Darwin also expressed conventional views on the superiority of the civilized "Anglo-Saxon" nations over other countries and regarded "savages" as examples of mankind arrested at its most primitive stage of development, while being convinced of the intellectual superiority of men over women. (1997:36)

Some men, like Josiah Strong, openly incorporated Social Darwinism in their view of American Christian expansion, saying that world history was entering a period of "the final competition of the races" with "the survival of the fittest" (1893:79). According to this philosophy, the strongest race would be the Anglo-Saxons who were destined to dominate the world. Strong maintained that the Anglo-Saxon race "is destined to dispossess many weaker ones, assimilate others, and mould [*sic*] the remainder, until ... it has Anglo-Saxonized mankind" (1893:80). For Strong, making America powerfully Christian was the best way to accomplish the Christianization of the entire world.

Charles Loring Brace was, like Strong, an early proponent of the Social Gospel, having spent thirty years using Christianity to cure "certain social evils in the City of New York" (1886:v). He too supported Social Darwinism, equating Christianity with the most evolved form of religion now allied with the most evolved race. He had no doubt the "Aryan races" would succeed in the task of perfecting not only America, but the whole world:

> In the struggle for existence, a perfected race like this will be as much beyond the races which history has known, as the Aryan races now are beyond the African … If driven to physical contest, it would conquer them … But its final triumph would be like those of civilization—gentle, profound, and full of blessings to all others. (1886:472)

Although evangelicals were opposed to Darwin's theories of evolution, their predilection for postmillennial optimism about the role of the United States in the world predisposed them to accept Social Darwinism since it lauded the Anglo-Saxon race as naturally superior to all others. Even in 1849, Alexander Campbell stated that English was the noblest language in service of the noblest religion, Christianity:

> For all over the earth there will be but one Lord, one faith, one hope, and one language … No event in the future, next to the anticipated millennial triumph, appears more natural, more probable, more practicable, or more morally certain and desirable, than this Anglo-Saxon triumph in the great work of human civilization and redemption. (1863a:44-5)

Southern Baptists meanwhile came out of the Civil War defeated militarily, but ideologically undefeated. They "refused to admit that secession or slavery were wrong in any way" (Spain 1961:20). They rejoined the union, however, and saw the United States as the hope of the world. A report to the Southern Baptist Convention in 1866 indicated this optimism, as quoted by Robert T. Handy:

> God has given our country a great and growing influence, and the propagation of the Christian religion here must exert a vast reflex influence upon the destinies of mankind. America is the radiating center whence high and ennobling influences beam upon the world; and we are enlightening mankind in brightening the radiance of our own piety. (1971:67)

A later report in 1890 mixed this optimism with Social Darwinism: "The religious destiny of the world is lodged in the hands of the English-speaking people. To the Anglo-Saxon race God seems to have committed the enterprise of the world's salvation" (Handy 1971:106-7).

Not coincidentally, the rise in feelings of national and racial superiority corresponded to the era of high imperialism when European powers carved up the continent of Africa for colonization. Brian Stanley explained, "Imperialism now meant, in the words of Kipling's famous poem of 1899, the willing assumption of 'the white man's burden' to conquer and civilize 'the dark peoples of the world' for their own good" (1990:36).

American Imperialism

The convergence of Social Darwinism, Manifest Destiny, and American nationalism culminated in the emergence of imperialistic methods in American foreign policy. During the Spanish American War of 1898, President William McKinley described the capture of the Philippines from Spain as a Christian duty: "There was nothing left for us to do but to take them all and to educate the Filipinos and uplift and civilize and Christianize them, and by God's grace do the very best we could by them, as our fellow men for whom Christ also died" (Hudson and Corrigan 1999:309).

Senator Albert J. Beveridge of Indiana made a speech in 1900 that gained national attention:

> [God] has made [Anglo-Saxons] the master organizers of the world to establish system where chaos reigns ... He has made us adepts [sic] in government that we may administer government among savage and senile peoples ... And of all our race, He has marked the American people as His chosen nation to finally lead in the regeneration of the world. This is the divine mission of America. (Sullivan 1927:47-8)

He added, according to Albert K. Weinberg, a "new theory" of imperialism: "They [Filipinos] are not capable of self-government. How could they be? They are not a self-governing race" (1935:307).

American Christians were both delighted and bellicose in response to American victories in Hawaii, Cuba, and the Philippines. Spain quoted the Southern Baptist periodical, *Christian Index*, of Atlanta of 3 August 1899:

Every victory for American arms means in the Philippines, as it did in Cuba and in the conquering of the savage Indians, an advancement of the plans of God in the calling out of his sheep which shall hear his voice and follow him … Oh, let the stars and stripes, intertwined with the flag of old England, wave o'er the continents and islands of earth, and through the instrumentality of the Anglo-Saxon race, the kingdoms of this world shall become the kingdoms of our Lord and his Christ! May the Eagle's scream and the Lion's roar echo and reverberate over earth's mountains and valleys, sending terror to the heart of tyranny and freedom to the shackled slave. (1961:126)

This view was in line with general American sentiments of the time. Evangelical Christianity was being reshaped by the sweeping tide of nationalism, postmillennialism, Social Darwinism, and Anglo-Saxon imperialism. Churches operated on the assumption that American culture had already absorbed Christianity so thoroughly that it reflected that faith more and more. Handy summarized:

In the earlier period, the priority of the religious vision was strongly and widely maintained … In the latter part of the century, however, … the real focus had shifted to the civilization itself, with Christianity and the churches finding their significance in relation to it. Civilization itself was given increasingly positive assessment, chiefly because it was understood to have absorbed much of the spirit of Christianity. (1971:110)

Handy explained how this shift took place in American Christian thinking by the end of the nineteenth century:

Because [churches] assumed that religious freedom and the separation of church and state had eliminated the possibility of too close ties between religion and culture, they were often oblivious as to how far they had moved toward a religion of culture. (1971:115)

This "religion of culture" in the age of imperialism would help to create long-term dependency in the peoples whom American missionaries converted, since the assumption was that the culture of the missionaries was superior and the converts were probably incapable of self-government.

Conclusion

Historically, American missions associated closely with British missions, especially in their concept of Christendom: a Christian Anglo-Saxon culture extending over the globe. From the beginning of outreach to Native Americans in the 1640s, American missions pursued the strategy of civilization with evangelization. This strategy envisioned a world dominated by one Christianized culture, contrary to New Testament teaching. In Acts 15, at the Jerusalem Council, the apostles and church leaders decided against such a strategy under the guidance of the Holy Spirit. If any human culture had a right to claim world dominion, it would be that of God's chosen people, the Jews of the Old Testament. Yet that is precisely what was rejected in Acts 15, opening the way for Christianity to enter each culture without forcing conformity to a foreign culture, not even to one shaped by God himself.

The ideal of civilization with evangelization was bolstered by powerful theologies and ideologies that seemed to spring from Christian history. Giddy with the success of the new nation in achieving independence in a vast continent, American Christians embraced the historical currents then blowing around them as the will of God. These currents included:

1. *Manifest Destiny:* the God-given mission to conquer the wilderness of North America and to rule over its inhabitants for their own good.
2. *Postmillennialism:* the optimistic belief that Christian missions will be so successful in bringing the world to Christ that there will be a millennium of global harmony before Christ returns.
3. *Christian Social Darwinism:* a social interpretation of the theory of evolution that believed that Christianity is the highest form of religion and Anglo-Saxons have the highest form of civilization; these two in combination will inevitably dominate the world.
4. *Imperialism:* Americans came to agree with Great Britain about "the white man's burden," granting the obligation to conquer, civilize, and Christianize other nations.

However, there was nothing inevitable or godly about this combination of doctrines. Rejecting the New Testament principle of servant leadership, these ideologies preferred domination. Mellowed by Scripture, the form of domination envisioned would be benign and so attractive that people of other cultures would gratefully accept and yield to it. For all that, domination can never be the type of leadership the New Testament envisions for Christian leaders. Even Augustine, who is often cited as the author of the concept of Christendom, stated that God originally "did not wish the rational being, made in his own image, to have dominion over any but irrational creatures, not man over man, but man over beasts … Hence the first just men were set up as shepherds of flocks, rather than as kings of men" (1984:874).

Domination, even if benign, breeds dependency. In fact the two are but sides of a single coin. Historian Eric Hobsbawm stated that the age of imperialism (1875-1914) produced a world divided into "two sectors combined into one global system: the developed and the lagging, the dominant and the dependent, the rich and the poor … The (much larger) second world was united by nothing except its relations with, that is to say its potential or actual dependency on, the first" (1987:16). Hobsbawm said that part of his reason for writing about this period of history was that "the Age of Empire cries out for demystification, just because we … do not know how much of it is still in us" (1987:5).

Twenty-first century Christians inherit the world our ancestors shaped, for better or worse. The fact that dependency is still alive and flourishing is a strong indication that their thinking is still with us American Christians despite major changes in the past century. We are still tempted to believe in our own cultural superiority to the extent that we may support a continuation of civilization with evangelization, even unintentionally. We have fewer excuses though to think that way. Beside the testimony of New Testament mission principles are significant voices from the nineteenth and early twentieth centuries that objected to this instinctive combination of evangelism with civilization. Although largely unheeded at the time, these voices would prove prophetic in the battle to overcome dependency.

2

EARLY VOICES OF WARNING

I N THE NINETEENTH CENTURY, DESPITE THE GENERAL trend toward paternalism in missionary activity, significant voices were calling for a different approach. Two of these were the heads of the largest mission agencies of their day, the British Anglican Church Missionary Society (CMS) and the American Board of Commissioners for Foreign Missions (ABCFM). These two men, Henry Venn and Rufus Anderson, represented the second generation of the modern missionary movement, and to this generation fell the task of clarifying the goals and methods of missions. Venn and Anderson independently came to the same conclusion that the aim of missionary work should be to plant self-supporting, self-propagating, and self-governing churches, so the missions could avoid creating dependency and hence could send the missionaries to virgin fields as soon as possible (Shenk 1981:168-72). This strategy came to be known as the Three-Self formula, and it reflected a greater optimism about the abilities of new churches planted by the missions to assume full responsibility for their own affairs in a short time, so that foreign missionaries would not need to become local pastors.

Henry Venn

Englishman Henry Venn was secretary of the CMS from 1841 to 1872. He expounded his philosophy of missions in three papers presented in 1851, 1861, and 1866 (Hanciles 2002:26); but the core of his policy was expressed in the first paper, entitled "Employment and Ordination of Native Teachers." According to Colin Reed, Venn stated his policy as follows:

> The object of the Church Missionary Society's Missions, viewed in their ecclesiastical aspect, is the development of Native Churches, with a view

to their ultimate settlement upon a self-supporting, self-governing, and self-extending system. When this settlement has been effected the mission will have attained its euthanasia and the missionary and missionary agency can be transported to the regions beyond. (1997:5-6)

Venn viewed the missionary agency as removable "scaffolding" while the indigenous church was the edifice being constructed. The "euthanasia" of mission did not imply that missions would die out, since the indigenous church would become self-propagating, but rather that the missionary apparatus would be free to move "to the regions beyond."

Venn thus distinguished between the temporary nature of the missionary's task in a certain location and the local pastor's work. His biographer summarized this approach:

The missionary was not to stop to shepherd sheep that could feed themselves while others perished in helplessness. ... The missionary's unique vocation is to cross cultural boundaries in order to preach the gospel of Jesus Christ and extend the church. Never a regular part of the local church, the missionary is appointed to continue founding churches. (Shenk 1983:41-42)

Shenk noted that Venn emphasized self-support since the CMS was experiencing a financial crisis (1990:29), which

emphasized the importance of freeing young churches from dependence on the missionary society. Evidence suggested that the present system made the local church dependent on the missionary society ... In 1841 the CMS issued a statement announcing that they intended to place greater responsibility on local resources. (1983:25)

The possibility of self-support was driven home to Venn when he hosted a wealthy Sierra Leonean merchant at his home. Noting that the man had been traveling around Europe with his whole family, Venn mentioned that it should also be possible for Sierra Leoneans to support indigenous clergy. The merchant replied, "Of course we could, Mr. Venn; but so long as you treat us like children we shall behave like children. Treat us like men and we shall behave like men.

We spend our money on ourselves because you don't invite us to support our clergy" (Shenk 1983:43).

Venn embraced the Three-Self formula as a pragmatic approach that aimed to extend Christianity rapidly throughout the world in a reproducible and inexpensive manner. He used the formula as a criterion for independence of local churches in his endeavor to untangle missionaries from those churches. Above all, he looked for indigenous leadership to arise in the place of missionaries.

In his second paper of 1861, Venn warned about the dangers of settling down in mission stations. Missionaries would be drawn inexorably into pastoral work at the expense of evangelism. Furthermore, with the missionary assuming local church leadership, converts would "naturally imbibe the notion that all is to be done for them—they are dependents upon a foreign Mission, rather than members of a native Church" (Shenk 1983:121). Missionary work would become bogged down in ecclesiastical details with needless expense. "Instead of advancing to 'the regions beyond,' [the Missionary Society] is detained upon old ground; it is involved in disputes about native salaries, pensions, repairs of buildings, etc." (Shenk 1983:121).

Field missionaries of the CMS in West Africa failed, however, to heed these principles; they began to settle down permanently in mission stations to the detriment of the maturation of the new churches. Jehu Hanciles emphasized that "four decades of dependence on CMS aid and European patronage [in Sierra Leone] had induced an inertia that could not be overcome without difficulty and careful teaching ... The spirit of missionary enterprise at the time ... favored foreign domination and created dependency" (2002:40-1). Sierra Leone became something of a test case for Venn's principles, as it was an early field for CMS missionaries sent to minister to freed slaves who were off-loaded in Freetown from all over West Africa whenever the British navy captured slave ships on the high seas.

Venn tried to push through the idea of indigeneity by ordaining the first African Anglican bishop, Samuel Adjai Crowther (Neill 1964:377). As a young man in 1822, Crowther found himself on a slave ship bound for the Americas after Muslim raiders captured him in his native Nigeria and sold him to Portuguese traders. The ship was intercepted, however, by the British navy's antislavery patrol. With thousands of other freed slaves, he was released at Freetown, Sierra Leone (Anderson 1998:160). Crowther soon became a Christian and was the first student at Fourah Bay Institute, a school established by the CMS in Sierra Leone to train indigenous church leaders (Neill 1964:306). After further study in London, Crowther was ordained to the clergy in 1843 and sent to serve at Abeokuta, near his home in Nigeria (Neill 1964:309).

Sensing the vindication of his indigenous principles, Venn made Crowther the head of an all-African mission to the Niger River in 1857. In 1864, he appointed Crowther "Bishop of the countries of Western Africa beyond the Queen's dominions" (Walls 1992:19). The awkwardness of this title reflected the refusal by English missionaries to have an African bishop over them; Crowther could only be assigned to territories where there were no Englishmen. Nevertheless, African leadership was affirmed, even if only to lead other Africans.

Unfortunately, much of this bold experiment ended in tragic failure as the prevalent currents of imperialism and racism gathered steadily against the implementation of Venn's indigenous church principles. New CMS missionaries affected by a combination of Keswick spirituality (coming from popular conferences on sanctification held in England's Lake District each summer) and high imperialism began to undermine those principles. In this case, the result was a mixture of self-righteousness coupled with an air of racial superiority. J. F. Ade Ajayi explained:

> Young, intemperate European missionaries from the Keswick Convention were drafted into the Niger Mission. They discredited Bishop Crowther's staff *en masse* and accused the aging bishop of being a weak disciplinarian, lacking in the highest spiritual qualities. Crowther resigned control of the Niger Mission to them in 1890. (1999:54)

Shenk lamented "the takeover of the Niger Mission by this new generation, sending Bishop Crowther to his grave discredited and broken" (1983:112). When Venn died in 1873, Crowther was powerless in the face of younger Englishmen who accused him of leading a corrupt administration. The white missionaries conducted a thorough purge of the Niger Mission, replacing Africans with Englishmen. Not only did this create tension with African churches, but many Nigerians also left the Anglican Church to form indigenous churches (Ajayi 1999:55; Shenk 1983:113), the first among many African Independent Churches (AICs). Hanciles attributed the rise of AICs partially to Venn's emphasis on the importance of selfhood for indigenous churches: "The 'three-selfs' ideal ... acted as a potent stimulus for such convictions," referring to Ethiopianism, a form of AIC (2002:155).

Mark Noll summarizes:

> In world-historical perspective, Crowther's Niger Mission, along with Venn's three-self principles, were swept away by an avalanche, the European scramble for African colonies. If that avalanche was not enough, other bombardments out of Europe would have done the job—for example, the intensification of racialist understandings of history and the rise of Social Darwinism. (2009:57)

Rufus Anderson

Born in 1796, the same year as Venn, Rufus Anderson was one of only two American missionary leaders before 1848 (the other being Archibald Alexander), who "deplored the tendency of the missionary movement to exceed its evangelistic commission by interfering with the social and economic environment of its converts" (Bodo 1954:246). As secretary of the ABCFM from 1832 to 1866, remaining active until 1875 (Beaver 1967:10-1), Anderson was later referred to as "the most original, the most constructive, and the most courageous student of missionary policy whom this country has produced" (Speer 1914:237).

On the one hand, Anderson agreed with other men of his time:

> The civilization ... that is connected with modern science, is all connected also with Christianity ... The civilization which the gospel has conferred upon our New England is the highest and best, in a religious point of view, the world has yet seen. (1967:73)

Unlike other men of his time, however, he saw this as a hindrance to "a purely spiritual character to missions among the heathen" (1967:73). In just a few years, American Christians and missionaries expected to establish a replica of American values and society, and Anderson saw this not only as unrealistic, but also as a distraction from the spiritual aim of missions. He stated, "The sole object [of missions] is the reconciling of rebellious men in heathen lands to God" (1967:81).

The two main reasons that Anderson advocated the separation of evangelism and civilization were simple. Pragmatically, he understood that world evangelization would be hopelessly drawn out if civilization were an aim; biblically, he saw that the apostle Paul's methods prioritized evangelism. He affirmed, "This is the only effectual way of prosecuting missions among the heathen–holding up Christ as the only Savior of lost sinners. It requires the fewest men, the least expense, the shortest time" (1967:85).

Anderson decried the tendency to judge "uncivilized" new converts by Western standards:

> If we discover that converts under the torrid zone go but half clothed, that they are idle on a soil where a small amount of labor will supply their wants, that they sometimes forget the apostle's cautions to his converts, not to lie one to another, and to steal no more, in communities where the grossest vice scarcely affects the reputation, and that they are slow to adopt our ideas of the rights of man; we at once doubt the genuineness of their conversion, and the faithfulness of their missionary instructors. (1967:74)

Furthermore, he foresaw social uplift of converts as a by-product of evangelism. Just as Nehemiah concentrated his efforts on rebuilding the walls of Jerusalem, expecting that the rebuilding of other structures and institutions would naturally follow, so missionaries should concentrate on pioneer evangelism and trust that their converts would establish the other transformations their societies needed. The depravity of the pagan world was so deep that missionaries could never accomplish its total transformation in one generation. After seeing people reconciled to God, however, missionaries could confidently expect social improvement to follow in time. Anderson summarized, "There is no way so direct and effectual as this, to remove the social disorder and evils that afflict the heathen world; indeed, there is no other way" (1967:85).

Thus, the missionary's first task is winning people to Christ, and this can only be done by preaching the cross. From the apostle Paul, Anderson learned:

> The weapons of our warfare must be spiritual. The enemy will laugh at the shaking of a spear, at diplomatic skill, at commerce, learning, philanthropy, and every scheme of social order and refinement. He stands in fear of nothing but the cross of Christ. (1967:84)

Nothing less than total dedication to the cross could sustain the missionary movement in its difficult task of winning the world for Christ. This is why Anderson insisted on a "purely spiritual character to missions among the heathen" (1967:73), as opposed to a civilizing mission that would export American values.

Anderson's emphasis in the Three-Self formula was on the self-governing aspect, as he sought to develop indigenous leaders. Like Venn, he understood that local pastors should be trusted and trained to assume the government of new churches (Shenk 1990:29). Commenting on the way the apostle Paul had ordained leaders to take over his work so he could continue to itinerate as a missionary, Anderson concluded, "In this way, the gospel soon became indigenous to the soil, and the gospel institutions acquired through the grace of God a self-supporting, self-propagating energy" (Shenk 1981:170). He sought to duplicate the same energy that Paul's ministry had in order to spread the gospel rapidly across the world.

William Taylor

Less well-known is this Methodist Episcopal missionary bishop born in Virginia in 1821 and converted at a Methodist camp meeting in 1841 (Anderson 1998:660). He began his missionary experience in California in 1849 during the gold rush and supported himself by writing and selling his books, eventually authoring a total of seventeen (Anderson 1998:660). From such self-supporting beginnings, he became a worldwide bishop holding to "Pauline methods," which he described as follows:

> The Pauline plan of planting the gospel in heathen lands was 1. To plant nothing but pure gospel seed ... 2. Paul laid the entire responsibility of Church work and Church government upon his native converts under the immediate supervision of the Holy Spirit, just as fast as he and his tried and trusted fellow missionaries could get them well-organized ... 3. Paul "endeavoured to keep the unity of the Spirit in the bond of peace" with the Jerusalem churches ... 4. He went and sent, according to the teaching of the Master, without "purse or scrip," or an extra coat or pair of shoes above the actual requirements of their health and comfort ... 5. He uniformly commenced in Jewish communities which had become indigenous in all the great centres of population throughout the Roman Empire ... 6. He remained in each centre of work long enough not only to effect a complete organization, with administrative elders, but to develop the Christian character of each member up to the standard of holiness indicated by his oft-repeated exhortations and prayers as recorded in his epistles. (1879:3-7)

Taylor saw direct parallels between the environment where Paul worked as a missionary and his own. In place of the Roman Empire of Paul's time, he now travelled in an "Anglo-Saxon Empire," which had greater advantages for missions because it was "part of a Providential programme for the permanent establishment of universal Christian Empire in the world" (1879:10). Instead of using the Greek language, Taylor could use English "which is manifestly a God-ordained medium, through which He will flood the nations with gospel light" (1879:11).

In addition, the commercial fleets of the Anglo-Saxon Empire had deposited strategic resources in manpower and wealth in every part of the globe, just as Paul found fellow Jews throughout the Roman Empire to help his work (1882:37). By this, Taylor meant that "vast resources in men, money and merchandise" from transplanted English-speaking merchants who called themselves Christians were now available for missions like his (1882:37). Paul, with a commission to reach the Gentiles, always started with the Jews first and "largely utilized those resources in the establishment of self-supporting and propagating missions throughout the Roman world" (1882:38). Similarly, Taylor would begin his mission in various parts of the world with local Europeans or people of mixed race who could speak English and had resources for the mission.

He described how this worked in India: "I commenced in Bombay in 1972, and in less than four years, the Holy Spirit thus planted powerful, self-supporting mission Churches in Bombay, Calcutta, Madras, and many other principal capitals of the Indian Empire" (1979:37). This emphasis on self-supporting churches characterized his mission as it had the apostle Paul's:

It seems never to have entered the minds of inspired apostles, nor of their people, that the great work of their "high calling," the salvation of the world, required the construction of costly edifices with their expensive appendages, to be called Churches, involving a vast outlay of funds, making dependence on rich men a necessity. (1879:31)

In a book published in 1882, after ten years in India, Taylor discussed three key financial principles that "the Lord has incorporated in his system of gospel work" (1882:44). First was "a pioneer principle, represented by men who, at their own cost, without any guarantee of compensation, open up new resources and new industries" (1882:44). Taylor took this common business principle as parallel to pioneer mission work. Men like Paul and Barnabas went out fully prepared to support themselves in order to preach the gospel free of charge, and Taylor followed this principle through his book sales as he traveled around the globe. He reminded Methodists that their founders followed this principle too: Thomas Coke lived on an inheritance and John Wesley sold books (1882:48).

The second principle was "'the laborer is worthy of his hire,' to be paid by the people who get the benefit of his labors" (1882:50). Here the gospel worker exceeded the business principle of supply and demand, since "he bears in his hands a gospel message infinitely more valuable than any thing that could be given in return" (1882:51). Using the first two financial principles, "the apostles and their coadjutors conquered the Roman world" (1882:51).

The third principle was "a charity principle" (1882:52). Taylor understood that "all the missionary societies are based on this heaven-born principle number three. They constitute the greatest benevolent institutions in the world; tending not only to alleviate the physical woes of millions of the human race, but to rescue their souls from destruction" (1882:53). Taylor appears to place himself outside these missionary societies, but he clarified that there should be no antagonism between benevolence and self-supporting missions (1882:54). Nevertheless, "the proper disbursements of charities in all their variety, to individuals, is one of the most perplexing problems of the age in which we live" (1882:55).

He supplied a graphic example of this perplexity from his experiences in places like Wyoming, where farmers raised cattle that could easily die in the cold winters. Indeed, those cattle that had easy access to haystacks would invariably die in winter, because as soon as the hay was finished they no longer knew how to find native grasses (1882:56). By refusing to overfeed their cattle, farmers ensured that only 3 to 5 percent would die because the cattle could forage for themselves, even in winter. He asserted, "That was a rigid application of the principle of self-support, but that is the way they develop the hardy herds which require no feed in winter" (1882:55).

Similarly, Taylor saw a need for charity for the poorest people, but he cautioned that charity should "not be allowed to cripple the energy and operations of self-support" (1882:57). Therefore, he followed the practice of involving local people of some means in his mission work. He maintained that the apostle Paul did the same: "Paul's plan was to reach the educated, influential people of the great cities of the Roman world" (1882:64). These were the people who held enough resources for self-supporting missions anywhere in the world, and it would be totally wrong to approach such people as if they needed benevolence. Taylor advised: "Meet the man of means on the platform of independent personal equality, call his attention to something that will commend itself ... as a thing of great value to him … and he will invest his money in it, and become an interested party in its dissemination" (1882:63).

For William Taylor, self-supporting mission was normative, and he practiced it in an age when it was not common; the great mistake he saw in most mission societies was to regard local people as uniformly in need of benevolence instead of drawing on the resources they held for mission. His reliance on business principles in the cause of worldwide mission made him a precursor of those who seek to harness globalization for the cause of Christ.

John Nevius

In Korea in 1890, John L. Nevius was able to train new Presbyterian missionaries in a variation of the Three-Self formula that came to be known as the "Nevius method" (Neill 1964:343). He had not seen great church growth in his own field of China because missions there used various methods, including some that Nevius opposed. When the Presbyterian missionaries in Korea faithfully applied his principles from the outset, however, they achieved dramatic results. Roy E. Shearer indicated that from a few hundred baptized believers in 1895, the Presbyterian Church grew to 9,000 by 1905 and to 100,000 by the early 1930s (1966:50).

The Nevius method concentrated on self-support, stating that missionaries should not employ local church workers or evangelists (Nevius 1958:19). Nevius warned emphatically, "The Employment System tends to excite a mercenary spirit, and to increase the number of mercenary Christians" (1958:15). Not only did the mercenary spirit create a ripple effect in the expectations of new converts that they might be paid to evangelize, but non-Christians also assumed that missionaries were buying converts. Furthermore, this system tended to stop unpaid volunteers from witnessing at all.

For these reasons, Nevius advocated that all converts should remain in the social setting and secular vocation that they had before conversion, each one being a witness in that setting. To this end the Nevius method stressed times of intense Bible study and training for witness. Church programs should develop only so far as the local churches could care for and manage them so the newly planted churches would provide their own workers and support those best qualified to evangelize. Finally, the local converts should provide their own church buildings (Neill 1964:343).

This radical method was at odds with what Nevius called the "Old System" of heavy mission subsidy for local evangelists and buildings (Nevius 1958:12).

It achieved its aim of rapid self-propagation, however, and rapid church growth led to early self-government when the Korean Presbyterian Church became independent of the missionaries by 1907 (Shearer 1966:58). Shearer recognized that the Presbyterians grew because they had a reproducible indigenous pattern:

> They had an indefinitely reproducible pattern because it was indigenous and free of foreign funds ... The faith which burst into flower all over northwest Korea would have been crushed by dependence upon Western leadership or Western funds. (1966:188)

L. George Paik, a Korean scholar and statesman, wrote in 1929:

> Both self-propagation and self-government were the logical consequences of the self-support program. The persistence of the principle gave the Koreans the feeling that the whole enterprise was theirs ... It is the self-support principle that created the self-respect, self-reliance and independent spirit which are necessary for any successful movement, and that made the Korean Church active and endowed it with resources which sustained it through all its trials. (quoted in Noll 2009:155)

It is not surprising that with this healthy start, the Korean Presbyterian Church also became a major missionary sending denomination. Larry D. Pate listed six Korean Presbyterian mission agencies in 1988, with a combined total of 441 missionaries on all six continents (1989:184-9). By 2006, according to Rob Moll, South Korea had almost 13,000 missionaries serving as long-term missionaries around the world, making South Korea the second largest missionary sending nation after the United States. Moll projected that Korea will eventually deploy more missionaries than the United States because it is sending out more than 1,100 new missionaries per year, more than all Western nations combined (2006:30).

Nevius understood that Christian missionaries operated in a "commercial age" (1958:85) that brought a spirit of commercialism into the church. He warned strongly against this reliance on financial power rather than on spiritual power. The Nevius Method therefore tried to shift the emphasis from dependence on foreign funds to dependence on the Holy Spirit. This example, however, was not generally followed in other places then and the "Old System" remained the norm. Ironically today, Timothy Park, a Korean professor of missions, chastises current Korean missionaries: "Recent Korean missionaries have not always followed the indigenous church principle that made the first missionaries to Korea so successful" (Moll 2006:33).

Roland Allen

By the late nineteenth and early twentieth centuries a new "Age of Imperialism," characterized by racial prejudice, had dawned. "Conversionist" theories that peoples such as Africans could become equals of Europeans shifted to theories of "trusteeship," where "the superior races were duty-bound to come to the aid of the inferior peoples," but the latter were "inherently incapable of developing to the same level as the superior races" (Shenk 1983:107). Voices such as those of Venn, Anderson, Taylor, and Nevius, tended to be drowned out by rising racism, which Colin Reed defined as "essentially the refusal to ascribe to a people their true worth and dignity simply because of their race" (1997:138).

A solitary voice of that period that proved to be prophetic was that of Roland Allen, an Anglican missionary to North China whose career is mostly remembered for his 1912 book *Missionary Methods: St. Paul's or Ours?* Comparing the conduct of modern missions with Paul's methods, Allen delivered a shattering critique: "We have preached the Gospel from the point of view of the wealthy man who casts a mite into the lap of a beggar ... We have done everything for them, but very little with them ... We have educated our converts to put us in the place of Christ" (1962a:143).

Allen noted that the apostle Paul planted healthy indigenous churches in four Roman provinces in just ten years (1962a:3). The key question was whether Paul's was a unique ministry with unique circumstances, or whether his methods are applicable to modern missions. Allen found that the differences between the conditions that Paul faced and those faced by modern missions were not sufficient to make his methods irrelevant now. Even his use of miracles was not essential to his preaching, since miracles were not used to induce pagans to believe in Christ (1962a:41-8). Thus, we can still learn much from Paul's missionary methods.

One of the greatest contrasts between Paul and modern missions lies in finances. Allen found that Paul had three basic rules about money in missions: 1) He sought no help from his converts; 2) he gave them no financial help; and 3) he did not administer local church funds (1962a:49). Paul understood that money could either be a great help to missions or a huge impediment, so he always used wisdom and caution in this crucial area, even to the extent of working with his own hands to provide a good example to converts. The way missionaries use money speaks volumes to their new converts; if money is not seen to be the servant of missions, it may easily become the master of the converts.

In answer to the question of how Paul was able to leave healthy new churches after only a short time, Allen found that Paul trusted his new converts to the power and care of the Holy Spirit, so that he could move on to new fields. Paul saw his converts not as they were by nature, but as God would mold them by grace, even through their own mistakes. Allen concluded that "It would be better, far better, that our converts should make many mistakes, and fall into many errors, and commit many offences, than that their sense of responsibility should be undermined" (Allen 1962a:145). Allen realized that this would take faith like that of the apostle Paul, but such faith was essential to avoid the paralyzing dependency created by paternalism.

In the area of church discipline (1962a:111-25), Paul soon appointed elders in each new church and held them responsible for the conduct of church members. Although he was an apostle, he never issued decrees, but preferred to call church leaders to holiness and sound church government. He wrote letters of loving persuasion and admonition rather than making pronouncements, so that new leaders would learn to think prayerfully through issues guided by the Holy Spirit. When discipline was sorely needed at Corinth, Paul deliberately chose to stay away to let the Corinthians work out their own issues so that the pagans would not slander the name of Jesus. In Allen's words, "He disciplined the church; we discipline individuals" (1962a: 124).

In maintaining church unity (1962a:126-38), Paul again stayed away from issuing edicts or creating a central hierarchy for the new churches. Rather, unity was created by fellowship in Christ, sharing in the burdens of preaching the gospel, and caring for one another in practical ways. Each new church was regarded as equal with older ones, despite racial differences between Jews and Gentiles. Paul's practice of unity, based on respect rather than on decrees, created the inevitability of a variety of different local practices, a unity in diversity. This is the reason for most of Paul's letters, which contain specific admonitions for each church to which they are addressed. Thus, unity was maintained by frequent communication through letters, envoys, or in person.

Missionaries must avoid the temptation of assuming the role of Christ and the Spirit. Rather, they must let converts learn how to think and work things out by themselves with the Holy Spirit's help, even to the extent of learning through trial and error. The modern missionary must act "as though he would have no successor" (1962a:153), identifying with converts by sharing life with them, being open about finances and letting them manage the institutions that they deem necessary. For this reason, all teaching and organization must be at such a level that the converts can soon assume complete responsibility for them and reproduce them, as the missionary progressively retires (1962a:158).

In two later books, Allen tackled the issue of appropriate training of clergy, insisting that the current models no longer worked either in Britain or overseas in mission areas. In his first book, *Voluntary Clergy*, he began, "Everywhere at home and abroad there is a great dearth of candidates for Ordination" (1923:1). He attributed this shortage of ordained clergy to the requirements that candidates pass examinations "designed for young men fresh from school and for them alone" (1923:13). Tragically, these qualifications were required uniformly in Anglican churches worldwide (1923:18). This limited the priesthood to only well-educated professionals who expected stipends for their labor, so that "in India, China, and Africa no man is ordained unless he is dependent for his livelihood upon a clerical salary" (1923:26).

Such a system was not only bound to create severe shortages of clergymen, but, even worse, it was not according to the New Testament model of leadership training. As for the apostle Paul, "the men whom he desired to see ordained were all men who were capable of maintaining themselves and their families without any assistance from the Church" (1923:55). Indeed, the New Testament model for church leadership was voluntary clergy, but this was precisely the type of leader who would not be ordained in modern times. Allen denounced this unfruitful system with these words: "We abandoned the Apostolic conception of the ministry: we find that we have abandoned the Apostolic conception of the Church" (1923:72).

In a second book on this subject, *The Case for Voluntary Clergy*, Allen expanded on his reasons for calling for a voluntary clergy. The current system of selecting and ordaining clergymen was expensive and not reproducible in mission areas. Yet Anglican missionaries were using the same system overseas: "They soon began to train natives to work with them, as evangelists and teachers and pastors, and they paid them. Thus very early the native Christian community was divided into two classes, workers who were called mission agents, and the rest who were not" (1930:201).

Allen listed some of the dangers inherent in what he called "the stipendiary system" (1930:202). First, those in full-time service "tend to look upon an increase in the stipend or pay as the mark of progress in Christian service" (1930:202). Those who are more spiritually mature and productive, but do not qualify for ordination, are thus downgraded in the eyes of others. Furthermore, "Men tend to think of Christian service as the service of a mission, rather than as a service of Christ. The mission holds the purse strings, and pay is the mark of progress" (1930:203). Paradoxically, the initiative of a paid worker is less than that of an unpaid one, since the paid worker "is financially dependent upon the mission ... In relation to his own people, or his congregation, he feels no responsibility to them, and they feel no responsibility for him" (1930:209).

Perhaps the ultimate danger is that this system teaches Christians that "all growth depends upon money" (1930:212) and this causes rivalry between missionaries and local Christians in the effort to control funds. In this inevitable struggle, the missionaries remain dominant because of the system they operate with: "The native clergy depend for their livelihood, directly or indirectly, upon foreigners. We have made our position as secure as we possibly can. In the last resort, we are supreme" (1930:215). Such a system automatically creates dependency to the detriment of new churches. Allen lamented, "The world is not evangelized in that way, and Churches are not established on that foundation" (1930:212).

Allen stood squarely in the tradition of Venn, Anderson, Taylor, and Nevius in yearning for mission structures that were flexible and mobile, so that the task of world evangelization could be completed; however, his pleas went largely unheeded. This did not surprise Allen—in fact he had told his son that "his writings would come into their own about the year 1960" (1962a:i). He desired earnestly that colonialism would end and that indigenous church principles would once again be respected.

Conclusion

Once colonialism ended in mid-twentieth century, one might assume that the principles espoused and explained so forcefully by Venn, Anderson, Taylor, Nevius, and Allen would become standard procedure. To some degree, these men were more highly honored long after they died, as they had accurately foreseen a time when European and American missionaries would no longer be in control of mission churches. In spite of much lip service to their ideals, mission practice has lagged behind. Wilbert Shenk wrote, "missionary practice continually compromised this ideal [of the Three-Self formula]" (1999:42). He attributed this to "the Anglo-American bent toward pragmatism and disdain for theory. In other words, this reflects a cultural trait that values action over reflection" (1999:35).

At the same time, the Three-Self formula itself came under heavy criticism, for reasons we shall explore in a later chapter. Suffice it to say now, some wished to discredit what they saw as a Western formula that was used as a straitjacket for non-Western churches, while some wished to discard the formula to justify continued dependency as normal. Unfortunately, that failure to implement the Three-Self formula took a heavy toll on Western mission work both during and after the lives of the men who were such capable proponents of these radical ideals.

3

COLONIAL MISSION MODELS
IN AFRICA

O
UT OF THE HUNDREDS OF EARLY PROTESTANT missionaries to Africa, it is
difficult to name more than a handful who implemented the indigenous
church principles expounded by Venn, Anderson, Nevius, or Allen.
Consider the case of Anglican bishop Alfred Tucker. Consecrated Bishop of
Eastern Equatorial Africa in 1890, he arrived in Uganda late that year, serving
as Bishop of Uganda from 1897 to 1911. Tucker hoped to implement Venn's
Three-Self formula in his work; other European missionaries working with him
were more skeptical about the Ugandans' ability to be self-governing (Anderson
1998:682). Church growth was rapid through self-propagation, with Ugandans
eager to become evangelists and cross-cultural missionaries in their region. Tucker
proceeded to emphasize education of Ugandan church leaders for self-government
in anticipation of the euthanasia of the CMS mission there. He even sought a
church constitution that guaranteed equality between African and European
Christians, but missionary wrangling ensured that when the constitution was
passed in 1909, foreigners would retain effective control (Griffiths 2006).

While mission historian Stephen Neill strongly criticized what he considered
Venn's doctrinaire approach to the euthanasia of mission, he commended Bishop
Tucker: "He envisaged a Church in which African and foreigner would work
together in true brotherhood, and on the basis of genuine equality. For the most
part missionaries of almost all the Churches were blind to this kind of possibility"
(1964:260). Neill lamented the fate of Tucker's plans, which were "to a large extent
shattered on the inveterate opposition of the missionaries ... [who] appear to
have been incapable of the great imaginative effort involved in seeing themselves
as servants of the local Church in real fellowship with Africans" (1964:387).

What made it so hard to implement indigenous church principles? The problem was with the hardening of European and American attitudes when missionaries from those regions began to move in large numbers to Africa. The story of Christian missions to Africa coincides with the "Age of Imperialism," when European powers joined in the scramble to partition Africa into spheres of influence.

In the late nineteenth century, the German Chancellor, Otto von Bismarck, deliberately began to divide Africa on paper, with pieces of territory for interested European nations to take for colonies. He first laid claim to pieces intended for Germany and then called a major conference to parcel out the rest. Niall Ferguson reported that these powers met in Berlin from November 1884 to February 1885 ostensibly

> to watch over the preservation of the native tribes, and to care for the improvement of the conditions of their moral and material well-being and to help in suppressing slavery ... Christian missionaries, scientists, and explorers, with their followers, property, and collections, shall likewise be the objects of special protection. (2003: 236)

These words from the Berlin conference documents envisioned missionaries as agents of imperialism to be used for benevolent purposes. The real purpose of the conference, however, was to keep the European powers from fighting among themselves over the spoils of Africa, without regard for the existing African rulers. In fact, not a single African was present to express the wishes of the indigenous peoples. Ferguson called the conference "a true thieves' compact, ... slicing up a continent like a cake" (2003:237). Missionaries willingly participated in the stated imperial objective of civilizing the African peoples, although they usually had the ultimate goal of converting them to Christianity as well.

Civilization with Evangelism

The cradle from which the modern missionary movement to Africa was born was the awakenings that touched mainly Great Britain and North America. Mark R. Shaw noted:

> At the heart of these evangelical revivals were three powerful convictions. The first was the centrality of the death of Christ for salvation. A second

was the necessity of the new birth. The third was a new eschatology that envisioned the spread of Christianity around the world as a prelude to Christ's personal return. (1996:129)

This heady mixture of revivalism, confidence in progress, and the perceived divine commission of the Anglo-Saxon race caused missionaries to assume that Africans would respond fairly easily to the Western gospel as to an obviously superior way of life. But what in fact happened when European and American missionaries arrived in Africa? In the following sections, we will investigate the missionary movement's impact in Africa, with particular reference to Zimbabwe as a case study.

In West Africa, the Anglican Church Missionary Society took on Sierra Leone as their first main mission in Africa. At the time, "the British navy was patrolling the waters off the West African coast. Slave ships that were intercepted were forced to transfer their human cargo to the care of the British navy" (Shaw 1996:143). These rescued slaves were then transported to the new colony of Sierra Leone, and by 1846, 50,000 ex-slaves speaking 117 languages had settled there (Neill 1964:305). In this way, Freetown was populated, and British missionaries arrived to evangelize the new citizens of Sierra Leone.

Meanwhile, Americans were inspired by the Sierra Leone experiment and saw it as a possible model solution for freed American slaves before the Civil War. Samuel Mills helped this idea come to fruition with the formation of the American Colonization Society, which sent its first shipload of ex-slaves to the new colony of Liberia in 1821 (Bodo 1954:120). After many deaths of early missionaries due to tropical illness, Archibald Alexander reported by 1849, "Liberia not only exists, but is in a flourishing condition" (1971:6).

The Colonization Society's plan clearly implied that freed African American slaves really belonged in Africa, presumably because they had not yet reached the stage of civilization attained by white people. Since they had learned some traits of Western civilization in America, however, they were now well-suited to transform Africa. Thus, the repatriation of ex-slaves to Liberia made missionary sense, because ex-slaves could bring both the gospel and Western civilization to the pagan continent.

Observations made by the missionaries themselves reveal much about the general missionary attitudes of the time. The writings of Thomas J. Bowen are a good example. From 1849 to 1856, Bowen undertook a missionary journey into West Africa on behalf of the Southern Baptist Convention, traveling from

Liberia to Nigeria. His aim was conversion of Africans to Christ, because "the veriest savage on earth is not too inhuman to be capable of conversion" (1857:321). Evangelism would also require civilization as necessary and inevitable:

> The revival of letters and science; the great but still defective reformation of the sixteenth century; the extension of geographical knowledge; the American revolution; the recent going forth of the missionary spirit, and the labors which we are now performing, are all indispensable links in the chain of providence which is to fill the whole earth with the knowledge of God. (1857:325-6)

He recognized, however, that American civilization was not immediately suited for Africa, and that schools, industrial arts, mechanics, and trade were useful but "secondary means for the extension of the gospel" (1857:329). He said that slavery's time was past and that it should be replaced with "lawful commerce" (1857:330). He therefore advocated that the United States explore the Niger River and establish trading posts, since America was "raised up by Providence for the exposition and vindication of principles which are destined to govern the world" (1857:337). He believed that conversion to Christianity would mean a complete social transformation of African society, especially the eradication of polygamy, but he understood that this would all take time (1857:342).

Bowen epitomized the zeal and optimism of early missionaries about the contribution of their own culture to the missionary enterprise, as well as realism about the difficulty of long-term social transformation. Despite a high death toll, missionaries continued to come and plant mission stations, and Bowen was able to report three such stations in Nigeria manned by seven missionaries. He announced plans for a line of such stations "from Lagos on the coast, directly to the remote interior" (1857:350).

In South Africa in 1799, a Dutchman, Johannes Van der Kemp, represented the newly formed London Missionary Society (LMS) in this recently claimed British colony (Hastings 1994:199). Adrian Hastings described this eccentric man as a person of great spirituality and spiritual power, known to the Xhosa tribe as a rainmaker. Van der Kemp lived in "the most absolute poverty ... He walked bareheaded and barefoot, he fed on what was put before him, he was satisfied with the poorest of huts ... He lived on a principle of the most absolute human equality" (Hastings 1994:201). He married a Malagasy slave woman and had four children, and thus was certainly not typical of missionaries of this time (Hastings 1994:202).

The LMS missionary who helped launch Protestant missions into southern and central Africa was quite a different kind of man. Robert Moffat was born in Scotland in 1795 and became a gardener before taking up the call to missions. Hastings commented that while Van der Kemp was unconventional, "Moffat [was] the norm" (1994:206). Moffat set out for Africa at age 21 and served primarily at the mission station of Kuruman for fifty years, as missionary to the Tswana peoples. He turned his gardening skills to good use, by turning Kuruman into "an oasis ... near the southern edge of the Kalahari Desert" (Latourette 1970b:345). His major work was the translation of the Bible into Tswana (Tucker 1983:145).

Jane M. Sales criticized Moffat for his low regard of African traditional religion, his linking of Christianity and commerce, his emphasis on Western civilization for Africans, and his insistence on severe church discipline to enforce Christian conduct. For example, Moffat would explain to textile merchants in Britain how much the missionaries assisted their trade by insisting that Africans should wear Western clothes (1971:81). All these criticisms describe typical missionary attitudes of the time. Missionaries instinctively tied the task of evangelism to the task of civilization.

Moffat may be best known for his son-in-law David Livingstone, whom he helped recruit to come to Kuruman in 1840 (Moffat 1886:156). Moffat's wife, Mary, had tried vainly to talk Livingstone into taking a wife to Africa, writing in a letter, "I have done what I could to persuade Livingstone to marry, but he seems to decline it" (Moffat 1886:158). Instead Livingstone found his wife at Kuruman, and he married Mary, the oldest daughter of Robert and Mary Moffat (Moffat 1886:168).

Kenneth Scott Latourette called David Livingstone "one of the greatest and most influential missionaries in the history of mankind" (1970b:345). From a poor Scottish family, Livingstone was converted to Christ and went on to study theology and medicine. Moffat persuaded him to serve in Africa by describing the smoke from a thousand villages where Christ was not known in the interior of the continent (Mackenzie 1993:46). Livingstone ended up being as much an explorer as a missionary, but his motivation for exploration was always to open Africa for Christianity and legitimate commerce. He developed a passion for ending the brutal slave trade that he witnessed especially as it was conducted by Muslim traders in east and central Africa (Mackenzie 1993:137), and he deemed that British trade would be the antidote for slavery.

After his initial daunting journeys into the heart of Africa had made him famous, he gave a speech at Cambridge University in 1857. In it, he exclaimed, "I go back to Africa to try to make an open path for commerce and Christianity. Do you carry on the work which I have begun. I leave it with you" (Neill 1964:315). The link of commerce and missions was intended to make the slave trade less attractive to Africans, but certainly Livingstone assumed that British trade would be a natural ally of Christianity. Indeed, the Universities' Mission to Central Africa came into being in direct response to Livingstone's speech, and the agency attempted to carry out his vision (Latourette 1970b:388), impacting countries like Zanzibar, Tanzania, Malawi, Mozambique, and Zambia.

Livingstone's father-in-law, Robert Moffat, became the means of extending Christianity into the regions of southern Africa beyond British occupation by befriending the Ndebele king, Mzilikazi, in 1829 (Tucker 1983:146). At the time, Mzilikazi was fleeing across South Africa from his own king, the Zulu tyrant Shaka, on the way to his eventual new home in Zimbabwe. Even at their first meeting, Moffat expressed the desire to send LMS missionaries to live among the Ndebele, according to his son, John (1886:112). This desire was finally fulfilled in 1859 when Moffat escorted the new missionaries into Matabeleland, the southwest part of Zimbabwe now occupied by the Ndebele people. Moffat knew that Mzilikazi was wary of outsiders and would only accept missionaries based on their personal friendship. John Moffat, himself one of the new missionaries, noted that Mzilikazi "and his people shared in a deep conviction that the opening of the country to white men to come and settle would be the beginning of the end. They were not far wrong there" (1886:218).

The establishment of the Inyathi mission station of the LMS in 1859 marked the start of settled Protestant missions in Zimbabwe. At the time, the LMS was the only Christian mission in Zimbabwe since a much earlier Portuguese Catholic mission had disappeared by 1667 (Murphree 1969:6). As Mzilikazi and his people had suspected, white settlement, as insignificant as it initially seemed, marked the beginning of the end of the Ndebele kingdom. As far as the missionaries could see, civilization could take place only if European colonial power replaced the Ndebele kingdom. Furthermore, LMS missionaries working under Mzilikazi and his successor, Lobengula, found their work constantly blocked by these kings. After twenty-five years of ardent labor, the LMS could not claim a single convert (1886:233).

Ngwabi Bhebe noted that the LMS missionaries "had by the 1880s come to the conclusion that the Ndebele political system must be overthrown to pave the way for Christianity" (1979:82). By that time the British imperialist, Cecil John Rhodes, began to covet Lobengula's realm and to negotiate with the Ndebele king for the right to look for gold in parts of Zimbabwe occupied by his Shona vassals. Lobengula used the LMS missionary, C. D. Helm, as his interpreter and adviser in the negotiations with Rhodes's men. Mark R. Shaw claimed that Helm deliberately misinterpreted portions of the concession that gave Rhodes the prospecting rights he was seeking (1996:214). Bhebe, however, defended Helm, saying that Helm, Lobengula, and all his other advisers, "were in the dark regarding Rhodes's intention to use the agreement as a basis for the extension of the British Empire to Zimbabwe" (1979:83). Apparently, Helm believed that Rhodes would restrict his venture to mining, and that such commerce itself would open greater possibilities for evangelism.

In any case, within three years of the entry of Rhodes's British settlers into Zimbabwe in 1890, war broke out between the British and the Ndebele, resulting in the collapse of Lobengula's kingdom and the disappearance of the king as he fled north (Baden-Powell 1901). A further uprising in 1896-1897 of both the Ndebele and Shona peoples was crushed by the British, and colonial rule was established (Ranger 1967). In general, missionaries greeted this development with enthusiasm. A Jesuit priest called the 1896 rebellion "a war of heathenism against Christianity" (Zvobgo 1996:55). Chengetai Zvobgo stated, "Clearly, missionaries needed the support of a secular power if the evangelisation [*sic*] of Matabeleland was to succeed" (1996:2). With the establishment of British colonial rule in the 1890s, missionaries of many denominations flooded into Zimbabwe. Most would have agreed with the comments of George Eva, a newly arrived Wesleyan missionary: "The Matabele had never been thoroughly beaten by the White man, and until we give them a thrashing, we may experience periodical outbreaks" (Zvobgo 1996:27).

The Planting of Mission Stations

Missionaries in Zimbabwe now saw an unprecedented opportunity for winning the Ndebele and Shona peoples to Christ. Christian groups lined up to ask Rhodes for huge tracts of land on which to build mission stations. John Baur summarized, "The first twenty years [of colonialism] saw twenty different missionary groups establishing themselves in Zimbabwe ... It was a record number in early mission history" (1994:310). Although these missions established churches in the growing towns, they concentrated their efforts on their mission stations in rural areas where the vast majority of Africans lived. Baur noted that the willingness of Rhodes to donate large land tracts to missions "blurred the difference between settler and evangelizer in African eyes" (1994:310). Stephen Ndlovu, a bishop of the Brethren in Christ Church, stated that his denomination started their missionary work in Zimbabwe in 1898 when it was given 3,000 acres in the Matopo Hills. As Rhodes himself said, "Missionaries are better than policemen and cheaper" (Ndlovu 1997:74).

Christian missionaries were now generally optimistic about the future and agreed with Rhodes that mission work was "one of the best means for opening and civilizing a country" (Zvobgo 1996:11). Missionaries used education to train the younger generation in mission schools and to attack the African marriage system that was embodied in polygamy and *lobola* (bride-price) (Bhebe 1979:111). In both these areas they expected colonial assistance and used mission stations as a model of the civilization they expected the Africans to achieve. Marshall Murphree noted that some mission stations were so large and autonomous that missionaries became in effect "substitute chiefs" (1969:9). John Climenhaga, a Brethren in Christ missionary who arrived in 1921, agreed: "The native is held under, again because of necessity; he has no say in the affairs of state, since he is not ready for it … In Rhodesia, the missionary is the ruler of his realm so far as the native is concerned" (Wenger 2000:435-6).

Since the missionaries worked independently of tribal authority, they usually did not win tribal chiefs to Christianity. Thus, Christianity developed outside the mainstream of tribal life. Murphree noted, "Conversion to Christianity was usually individual, and at conversion the individual frequently moved out of his tribal milieu into the society of the mission station" (1969:9). Indeed, missionaries aimed primarily at extracting the youth from tribal society (Van Rheenen 1996:61-4), since they believed that the older generation was too steeped in pagan practices to contemplate change. A Jesuit missionary recorded, "As for the old people, one might as well preach to the cattle" (Zvobgo 1996:103).

In the artificial environment of the mission stations, missionaries continued to attack traditional marriage practices by educating both boys and girls who would produce Christian marriages and families. The Brethren in Christ Mtshabezi Mission established a Rescue Home for African Girls in 1908. According to Wendy Urban-Mead, missionaries saw traditional marriage customs as "licentiousness," so they were only too happy to provide refuge "for girls escaping arranged marriages, and … [the Rescue Home] sought to prepare these same girls for life as Christian matrons" (2002:4-5).

The colonial authorities steadfastly refused to legislate against tribal marriage customs because this constituted a "total condemnation of the traditional ways of life" (Bhebe 1979:111). They believed that such a move would destabilize the African culture, for "to abolish *lobola* and polygamy would be striking a blow at the whole African social and economic order, which was bound to provoke universal disaffection and dangerous unrest" (Bhebe 1979:113).

The colonial government did, however, assist missions in setting up an educational system for African youth because it needed semi-skilled manpower for the growing economy based on white farms, mines, and urban industries. The government insisted that missions teach vocational training and industrial arts because it did not want Africans to compete for jobs with European settlers. Africans themselves, however, began to see Western education as a route to greater prosperity, so they insisted on academic subjects as well (Zvobgo 1996:195). As a result, mission schools, which were all initially primary schools, offered industrial arts, academic subjects, and Bible knowledge. Soon they added teacher training as the number of schools outstripped the capacity of missionaries to staff them all. Not forgetting their ultimate goal of evangelization, missionaries undertook not only to convert their students but also to train evangelists.

In this way, mission stations chose the lengthy and arduous route to evangelism through civilization. By this method, they willingly partnered with colonial authorities whose priorities did not match their own. These authorities came increasingly to tie missionaries down to prescribed educational programs that would benefit the government. On the other hand, on the issue of African marriage customs, which the missionaries saw as "the greatest hindrance to Christianity" (Zvobgo 1996:104), the government refused to side with missions. Indeed, both polygamy and *lobola* persist to the present, and Christians now commonly accept *lobola*. Meanwhile, church growth was very slow.

Donald McGavran did a church growth study of the mission station approach to evangelism in Zimbabwe and Zambia. He concluded that this method "was not based on New Testament practices" (1970:23), adding:

> This narrow kind of church growth, which during the years 1880-1950 was developed to fit one kind of government and social structure, must speedily be transformed into one that fits the political and social realities of the last third of the twentieth century in southeast Africa. (1970:23)

The assumption of the mission station approach was that colonialism would continue, with Africans as second-class citizens. McGavran described the rate of church growth under this assumption as "glacial advance, which is all the school approach can deliver" (1970:23). Mission strategy in Zimbabwe had produced few people movements into Christianity, and "those that have occurred have been weak and quickly arrested" (McGavran 1970:22).

Rating Zimbabwean churches on five axes, McGavran found them to be heavily dependent on the founding missions, opting for individual over group conversions, leaving most of the country unevangelized, doomed to slow growth, and non-indigenous (1970:29). Baur confirmed the lack of spiritual impact of Christian missions in Zimbabwe: "Under the [Ian] Smith regime [during the 1960s to 1970s] ... eight out of ten Ndebele ... still held on to the faith of their ancestors" (1994:310). The Ndebele were listed as an unreached people group as late as 1983, after more than 120 years of mission work among them (Dayton and Wilson 1983:306).

African Responses to Christianity

There were encouraging signs for the early missionaries that Africans would welcome them and their message; the Africans were subdued by war and initially greeted white missionaries into their tribal lands, not just as representatives of the conquerors, but also "as friends–different from other white people" (Ndlovu 1997:75). Ndlovu noted, however, that the oppressive structures "that existed in the colonial regimes also existed in the missionary life-style as observed by the African ... Missionaries had a preconceived and negative attitude about the African people, the African culture, and the African land" (1997:76). Missionaries, in their desire to uplift the Africans, were often heavy-handed and paternalistic. John Climenhaga, noticing Africans working on a Sunday, "preached [to them] on observing the rest of the Sabbath day. Finding people drinking beer, he preached on the only liquid that truly satisfies, the water of life" (Wenger 2000:430). On one occasion, he fined an African for drinking alcohol on the mission farm, and a European policeman took him to court on a charge of extortion. The European judge, however, dismissed the case, chiding the policeman, "Hereafter I want you to do all you can to build up appreciation for the work of Matopo Mission. They are doing a splendid piece of work" (Wenger 2000:432).

The fact that missionaries chose African marriage customs as a primary battleground also alienated them from mature Africans. The initial welcome faded and missionaries met with marked resistance to the gospel. The missionary decision to target the younger generation through education also met with resistance at first. It was seen for what it was—an attempt to divide children from their parents, so tearing the African social fabric in two. At first, missionaries had to offer incentives to get students. Bhebe claimed that Seventh-Day Adventists "either bought or accepted into their care children offered by parents who were unable to feed them" (1979:132). For other missions, "missionaries had to resort to giving presents of sweets and clothes to induce those who came to school to attend regularly" (Zvobgo 1996:151).

Eventually, as the impetus toward civilization inevitably overtook the priority of evangelism, Africans began to flock to mission stations for the perceived benefits of learning job skills and receiving medical treatment. Since Christianity had not significantly penetrated tribal structures and cultural beliefs, Africans were able to claim church membership based on the mission station in their area, while continuing to hold to traditional beliefs and customs. Roland Oliver stated that for the rural African, "his denomination depended purely on the accident of which mission lay closest to his home" (1991:207). This attachment to Christianity for the material benefits it offered resulted in what Paul Hiebert, Daniel Shaw, and Tite Tiénou called "two-tier Christianity" (1999:15). Nominal Christians would attend church services while continuing to use the services of traditional healers, diviners, and exorcists. This "has sapped the vitality of churches and limited Christianity to a segment of people's lives" (Hiebert 1999:15). Furthermore, it helped to create dependency, since Africans tended to see Christianity primarily in terms of secular rather than spiritual benefit.

Christian missions acted as a bridge between rural Africans and the modern world, introducing them to Western education and medicine. Zvobgo noted, "Initially, the main objective of missionary education was religious" (1996:149). One missionary estimated that 80 percent of all converts were won first in mission schools (Zvobgo 1996:150). As time went on, however, government pressure pushed mission schools to become more secular.

Government objectives of supplying the economy with semi-skilled African workers did not always match missionary objectives, but the government exercised control through issuing financial subsidies to mission schools that met its standards. The colonial government was content to let missions perform the governmental functions of education and health care, while it imposed the standards and inspections. Missionaries cooperated with the government "in order to make their own educational work among Africans more fruitful" (Zvobgo

1996:188), even though they often resented government interference. Summing up the contribution of Christian missions, Zimbabwean nationalist Ndabaningi Sithole said, "It was the Christian Church that first introduced literacy which was to give birth to African nationalists, medical doctors, advocates, businessmen, journalists, and graduates" (Zvobgo 1996:372). Sithole, himself a Congregational Church minister, therefore saw the benefits of missions in secular terms. Thus, Christian missions unwittingly contributed to the rise of African nationalism through education and health care.

Revivals in mainline denominations tended to spawn African independent churches rather than to strengthen those denominations. Such revivals seemed to be most common among American Methodist Episcopal (AME) churches in eastern Zimbabwe, since American Methodist missionaries employed camp meetings similar to those that took place on the American frontier. Potential people movements arose from AME camp meetings in 1918 and 1928 (Zvobgo 1996:353; Moss 1999:122). Ranger analyzed this period of revivalism and found that it produced a two-tiered Christianity—the official missionary version and the African folk version. By the 1930s, he claimed the "missionaries themselves seemed to have lost what enthusiasm they had had for energetic manifestations of popular religion" (1999:179) and had turned their attention to improving education and training teachers.

Ranger argued that these conditions proved ripe for the birth of a potent form of African independent church in the very place where Methodist revivals were the strongest. Johane Masowe, founder of the *Vapostori* (Apostles) sect, was both "a critique and continuation of Manyika folk American Methodism" (1999:195). He was born in Gandanzara, a key AME mission station, and in contrast to the periodic AME camp meetings, he offered "continual rather than occasional rituals of repentance, exorcism, and protection" (1999:199). Ranger concluded, "Masowe's teaching struck deeper into Manyika society than American Methodism had ever done" (1999:199).

When missionaries challenged *Vapostori* evangelists, the latter referred to two serious deficiencies in mission Christianity: mission evangelists worked for money and could not cast out demons (Ranger 1999:200). Although lacking the resources of Western missionaries, the *Vapostori* planted their churches from South Africa to Kenya in Masowe's lifetime (Dillon-Malone 1978). Their zeal resulted in the people movements that had eluded Western missionaries, and the *Vapostori* were just one of many African independent churches that arose from the interaction of Christian missions with African traditional religion.

While Christian missions tried to stamp out traditional practices or to ignore them, African independent churches incorporated them into new understandings that were often syncretistic. Nevertheless, these churches stand as stark proof that rapid evangelization and church planting can take place under African leadership without dependency on foreigners.

Political Independence and Mainline Churches

The colonial period could not last forever, and the question for Christian missions was whether they could adapt to a changing political situation. Even if the mainline denominations were the first to change, this did not mean that change was quick or easy. Nathan Goto noted that during the colonial era:

The conspicuous missionary presence in the primary decision making process impeded the development of top level African leadership ... Issues of fear and insecurity, control and prestige, blurred the vision of many missionaries with respect to the future of the Church on the African continent ... The African was trained to be a dependent person. (1994:21)

Goto added that it took "over fifty years to produce an African graduate in the Methodist Church in Rhodesia, and fifty-nine years to have Africans appointed to responsible positions in administration" (1994:22). Stephen Ndlovu noted that it took almost that long for the first Africans to be ordained in the Brethren in Christ Church, and this coincided with the time when "missionaries began to accept the culture of those around them and learned better how to relate" (1997:76-7).

For the Methodist Church, Goto emphasized that the turning point in interracial issues came with the arrival of Bishop Dodge in 1956 (1994:22). Ralph Dodge was an American Methodist missionary who had already served in Angola since 1936, where there had been a "nonracially-segregated society" (Dodge 1986:115). He arrived in Zimbabwe determined to change entrenched missionary attitudes, because he noted that American missionaries "ate in separate dining rooms during Church conferences" (1986:117), and used their own vehicles while African pastors boarded buses. Because of his long experience in Angola, he was aware that change would come to Zimbabwe. He wrote, "The major blind spot of the total missionary program in Africa may well be the failure of white church leaders to foresee the approaching rebellion and to train nationals for administrative responsibilities" (1986:153).

Dodge immediately set out to transfer power and authority in the Methodist Church to Africans when Prime Minister Ian Smith was declaring, "not in a thousand years" would Zimbabwe be ruled by a black man (1986:153). Ironically, the first black prime minister in 1978 was Bishop Abel Muzorewa, whom Dodge had appointed as the first African Methodist bishop. For his racial activism, Dodge was declared a prohibited immigrant by Ian Smith's government in 1964. His African church members, however, were delighted, saying, "You have made the government recognize the position of the church. They are afraid of us" (1986:155).

The time had arrived when African Christians were demanding more control of their own churches as African nationalists were demanding greater control of their own nations. Now, in the words of Orlando E. Costas, the "world … is fed up with foreignness, imperialism, and colonization and is searching for life in terms of her [sic] own historical, cultural, social, economic, and political realities" (1974:163).

Thus, as political independence approached, the impact of Christian missions seemed to be greater in the secular realm than in the spiritual. Evangelical missionaries had adopted methods that produced ineffective evangelism and promoted dependency, because the churches that were planted were not indigenous. Furthermore, political changes were on the horizon.

In these political changes, mainline denominations were probably in a better position to adapt than either evangelical groups or the government. Oliver noted that these missions, "under constant pressure from their headquarter organizations, proved much more adept than colonial governments at transferring power to African leaders" (1991:212). This is not to say, however, that change came easily.

With the rising tide of anti-colonialism and anti-imperialism in the developing world, more missionary leaders of mainline denominations followed the example set by Bishop Dodge. They began to realize that they were on the wrong side of a changing political landscape, as it appeared that they had sided with colonial masters against the oppressed. Emerito P. Nacpil stated that the younger generation in developing countries was no longer fond of Western missionaries:

> When they see a missionary, they see green—the colour of the mighty dollar. They see white, the colour of Western imperialism and racism. They see an expert, the symbol of Western technology and gadgetry. They see

the face of a master, the mirror of their own servitude. They do not see the face of a suffering Christ but a benevolent monster. (1971:359)

Two factors caused the mainline denominations to cut back on foreign missions with the coming of political independence. First, they were under increasing pressure from emerging African church leaders to hand over control of local churches. Second, they were losing interest in evangelism. Mission was now seen as liberation of the oppressed rather than as salvation of sinners. Adrian Hastings noted the denominations that cut foreign missionary programs at the time of political independence in Africa were "precisely those bodies whose commitment to missionary work is anyway seriously diminishing" (1976:23). The time of the prominence of Western missionaries seemed to be fading rapidly as colonialism ended.

Conclusion

The heyday of Christian missions to Africa coincided with the era of high imperialism when Europeans began to assume that Africans and indeed all their subjects around the world were incapable of self-government. In that historical climate, missions became paternalistic and the indigenous principles expounded so clearly by Venn and Anderson were cast aside as too idealistic. For example, in India in 1908, an indigenous pastor referred to Venn's concept of foreign mission as temporary scaffolding for the construction of an indigenous church. He protested that Indian churches had been "taught to admire the ornate and ornamental scaffolding and to look upon that as the permanent structure" (Houghton 1983:219). Rare indeed was the missionary of that era who implemented the Three-Self formula; those who tried, such as Bishop Alfred Tucker in Uganda, found their plans undermined by fellow missionaries.

The missionary trend of those years was to establish mission stations as rural outposts of European civilization in competition with ancient tribal structures. Missionaries actively worked for European control through colonial governments so that they might receive government support for their aims. These aims included Western education and medical treatment, in addition to evangelization. Evangelism focused on the youth and attempted to extract them from their culture. Missionaries hoped for colonial government support for both education and for their proposed legislation against tribal marriage customs. Governments, however, came to use missions to teach secular education that would produce semi-skilled workers, but they did not approve of tampering with traditional marriage for fear of unrest.

The long-term impact of mission stations was to secularize rural Africans who flocked to the missions for education and health care, but continued to resort to African traditional religious customs. Paul Hiebert summarized, "In much of the world, people welcomed the schools and hospitals that were brought by missionaries and that were based on science, but rejected the gospel and the church. Consequently, modern missions often became a powerful secularizing force" (2008:154-5).

Inadvertently, missions promoted African nationalism as they acted as a bridge between traditional Africans and the modern world, promoting democratic values such as the worth of each individual. Many African political leaders were first educated on mission stations and some were even clergymen. As a result, many Africans viewed Christianity as a liberating but secular ideology, and they engaged it for the perceived benefits.

For Africans who desired a deeper spirituality, Christian revivals often spawned African independent churches (AICs) instead of producing people movements for the mission churches. These AICs were mixtures of Christianity and folk religions, but the largest of them proved that Africans could administer and finance well-organized, growing churches with active missions, something that the mission churches seemed far less capable of sustaining.

As political independence swept across Africa, mainline denominations belatedly decided it was time to indigenize. But this form of indigenization often amounted to withdrawal of foreign missionaries leaving behind dependent churches and institutions. They were dependent because they had relied too long on foreigners to manage them and because they were of foreign design, with little input from local Christians. Naturally, there was an indigenous backlash against western domination both in nation-states and in churches.

For many people in mainline denominations, the time of Western missionaries seemed to be passing, because those missionaries were seen as too closely identified with colonialism. Both from the mission field and from the sending churches, the cry came up, "Missionary, Go Home!" (Scherer 1964).

4

THE CALL FOR A MORATORIUM
ON MISSIONARIES

T HE CALL FOR WESTERN MISSIONARIES TO GO home evolved from a mixture of motives, including the general backlash against colonialism and imperialism, the loss of interest in direct evangelism, and the desire for greater self-hood of emerging churches in the developing nations. A primary motive was the desire to end the crippling dependency of African churches that had relied for too long on Western missionaries for life support. Nigerian E. Bolaji Idowu questioned "whether what we have in Nigeria today is in fact Christianity, and not in fact only transplantations from a European cult" (1965:1). He predicted that "the inherent urge to freedom and self-expression which resides in a man will bring about rebellion against any form of bondage" (1965:41).

In Congo, Kikama Kividi called on his fellow Baptists to recognize their "mission station mentality" and "to challenge the foreign and expensive model of church inherited from the missionary era" (1999:237). Mutombo Mpanya identified dependency as the basic problem of churches in Central Africa, and he expanded on the types of dependency that the mission station mentality had produced. In church administration, people were campaigning for office rather than reaching consensus through long discussion in the African way; in finances, people were fighting to reach the top levels of leadership to have access to foreign funds; in personnel, Africans seemed resigned to the fact that their destiny would always be in the hands of foreigners; in programs, the African churches simply maintained the institutions founded by missionaries; and in theology, Africans could not relate their faith to their traditional African background (1978:117-22). The need to end such dependency was at the heart of the call for a moratorium on Western missionaries and funds.

John Gatu's Moratorium

In 1971, John Gatu, General Secretary of the Presbyterian Church of East Africa, issued a now famous call for a moratorium on foreign missionaries and foreign funds. This call was repeated at Lusaka, Zambia, at the All-African Conference of Churches in 1974 (Hastings 1976:22). The aim was to give African church leaders time and space to decide their own priorities as they took stock of what the missionaries had bequeathed them. Glenn Schwartz called this bold action a "unilateral declaration of independence" (1989a:12), suggesting it to be a parallel political action to Ian Smith's in wresting Zimbabwe from British control. Schwartz indicated that, as a result of the moratorium, the Presbyterian Churches of East Africa began to build their own buildings, pay their own pastors, and do their own outreach (1989a:12).

Gatu's extreme stance, however, alarmed his fellow Africans who feared that the moratorium would isolate them. Mpanya warned, "The solution is not independence as it may be possible to think, but interdependence" (1978:117). Gatu himself saw the moratorium as the best route to interdependence. Alan R. Tippett quoted Gatu:

> True selfhood might be better achieved through a period of independence, rather than by a gradual modification of existing patterns. Thus the moratorium would be a dynamic process leading to true partnership and interdependence. Any initiative for a moratorium should be taken by "receiving" churches. (1973:275)

Therefore Gatu intended for the abrupt nature of the unilateral moratorium to send a strong signal about the African desire for self-hood to all parties.

Wade T. Coggins noted that Gatu influenced the 1974 International Congress on World Evangelization at Lausanne, Switzerland (1974:7). Some of Gatu's ideas were incorporated into the final draft of the Lausanne Covenant: "A reduction of foreign missionaries and money in an evangelized country may sometimes be necessary to facilitate the national church's growth in self-reliance and to release resources for unevangelized areas" (1974:7). This covenant framed the issue in terms of the needs of the unevangelized world, recognizing that past missionary patterns of operation had tied up much-needed resources in order to cater to dependent national churches. The issue of dependency was finally recognized as widespread in the developing world and as detrimental to world evangelization.

African Reactions to the Moratorium

Pius Wakatama wrote his views of American missions based on his own experience and in reaction both to John Gatu's call for a moratorium and to the Green Lake Conference on church-mission tensions, held in 1971 at Green Lake, Wisconsin (1976; Wagner 1972). Wakatama was converted to Christ and educated at a mission station in Zimbabwe. He graduated from Wheaton College in Illinois and later returned to Zimbabwe to teach at a Christian college.

He noted that in Zimbabwe, "there was a marked employer/employee relationship between the missionary and the pastor" (1976:31). He agreed with Gatu that "the American dollars crippled indigenous initiative and saddled the churches with expensive programs which they can never dream of financing themselves" (1976:36-7). Citing the New Testament example of interchurch cooperation to alleviate specific needs, Wakatama acknowledged that wealthier churches should assist poorer ones, adding "However, this [New Testament] assistance did not carry with it the crippling paternalistic control which often follows some missionary largess today" (1976:37). Furthermore, he criticized the Green Lake Conference despite its timeliness because "it was an Americans-only conference ... [Thus] the structure of this conference reflected the same paternalism and short-sightedness which makes some nationals call for a moratorium" (1976:106). He claimed that the nationals most affected by the issues were not included in the discussion, so it was another case of missions deciding the course of action without consulting the national churches.

On the key subject of the moratorium, however, Wakatama differed from Gatu, calling only for a "selective moratorium" (1976:11). By this, he meant highly qualified missionaries were still needed "to meet specific needs, especially in the area of training nationals at a higher level" (1976:11). The Nigerian church leader, Byang Kato, took a similar position in opposing the moratorium. He also called for the training of nationals: "The training of national leadership should have the overriding consideration. In this aspect, theology is being given the top consideration ... At this initial stage, ... a number of nationals must be sent abroad for sound evangelical scholarship" (1972:199-200). As evangelicals, both Wakatama and Kato opposed the moratorium on biblical grounds that the Great

Commission has "only one limitation ... We should go until the end of the age" (Wakatama 1976:20).

The Meaning of the Moratorium

The call for a moratorium could be misconstrued to mean that the age of missions is over. The wording of the Lausanne Covenant in response to Gatu's proposals instead reflected evangelical determination to maintain or increase the level of evangelism (Coggins 1974:7). Evangelicals were skeptical of any interpretation of the moratorium that would redefine mission work. Tippett objected to replacing "missionary" with "interdependence," "if it reflects the current mood of reaction against the biblical idea of mission" (1973:277-8).

While Gatu was apparently operating with genuine motives of developing self-hood in East African churches, others picked up the call for a moratorium for other reasons. Mainline denominations combined it with rhetoric that changed missions from evangelism to political and social liberation. This was reflected in the wording of the resolution that came out of the All-Africa Conference of Churches (AACC) in Lusaka in 1974:

> To enable the African Church to achieve the power of becoming a true instrument of liberating and reconciling the African people, as well as finding solutions to economic and social dependency, our option as a matter of policy has to be a moratorium on external assistance in money and personnel. (Coggins 1974:8)

Coggins noted that "this call has proved very attractive to some large denominational missions that are already in trouble because lay revolt against their radical political adventures has dried up a large part of their missionary resources" (1974:8). Peter Wagner also said that some mainline denominations were "using the moratorium proposal as a smoke screen to hide some much more fundamental problems in their missionary programmes" (1975:170). Halting classical Western missionary work was the agenda for these denominations, but this was unacceptable for evangelicals.

The suspicion also arose that the call for a moratorium meant a reduction in missionaries only, but not in funds. It became apparent that the AACC general secretary, Burgess Carr, viewed the moratorium as "a demand to transfer the massive expenditure on expatriate personnel in the church in Africa to programme activities manned by Africans themselves" (Wagner 1975:167). This amounted to a rejection of missionaries but not Western funding, an idea that was to gain prominence.

Some African evangelicals, on the other hand, opposed the moratorium out of fear of cutting the umbilical cord that tied them to the Western churches. For example, S. O. Odunaike stated, "We completely resist the idea of a moratorium on missionaries in Africa. How can we talk like this when our own governments are actively soliciting economic, technical, and educational aid from overseas?" (Wakatama 1990:128). Long-term dependency was not going to be easily overcome by mere resolutions.

In effect, the moratorium signaled that times had changed. The postcolonial world demanded new missionary approaches, as the incompatibility of Western dominance and indigenous initiative in leadership was recognized. Lesslie Newbigin stated emphatically:

> We are forced to do something that the Western churches have never had to do since the days of their own birth—to discover the form and substance of a missionary church in terms that are valid in a world that has rejected the power and influence of the Western nations. Missions will no longer work along the stream of expanding Western power. They have to learn to go against the stream. (1995:5)

The whole concept of missions from west to east or north to south was changing, since the unevangelized appeared to reside everywhere. Furthermore, the missionary force now came from everywhere, as emerging churches from the developing world began to take the call to self-hood and world evangelization more seriously. It was now missions to and from all six continents. David Howard has analyzed the history of the modern missionary movement in three stages: the era of dependence during colonialism (1793-1945); the era of independence from the end of colonialism until the calls for a missionary moratorium (1945-1974); and the current era of interdependence (1974-present), dated from the Lausanne Congress where Christians from all six continents committed themselves to planting churches among the 2.7 billion unreached peoples (1997:27-8).

Evangelicals assessed the moratorium for its effect on the progress of world evangelization. Wagner admitted that while his initial reaction to the moratorium was negative, he later decided:

To the degree that a moratorium on missionaries facilitates the fulfillment [*sic*] of the Great Commission of our Lord, it should be supported by Bible-believing Christians ... The reverse equally holds; if a moratorium on missionaries hinders the progress of world evangelization, it should be opposed. (1975:165)

He concluded that a moratorium would help in four areas. "There should be a moratorium on missionaries who 'continue to indulge in theological and ethical imperialism, ... are dedicated to paternalistic interchurch aid,' and 'on unproductive missionaries'" (1975:171-4). In short, Wagner argued for a change in the missionary attitudes that had caused the call for a moratorium. A new kind of postcolonial missionary was needed for world evangelization to succeed.

Evangelical Churches in the Postcolonial Period

Despite the discussions surrounding the call for a moratorium, in actuality it had little impact on evangelical missionaries. As Adrian Hastings noted, conservative Christian organizations "tend to reject the appeal [the moratorium] out of hand as theologically unjustified: the obligation to preach the gospel is an absolute one which cannot be abandoned on any grounds" (1976:23). In fact, as political independence approached and mainline denominations began to downgrade their missions, there was a veritable flood of new missionaries from evangelical and Pentecostal backgrounds into Africa. For example, the German evangelist, Reinhard Bonnke, began to hold mass crusades all over Africa with great success. Steve Brouwer, Paul Gifford, and Susan D. Rose commented, "Both Bonnke and TBN [Trinity Broadcasting Network] are contributors to a Protestant wave of conversion in Africa," which they estimated at 20,000 conversions a day (1996:151).

Brouwer, Gifford, and Rose calculated that by the 1960s nonecumenical evangelical missionaries outnumbered mainline Protestant missionaries, and "these new missionaries to Africa are normally not working in development or schools or clinics; the vast majority are concerned with evangelism pure and simple" (1996:153). A shift was starting to occur among evangelicals in the postcolonial period as they began to turn away from the old mission station approach toward more evangelism and church planting. Missionaries perceived that large institutions required so much care that they could be a hindrance to evangelism. Moreover, governments had assumed the role of providing education and health care, so the original need for missions to provide such services was now fading, and missionary strategy could shift back to the priority of evangelism. Despite this shift in missionary thinking, many other old colonial patterns of thinking remained. American missionaries came from the richest and most powerful nation in the world, so it was hard for them to think of the African churches as equal to American churches. Furthermore, they perceived that the African population continued to have enormous needs that they could help to meet. Brouwer, Gifford, and Rose observed:

Although the missionaries often claim they are working for the local churches or networks, or are "partners" with them, one must make full allowance for the disparity of resources and education. The missionaries and the pastors they link with do not meet as equals; and the effect of this on the Africanness of the African churches needs to be researched. The claim that churches are "independent" or "autonomous" may sometimes disguise foreign influences that are increasing rather than diminishing. (1996:153)

Leslie Goffe of the British Broadcasting Corporation was similarly shocked by the implication of large-scale American missionary intervention. He warned, "Africa is being colonised and Christianised all over again. The colonisers this time are Americans, not Europeans, and the brand of belief they are bringing to Africa is Evangelical Christianity" (2005:11). He emphasized that the growth in the number of converts from 17 million in 1970 to 125 million, which was 19 percent of the population, has "not come by faith alone. Evangelicals have won the hearts and minds of people by building thousands of churches, medical clinics, HIV/AIDS centers and schools across the continent" (2005:12). He quoted a Ugandan, "This is not so much a colonising of land as it is a colonising of the mind" (2005:12).

In 1962, the Evangelical Fellowship of Zimbabwe (EFZ) was established. According to Frans J. Verstraelen, its purpose was "to express unity, fellowship, and combined action among churches and organizations of evangelical persuasion, ... [especially] the promotion of effective evangelism and church growth" (1995:192). In the 1980s, the EFZ adopted Jim Montgomery's Discipling a Whole Nation (DAWN) program, which was called Target 2000, in Zimbabwe (Verstraelen 1995:198; Montgomery 1989). Target 2000 consisted of an evaluation of the current status of evangelical churches in Zimbabwe and setting a goal to plant new churches until every Zimbabwean could be within walking distance of an evangelical church. Verstraelen noted that Target 2000 adopted a goal of planting "10,000 new churches by the year 2000, ... the minimum numbers of churches needed to put a church within easy reach of every person in the country" (1995:198).

What alarmed Verstraelen was the participation in this effort of what he called New Religious Movements (NRMs), defined as "a special brand of Christianity largely from the fundamentalist stream ... Most of these groups are American of origin and reflect views espoused by the Religious Right in the United States of America" (1995:193). He claimed that "the NRMs have mushroomed in Zimbabwe as from 1982," citing Campus Crusade for Christ, Youth With a Mission, World Vision, Christ for All Nations, Rhema, and Jimmy Swaggart Ministries as examples (1995:193). He criticized these and other similar missionary groups: "With their strong foreign orientation and foreign control they represent a rather neo-colonial type of mission which seems to be anachronistic in the post-independence era of Africa" (1995:194). He characterized NRMs as teaching dispensationalism, a prosperity gospel, and a dualism of simplistic alternatives that "ignores all political and economic factors affecting the lives of the people" (1995:199). By dualism, he meant the emphasis on conversion to Christ as opposed to the more complex transformation of society. Conservative evangelists gave potential converts the simple choice of accepting Christ or rejecting him without being instructed in how to impact their society. He claimed to reflect the view of the Symposium of the Episcopal Conferences of Africa and Madagascar, or SECAM, which stated that simplistic dualism "is hardly calculated to promote self-help, self-reliance, self-esteem, self-determination, responsibility, and autonomy" (1995:199).

Although Verstraelen may have been an alarmist, he emphasized an important issue—that Zimbabweans are susceptible to the lure of American prosperity that is sometimes embodied in current missions. American missionaries from conservative evangelical and Pentecostal groups have now taken the lead in Zimbabwean missions. Yes, they did move away from establishing the institutions traditionally associated with mission stations, focusing instead on evangelism and church planting. However, their position of financial strength unwittingly contributed toward continued dependence of local churches on foreign funds, particularly because of the rapid decline of the Zimbabwean economy.

Economic Collapse in Africa

One of the general trends of postcolonial Africa as a whole has been economic decline. Joseph E. Stiglitz and Lyn Squire showed that per capita income in sub-Saharan Africa declined steadily from 1970 to 1995 to about US $500 per annum. By contrast, per capita income in East Asia climbed dramatically from about the same starting point as Africa in 1970 to about US $2,500 by 1995 (1998:143). Zimbabwe is no exception to this trend of increasing poverty. Since independence in 1980, Zimbabwe's socialist government has concentrated on "rectifying the social and economic inequities of Zimbabwe's colonial past" (Grant and Palmiere 2003:215). Initially, "in the 1980s Zimbabwe experienced some of the most rapid improvements in health, nutrition and population indicators in all of sub-Saharan Africa ... However, while social indicators improved, per capita income stagnated" (2003:215).

By the early 1990s, the poor performance of the Zimbabwean economy led the International Monetary Fund to sponsor the Economic Structural Adjustment Program (ESAP). Grant and Palmiere said that the economy grew at an average rate of one percent every year during ESAP from 1991 to 1995 (2003:215). At the same time, persistent severe droughts and the HIV/AIDS epidemic took a heavy toll on the economy.

Patrick Johnstone and Jason Mandryk noted that these factors plus military adventures into the Democratic Republic of the Congo and the seizure of many white-owned farms from 1999 to 2000 have sent the economy into free fall. Over 60 percent of the population is unemployed; poverty and malnutrition are steadily rising. The HIV virus has infected over 25 percent of the adult population, causing 700 deaths a week and creating nearly a million orphans in a country of only about twelve million people (2001:689-90). Life expectancy has plummeted and many who die young are skilled and semi-skilled workers. As a result, whatever gains in health care and education for the masses were made in the 1980s have been reversed. Grant and Palmiere's comment about HIV/AIDS sufferers is now applicable to the general population: "Tea, bread, sugar, mealie meal—the very staples of life—have indeed become scarce luxuries. Access to basic health care, school and shelter are in jeopardy" (2003:238).

Throughout the first decade of the twenty-first century, Zimbabwe's economy continued to plummet dramatically. From being the breadbasket of the region, the country experienced starvation and disease with record high inflation. *The Economist* reported in 2008:

Cholera sweeps across the country. Mass hunger looms: the UN's World Food Programme reckons that, in the new year [2009], it must provide food for 5.5 million in a population that has shrunk, through disease and emigration, from about 12 million probably to less than 9 million ... The local currency is worthless, so swathes of public services have ceased to function. Zimbabweans have been reduced to subsistence (some survive on roots and berries), barter, and remittances and handouts from abroad. A true humanitarian disaster beckons. (2008:17)

Into this rapidly increasing poverty, American missionaries have entered with their ample resources. Such a situation invites dependency. Brouwer, Gifford, and Rose noted:

Given Africa's phenomenal economic and social collapse, and the state of dependency this has created, Africans are vulnerable to resourceful outside interests that radiate success, professionalism, and enthusiasm. Thus the continent has become receptive to a new form of Christianity that derives primarily from the United States. (1996:151)

Like Verstraelen, they were alarmed at the spread of American fundamentalism, and they included Pentecostals, charismatics, and Southern Baptists in this category. They claimed that this Christian fundamentalism "rivals Islamic fundamentalism in its global scope and is very likely more potent in its cultural influence" (1996:2). The frightening aspect for them was that "Christian fundamentalists in the United States ... also believe in the Manifest Destiny of their country, in the God-given right to get rich, and in the necessary preeminence of U.S. military power" (1996:10).

The temptation in this situation is for African churches to seek an American partner. Brouwer, Gifford, and Rose claimed:

In their poverty, pastors and churches have been reduced to writing to U.S. churches in an effort to establish links with them—which most often means offering to become the African branch of the American church. ... In all these mergers (more correctly, given the economic reality, buyouts) the overriding motive seems financial. (1996:155-6)

They openly wondered what the convergence of American Manifest Destiny with the Christian desire to fulfill the Great Commission would produce in places like Africa: "What does this portend? Actual conquest, the literal extension of U.S. frontiers and direct political control? Or something different, something new in the annals of cultural conquest?" (1996:247).

American missionaries in Africa almost automatically seem to be preaching a prosperity gospel even if this is not their intention. The economy is so bad and the scale of dependency is so deep that a missionary with means is seen as a potential financial benefactor. In such a situation, missionaries need a strategy just to avoid adding to dependency. This is why forming true partnerships between American missions and African Christians is so difficult. Douglas Waruta called the situation "a new scramble for Africa" (1997:24), likening the current influx of new foreign missionaries to the aftermath of the Berlin Conference of 1884-1885. He continued, "Sadly, these new religious groups are contributing to a new form of slavery, more devastating than the literal enslavement of Africans in the past. Yet Africans are embracing them with zeal, especially when they have the promise of financial advancement" (1997:24-5).

Conclusion

John Gatu's call for a moratorium on foreign missionaries and funds in 1971 marks a historical milestone in mission history as the symbolic dividing point between colonial and postcolonial models of mission. For the first time, Africans in mission churches spoke out forcefully about the need to take charge of their own churches and programs. The dependency syndrome had been brought to international attention. That fact was recognized at the 1974 Lausanne Congress on World Evangelization as evangelicals officially noticed the damage dependency could cause to the spread of the gospel when they incorporated Gatu's ideas in the wording of the Lausanne Covenant.

Although Gatu himself did not envision a permanent break between Western and non-Western churches, others took the moratorium to imply potential isolation in worldwide Christianity and the possible termination of mission itself. While mainline denominations interpreted the moratorium in various ways that produced a reduction in the Western missionary force and a reinterpretation of the meaning of mission, evangelicals could not envision such drastic changes. For them, the Great Commission remained as it had always been and, ignoring the moratorium, they took advantage of the withdrawal of mainline missions to flood the developing world with new Western missionaries.

The timing of this new influx of missionaries coincided with the end of colonialism, just as Christians of the developing world were trying to take control of their churches and institutions. Western evangelicals, however, still operated predominantly under the colonial mindset of cultural superiority. As they pursued their main objective of evangelization, they also witnessed massive human need in the developing world and used their abundant resources to alleviate these needs. This ensured that dependency would continue unabated into the postcolonial period.

Despite the end of colonialism, Western dominance continues through the allocation of resources. The colonial legacy of dependency continues unwittingly through well-meaning missionaries who desire to help churches in the developing world. Financial domination has replaced colonialism with the same debilitating effects on the initiative of emerging churches. Dependency prevents such churches from having a positive role in the spread of Christianity. Thus, dependency has not only failed to disappear in the postcolonial period, but has become even worse. How and why does this happen in practice? Real-life examples of the dependency syndrome at work in southern Africa and South America may help to explain some of the reasons behind this complex problem.

5

THREE CASE STUDIES IN
DEPENDENCY

———————

THIS CHAPTER DEMONSTRATES HOW DEPENDENCY CAN CREEP into missionary work for many practical reasons. Some dependency is, of course, the result of colonial mission methods as the first case study illustrates. In this case, once precedents are set, change is difficult, so that colonial problems continue into the postcolonial period, sometimes indefinitely. In other cases, missionaries are warned of the dangers of creating dependency, but still apparently cannot avoid it. The second case study illustrates this and is a personal confession, as the story is that of my own mission work. Finally, some people groups are so isolated from the outside world that they are highly susceptible to becoming dependent once Westerners enter their domains. The third case study illustrates this problem, showing that the desire to protect and help such peoples may produce dependency.

These case studies are presented not with the desire to cast blame on missionaries or their methods, but to learn the subtlety of the dependency syndrome from actual situations so that remedies can be found. We begin with the work of Southern Baptists in Zimbabwe. The kind of bitter experience described here has helped to shift missionary policy of this denomination away from methods that create dependency.

The Baptist Convention of Zimbabwe

Southern Baptist mission work in Zimbabwe (then called Southern Rhodesia) began in 1950. The churches planted came to be called the Baptist Convention of Zimbabwe. Clyde Dotson was the pioneer missionary for Southern Baptists in Zimbabwe; he and his wife arrived around 1930 when Dotson was only twenty-four years old, working under another mission and using colonial mission methods (Dotson n.d.:27). Dotson acknowledged the validity of the famous Three-Self formula: "The ultimate aim of all mission work is the establishment of self-propagating, self-supporting, and self-governing Christian churches." He understood this, however, to be a long and difficult process in Africa where "the powers of darkness do not vanish immediately when the Light of the World comes." It could therefore be "the work of a lifetime, or in some areas of several lifetimes" (n.d.:46). Dotson considered that both medical and educational work would be essential in this process.

The fact that Dotson perceived mission work as a gradual process of changing the African worldview through Western medicine and education is not surprising, as it was the method followed by virtually all missions in Zimbabwe. Dotson was, however, more of a spiritual giant and zealous evangelist than most missionaries. Following a long period of service with another mission organization, Dotson worked briefly as an independent missionary. During this time, he established an extensive network of allies, evangelists, and churches in several Zimbabwean towns. He had also already secured the site for a permanent mission station. By 1950, he had persuaded the Southern Baptist Foreign Mission Board to accept responsibility for mission work in Zimbabwe, and to appoint his family as the first Southern Baptist missionaries there (Dotson n.d.:67). Now the Baptist Mission could begin funding these rapidly growing projects.

As the Baptists started to pour new missionaries into Zimbabwe, Dotson's leadership and methods were naturally adopted. Baptist Mission historian Davis Lee Saunders commented:

> In the beginning period, the dominant role was played by Dotson, in lieu of a mission organization. Most of the decisions relative to both funds and plans were conducted by personal correspondence with Richmond [Virginia, headquarters of the Foreign Mission Board]. (1973:83)

At first, the Baptist Mission supported all pastors and schoolteachers and owned all church buildings. The rapid expansion of the work was a testimony to Dotson's zeal. Within little more than a decade, the Baptists established a school, hospital, seminary, and publishing house as well as numerous churches. For each church planted, the Mission would be responsible for constructing the church building and hiring a pastor.

This method of church planting, however, required the missionaries to be paymasters. Saunders noted that, as early as 1954, "the missionaries worked out a carefully balanced system of grading for pastors, including a centralized method of equal subsidization of salaries and allowances complete with salary scales and terms of service" (1973:86-7). The system conformed to the colonial model that placed the white man in charge and perceived the African church leader as an employee.

At this stage, it seems clear that the local churches gave nothing to their own pastors, because the Annual Meeting of the Baptist Mission of 1957 asked: "Is it time for our churches to start giving gifts to the pastors?" The decision was taken that local churches should indeed start giving, with gifts for their pastors to "be paid in to the mission and paid to the pastor as part of his regular salary" (Reese 2005:85).

Such a system was destined to create friction between missionaries and the local pastors and converts, since the local Christians had so little authority in running their own churches. Furthermore, the winds of political change were blowing in southern Africa, as Africans began to demand an end to colonial domination. This indicated to the missionaries also that their role would need to change with the times. They had started to see that indigeneity was a preferable system to the one under which they were operating. Indigeneity implied the Three-Self formula, so subsidy for local pastors would have to be terminated.

Saunders noted that the Baptist Mission, meeting in January 1960, "presented a ten year plan whereby all organized churches would become responsible for the salary of their pastors within that period" (1973:95). Neither the Mission nor the churches, however, fully appreciated the pain that the phase-out of subsidy would cause. A 10 percent reduction per annum spread out over ten years seemed fairly painless and reasonable. The Southern Baptist Convention in the United States saw the Ten Year Plan as significant: "The national pastors of the churches of Southern Rhodesia [Zimbabwe] agreed upon a new plan of church support in which the local congregation will increasingly assume full responsibility for the pastor's salary" (SBC Annual 1961:167).

At the same time, the Mission was also intent on the formation of the indigenous Baptist Convention. In September 1963, the Baptist Mission magazine, *The Commission*, reported that representatives from thirty-nine churches attended the inaugural annual meeting of the new Convention in July that year (1963:31). Announcing the impending formation of the new Convention, the Southern Baptist Convention Annual noted:

In a significant step toward full self-support, all Rhodesian [Zimbabwean] pastors were made directly responsible to a local congregation and any financial assistance on pastors' salaries granted from mission funds will be channeled through the local church, rather than being paid directly to the pastor. (1963:144)

The Baptist Mission was intent on moving toward indigenous, self-supporting churches; the churches themselves were not so eager.

In 1964 the new Zimbabwean church leadership conveyed some questions to the Baptist Mission, asking for joint meetings to discuss the Ten Year Plan. The missionaries replied, "The Mission E. C. [Executive Committee] does not wish to have any combined E. C. or Mission meetings with the Convention E. C. to discuss matters relating to the 'ten year plan' of the Mission or the one proposed by the Convention E. C." (Reese 2005:89). This implies that the Ten Year Plan was a unilateral decision by the Mission with major reservations coming from the Zimbabweans.

The Commission of September 1964 reported that at the Zimbabwean Convention's annual meeting in July that year, President Abel Nziramasanga complained, "Whereas we have had showers of blessing in the past, today we are having showers of stones" (1964:31). Saunders noted that this partly referred to the tense political situation, but "primarily to an awareness of the full impact of the ten year plan" (1973:98). Relations between the Baptist Mission and its daughter Convention were heading toward a deeper crisis; the Convention rejected the Ten Year Plan and offered its own plan instead.

The Convention's plan recognized the importance of the Four Selfs—self-government, self-propagation, self-support, and self-expression—as the goal for the local churches. The Convention stated, however, "We believe the local churches need more time in which they receive financial assistance from the Mission in order to improve their organization through training the membership and assembling their resources" (Reese 2005:90). In principle, the Convention and Mission agreed on the ultimate goal of indigeneity, but disagreed on the timing. The Ten Year Plan made the Convention feel it was being forced prematurely into indigeneity.

By November 1965 the gulf between Mission and Convention was widening. Convention leaders had complained to H. Cornell Goerner, the regional secretary of the Foreign Mission Board, that the missionaries "refuse to cooperate and ...

do not know our customs" (Reese 2005:90). These missionaries asked Goerner to explain to the Convention leaders that:

> If missionaries leave, the money for their salaries will not go to the pastors; … that when subsidy is decreased the money does not go into the pockets of the missionaries; … that at the end of ten years the missionaries will not leave. They will continue to give financial help in building, etc. (Reese 2005:91)

Missionaries were trying vainly to rectify some misconceptions held by Africans. Apparently, leaders of the Convention were already calling for or expecting the departure of all Baptist missionaries, and were contemplating the possibility of receiving the funding that had been allocated to them. Missionaries, for their part, asked Goerner to clarify that they were not personally benefiting from the reduction in subsidies to local pastors, nor were they leaving and that, even if they did, their salaries would not be transferred to the Convention. For his part, Goerner urged the missionaries to dispel the rumor that they were "throwing away the pastors" (Reese 2005:91). The Mission and the Convention were headed toward a complete rift.

The Southern Baptist Convention Annual of 1966 reported this rift with some understatement:

> Rhodesian Baptists experienced growing pains. Officers of the recently established Convention of Central Africa were voted out and replaced by a new set who proved to be somewhat non-cooperative toward the Baptist Mission. The basic issue was the Mission's policy of subsidy reduction and insistence that the churches gradually become self-supporting. Communication between convention leaders and missionaries was made more difficult by the nation's political crisis. (1966:147)

This last reference was to the 1965 Unilateral Declaration of Independence made by Ian Smith's white government against the colonial power, Great Britain. This served to fuel African nationalism further and to underscore the grievances Africans had for the ill-treatment they had received at the hands of white people.

Despite the growing tensions, Goerner had some success in mediation between the two groups. He proposed that the executive committees of the two bodies meet. The missionaries agreed to this proposal, provided that such a meeting would focus on "the purpose of planning simultaneous revivals." The Convention expressed a desire to meet, but "pointed out that there could be no true and lasting revival until first there was a clearing up of misunderstandings between the Mission and the Convention" (Reese 2005:92).

With a broader agenda, then, the two Executive Committees met in December 1966. The Ten Year Plan was cited as the main cause of the breach between the groups. The Convention representatives described that plan as unilateral, unbiblical, and unworkable. They claimed, "It was planned by the missionaries for the people; the Mission and churches did not plan together." The missionaries countered, "The Mission was doing harm to the churches by continuing full support of the pastors." They described the financial help offered under the Ten Year Plan as a gift and emphasized, "The giver has the prerogative to decrease his gift" (Reese 2005:92). The goal was to have churches that would be financially independent, and reconciliation between the two groups would make the plan more workable. This meeting achieved enough common ground that the two parties could consider moving beyond the Ten Year Plan and focus instead on promoting stewardship and joint revivals.

By 1968, the Convention and the Mission had agreed to go ahead with a joint evangelistic campaign that year, with a similar nationwide effort scheduled for 1970. *The Commission* of February 1969 reported on the campaign and noted the observations of one of the revival speakers, S. M. Lockridge, an African American pastor from San Diego:

> The missionaries are doing a tremendous job, but the nationals have to be motivated, and when one does see the light, the rest of them often discourage him and hold him back. They tend to be dependent. They don't take hold of responsibilities too fast … They are afraid to venture out on their own. They seem to need somebody over them so that "If I fail, he can pick me up." I noted that very strongly. (1969:2)

Lockridge also noticed, approvingly, the fact that the local churches were copies of Southern Baptist churches in America: "In Africa, all that they know about the church and Christianity was handed to them by Southern Baptists, and naturally they just pick up Southern Baptist ways" (1969:2). Essentially, he was acknowledging that the Convention was nonindigenous and dependent. Despite the progress toward reconciliation, it appeared that the initiative for joint efforts still came primarily from the Mission.

Meetings held in 1969 confirmed that the Convention was having difficulty raising funds from its local churches. Out of its forty-four churches, however, twenty-one were listed as self-supporting, with twenty-six Zimbabwean pastors active (Reese 2005:93). Missionaries were urged to help motivate local churches to support their Convention. In 1969, a Joint Study Committee of the Baptist Convention and the Baptist Mission began to meet to explore ways of greater cooperation.

The local pastors seemed to resent the "parallelism" of Convention and Mission committees, saying they should merge. When a missionary replied that parallelism was necessary "because work is being supported by American money," a local pastor then said, "Until the Ten Year Plan is complete, it seems unlikely that the working together will be effective." Another added, "The Mission is satisfied with money—they have it, but the churches do not have it." When a missionary reiterated that the goal was to build indigenous churches, a local pastor responded that this could only be possible if the Mission dissolved committees that overlapped the functions of Convention committees. "Missionaries who would be members of the churches within the Convention can be elected to committees by the Convention." This sounded like a call for the Convention to absorb the Mission, at least in areas where their concerns overlapped. While the missionaries regretted the way that they had started the Convention, the local pastors regretted that "our churches were prematurely loaded with indigenous responsibility before they had been prepared to carry the load" (Reese 2005:94).

The dependency syndrome rendered the Zimbabwean Baptist churches powerless to decide their own future. They rightly saw that as long as the Baptist Mission held the purse strings, their own efforts to indigenize would be thwarted. True indigeneity would necessitate the removal of mission oversight and transfer of responsibilities to local churches. Yet they also could see no way to fund their own efforts apart from subsidies coming from the United States.

Subsidy to pastors was phased out as scheduled in the early 1970s. More evangelistic campaigns were carried out, and the Convention reported improved relations with the Mission in 1972. New churches were planted; by 1974, the Convention listed sixty-three congregations with 8,816 members and thirty local pastors (Reese 2005:95). The questions remained: What would be the long-term effect of the prolonged crisis of the Ten Year Plan? Would the phase-out of subsidy succeed in its goal of producing indigenous churches? What would be the future relationship of the Mission and the Convention?

Although subsidy to pastors had ended, various other subsidies continued for a long time. A contributing factor was the deteriorating political situation of the 1970s, when many rural church buildings were damaged or destroyed in the guerrilla war that led up to independence and majority rule in 1980. The Annual Meeting of the Baptist Mission of Rhodesia of 1976 indicated the existence of a disaster relief fund, which was used to assist the Convention during those troubled years (Reese 2005:95). In 1977, the Joint Study Committee of the Baptist Convention and the Baptist Mission indicated that "not enough progress has been made in turning over more of our Baptist work to Nationals" (Reese 2005:95). At that meeting, a local pastor moved:

> That the Baptist Mission seriously consider the rapid nationalization of our total Baptist work in Rhodesia. To be included in this nationalization are such vital matters as transportation for Nationals and better communication between Nationals and missionaries. (Reese 2005:95-6)

Even in 1985, Mission documents indicated numerous subsidies. Periodic droughts in Zimbabwe had resulted in a plan called "People Who Care" that assisted with food distribution, well-drilling, nutrition, and a revolving fund to pay for seeds. Churches continued to request and receive loans from the Mission. The Mission listed the following capital needs that it intended to supply to the Convention: a duplicating machine, a copy machine, ten church buildings, eight pastor's houses, a pastor's pension scheme, and an educational farm (Reese 2005:96).

The seminary in Gweru continued to be a focus of subsidy and remains on Baptist Mission subsidy at the time of this writing. In 1976, the Mission initiated a policy of full student support, under which students paid only for their own food, clothes, personal items, and any hospital fees. In 1985, the seminary sought accreditation from the Accrediting Council for Theological Education in Africa, but this was initially withheld pending approval of a constitution which included a "proposed change in the board structure to include more representation from the convention" (Reese 2005:96). Evidently, missionaries still dominated the seminary's board.

In a visit to the seminary in July 2004, I was told that the Convention had not yet received the title deeds to the seminary property. In October 2004, I verified this at the International Mission Board in Richmond, Virginia, and was told that the Baptist Mission continues to give a subsidy to the seminary that is on a decreasing scale to end in 2012 (Reese 2005:96-7). Isaac Mwase, in a provocatively titled article, "Shall They Till with Their Own Hoes?," castigates the International Mission Board for relegating the seminary to a low priority at a time when the Zimbabweans were still unable to "get the job done" on their own (2005:74). He cites the personal hardships this has forced on the current seminary principal, Henry Mugabe (2005:75).

Thus, once the subsidy was introduced, it proved difficult to terminate. This is the first legacy of the original subsidy and of the Ten Year Plan that sought to phase it out. Various circumstances such as wars, natural disasters, and economic decline combined with the compassion of missionaries to prolong subsidy in various alternate forms. Once dependency had been set as a pattern, it became hard to eradicate.

In 2004, I interviewed a few of the Baptist pastors who had been affected by the Ten Year Plan. Johane Neganda became pastor of the Gutu Baptist Church in 1965, but he could not remain there when the Ten Year Plan reduced his salary steadily. Neganda said that the church members in Gutu still have difficulty supporting a full-time pastor because they are farmers who reap a harvest once a year. He moved to another church which had no mission subsidy, but the area missionary was a member of his church and supported him personally in various ways. Neganda stated that although he worked well with that missionary, in general, the missionaries did not treat him as an equal. He summarized, "In speaking, they said that we are equals. But physically, especially financially, we were second class. If you go against the missionary who is your local church member, he may withdraw his offering" (Reese 2005:97). Neganda insisted, however, that the phase-out of subsidy was good for the Convention, because the Zimbabweans have taken ownership of their own churches, learned to give, and have now achieved indigeneity.

In Bulawayo, I met with Pastors Hugo Bonda and Moses Hlabano, both of whom said they were compelled by the Ten Year Plan to seek secular employment. Hlabano said the subsidy phase-out made life hard and forced him to be a weekend pastor. He regretted the inability to travel for evangelism, as he had to leave some earlier contacts stranded in outlying rural areas. Bonda claimed that some area missionaries helped him personally during the Ten Year Plan and even afterwards. Both men, however, said that they still had "no power" (Reese 2005:98). They pointed to urgent repairs that their church facilities needed and said that they would welcome outside help even today.

Thus, the second legacy of the Ten Year Plan is the painful memory it has left with all who were involved in it. I contacted missionaries from that time who uniformly acknowledged that the local pastors opposed the plan and felt a sense of betrayal at the hands of the missionaries. One missionary said:

> For the most part they felt betrayed and rejected by me, as one of the missionaries of the Baptist Mission. I personally never felt severed from them ... I believe the underlying fear of the pastors was dependence upon the churches, rather than the mission. They had felt security in being "employed" first as evangelists and later as pastors. (Reese 2005:98)

The missionaries also said that they enjoyed warm personal relationships with local pastors on an individual basis, and it seems clear that some of them found ways to cushion the effects of the Ten Year Plan through personal gifts to local pastors. Overall, however, the Ten Year Plan damaged working relationships between the missionaries and local pastors, especially those at the national level of leadership.

The third legacy of that plan is that relations between the Mission and the Convention have never fully recovered. One missionary family said, "The relationship between the Baptist Mission and the Baptist Convention was not good when we arrived in 1972 and it was not good when we left in 2001" (Reese 2005:99). Gordon Fort, who was the Regional Leader of the International Mission Board for Southern Africa from 1996 to 2004 based in Harare, confirmed that the relationship remains strained. He described the current missionary role as "respond as requested," whereby the Convention may request anything and the missionaries respond but take no initiative in Convention affairs (Reese 2005:99).

Stan May, a church planting missionary in Zimbabwe from 1989 to 1995, experienced the continuing rupture between the Convention and the Mission. His family's missionary service was prematurely ended through the loss of their work permit; work permits of twenty-four other Southern Baptist missionary families were likewise terminated between 1995 and 1996. May stated that a pastor who had become embittered during the Ten Year Plan gained a position with the Zimbabwe Immigration Department, and was then instrumental in reducing Southern Baptist missionaries on the field from thirty-four units down to only nine units (Reese 2005:99). May did not see this punitive action as merely the work of one disgruntled man, but as typical of a number of pastors who had been adversely affected by the Ten Year Plan and who had come into positions of leadership in the Convention.

The fourth legacy of the Ten Year Plan is that, despite progress toward becoming independent, the Baptist Convention of Zimbabwe remains dependent. While the seminary in Gweru is the central focus of dependency, it can also be seen in local churches, such as in the appeals of Bulawayo pastors for outside help to repair church facilities. The Baptist Convention of Zimbabwe remains more of a "receiving" denomination than a "sending" one. The original pastor subsidy alone does not fully explain the Convention's current dependency, since short-term missions and "partnerships" have also contributed to it, but it set a tone that the Ten Year Plan was unable to eliminate.

Important lessons are available from such stories, but some assume that these are lessons from bygone days. The problems the Southern Baptists faced resulted from the use of colonial paradigms just as colonialism ended. This caught them unprepared for the rising aspirations of African Christians. They first tried to subsidize everything for the churches they planted and then tried to withdraw subsidies selectively without thorough consultation with African church leaders. Throughout the implementation of the Ten Year Plan, the missionaries remained in the driver's seat, deciding what the next step for the Zimbabwean churches was going to be. Zimbabweans felt forced to accept their decisions because power and money was in the missionaries' hands, not theirs. Now that colonialism has ended we are in a position to avoid such mistakes. The next case study shows, however, that things are not that simple. Unfortunately, dependency remains a key issue long after colonialism ended because money and power still often reside in the missionaries' hands.

The Zimbabwe Christian Fellowship

My own missionary career did not avoid the problem of dependency despite our mission team's training in indigenous principles. We could not use the excuse that we were hampered by past traditions from colonialism. In fact, we were better trained in terms not only of seminary training, but also cultural awareness, by comparison with previous missionaries in our tradition. We knew to avoid the pitfalls of mission stations, schools, hospitals, and institutions so that we could concentrate on planting indigenous churches.

We focused on the Ndebele-speaking people in the province of Matabeleland around the city of Bulawayo, Zimbabwe. They were listed as unreached (Dayton and Wilson 1983:306). It later turned out that they were not unreached despite what our research in the United States had shown, but it was true that they were at their most receptive to the gospel in their entire history. We spent our first year learning the Ndebele language and culture and tried to delay entering into church planting until that phase was complete. But so many opportunities to start churches abounded that we were drawn prematurely into church work before we knew the local language and customs. This alone caused us to create some dependency.

An African evangelist had barely started a new church among a group of squatters on the edge of Bulawayo when he had to move away. He begged us to help make this motley group of new believers, who met for worship under a tree, into a viable church. So we jumped in fairly unprepared, although we did have considerable help from two other African evangelists who proved extremely reliable.

The first mistake we made and learned from was motivated by charity. As squatters, the Christians were very poor and lived in appalling conditions without running water or proper sanitation. Few of them had normal jobs and most were family groups. With good backing from our sending churches in the United States, we began to distribute free used clothing to all church members. We were not prepared for the fights that this caused. Some would complain that they received only a blouse while someone else received a dress. Jealousy and envy erupted among the new believers because of old clothing. We expected them to be grateful to receive anything, but we were simply ignorant of their mindset. When we started charging small fees for the clothing, however, all the fighting ceased.

We had a distinct advantage, with regard to avoiding dependency, over the Southern Baptists in that we were few in number as missionaries and therefore lacking in resources ourselves. Furthermore, we incorporated Zimbabweans on our Mission Board early on, to the extent that local Christians slightly outnumbered us. While this comforted us, it did not fool Zimbabweans who knew that real power rested with us. This came out, for example, at one of our board meetings in 1989, when we recorded that a Zimbabwean board member "stressed that decisions should be made jointly, and independent action avoided" (Reese 2005:102). The Zimbabweans knew that we held the purse strings and this inclined us to act independently.

With our lack of resources, we could only pay salaries for two evangelists and a secretary in the early stages. The justification for supporting evangelists was that they would soon become self-supporting with healthy churches behind them. We called this policy "priming the pump." By this we meant that mission funds could be used temporarily in limited ways to launch church work that would become healthy and indigenous later. While this showed the caution with which we approached the issue of dependency, in reality we were fooling ourselves.

As the Southern Baptists found out, temporary subsidies have a way of becoming permanent. And to date, there is no church among those we helped to plant that fully supports a pastor or evangelist. As Johane Neganda noted in the above Southern Baptist case study, rural churches in Zimbabwe, and probably elsewhere, will in all likelihood never be in a position to support full-time seminary trained pastors because they reap one harvest per year. Even urban churches must often rely on bivocational pastors. This is not the tragedy that we have made it out to be, and it should be embraced, as bivocational pastors or evangelists are entirely appropriate in many settings. Church workers who make their living like other people have increased credibility when people realize that they work for Jesus without any pay incentive. This was after all the case in New Testament churches, and it did not hamper indigeneity or strong growth at all.

The first of several crises in our mission work erupted in 1991, when some Zimbabwean church leaders decided it was time for a local church board to start taking over functions of the Mission Board. Minutes of a Mission Board meeting in February that year indicate that the missionaries had questions about this local initiative supported by one the Zimbabwean board members, Matthew Mpofu.

Mpofu was a forceful leader who had launched his own ministry to Bulawayo industries and he had considerable experience in several Christian organizations. There was concern that the proposed church board would duplicate the role of the Mission and that premature movement to self-government could lead to the rise of a bishop system as stronger local leaders like Mpofu exercised authority over less experienced leaders. Mpofu replied by reminding the Mission Board that churches were simply seeking greater cooperation and fellowship among the various congregations (Reese 2005:103).

In hindsight, several things are clear. The missionaries who feared the rise of an African "bishop" were already operating as bishops and continued to do so. Second, missionaries feared losing their own position if their roles were taken over by local people. What would they do? Could they continue with independence of action if they were subservient to local leaders? On what basis could they remain as leaders? Such concerns made it difficult to see that what the local leaders were proposing was a positive development that the missionaries could embrace and encourage. After all, the goal was to establish healthy indigenous churches.

Despite whatever misgivings the missionaries had, and some often heated meetings, the result of these discussions was the formation of the Zimbabwe Christian Fellowship, an association of churches that the missionaries and evangelists had planted. Through a series of meetings attended by delegates of all the churches, a constitution was forged that might prevent the rise of bishops through granting local congregational autonomy. On the other hand, a National Committee of seven leaders was also incorporated in the constitution to represent all the churches nationally.

During this process, Glenn and Verna Schwartz arrived at Mpofu's invitation to speak at his annual conference for industrial chaplains. Just before the Schwartz' arrival, Mpofu handed me a paper that Schwartz had written, entitled "Church and Mission in Central Africa: A Missiological Study in Indigenization" (1989a). It reminded me of all the basic principles I had learned from people like Venn, Anderson, Allen, and McGavran. Now that the Schwartzes were staying in our house during the conference, we had time to talk with them in depth about the transition we were going through. We invited them to talk to our Mission Board about some issues we faced because of the handover from mission to church.

Two years earlier, we had acquired a small farm to be used as a home for destitute elderly people. The impetus for this purchase came from two of our Zimbabwean board members who commenced to operate the home. Now at this critical moment when local churches were forming an association, the question arose about the relationship of the farm to the Zimbabwe Christian Fellowship. At our board meeting in September 1991, Glenn Schwartz advised that "the Farm [should] become a separate organization with its own Board and Constitution" (Reese 2005:104). Schwartz indicated that church leaders should focus on church issues, not the running of charitable organizations. Those who had the vision for and expertise in operating such organizations should run them. In that way, the farm property would never make its way onto an agenda for church leaders.

This solution adopted by the Mission Board was a relief to the Zimbabweans dedicated to helping the elderly who came from various nations and were destitute without the usual African extended family to help them. Now they could have a rural home that resembled African village life where they could farm if their health permitted, and they could receive medical attention and regular meals.

The founders of the home had worried that the formation of the Zimbabwe Christian Fellowship might mean arguments with church leaders over the use of the farm where the home was located. Now there were no further worries about the home's future.

Schwartz' advice proved sound. By taking the farm out of the discussion regarding the Zimbabwe Christian Fellowship, it has never been a subject for debate by church leaders. It continues to operate as an indigenous home for the elderly with no foreign funds or oversight. Schwartz' other advice, however, was not so easy to implement because it touched directly on the lives of the missionaries. He advised that the time was right for the mission to dissolve so the local churches could take full responsibility for all church matters. With some mixture of excitement and reluctance, the missionaries agreed to dissolve the mission after a transition period.

The Zimbabwe Christian Fellowship was thus established in 1991 with twenty-four member churches and a constitution that made membership voluntary and decisions nonbinding, while missionaries remained as advisors. The concepts of voluntary membership and nonbinding decisions were more American in origin than African, as Africans usually come to consensus by discussion and then expect universal compliance. The aim was to prevent the rise of a bishop system of church government. And although the mission technically dissolved, the missionaries continued to control the finances of the National Committee through subsidies for operating expenses. The new Fellowship had no assets other than the offerings of its own member churches and the subsidies of the missionaries.

Subsidies and greed proved to be the undoing of the arrangement worked out between the missionaries and the Zimbabwe Christian Fellowship. Since missionary subsidies dwarfed the contributions made by member churches, this meant the missionaries remained in effective control even without any constitutional authority. A series of severe droughts in the 1990s helped to ensure that local churches did not expand their giving to the National Committee. The droughts of 1992 and 1995 encouraged more foreign subsidies instead, which in turn encouraged fraud and corruption, although this went undetected until 1999.

In 1999, a series of crises rocked the young association of churches. The missionaries had noted the lack of success of the National Committee at raising funds locally. Indeed, it was becoming evident that the local churches had little confidence in their national leadership. When the missionaries brought this to the attention of the National Committee, it provoked a confrontation. At a meeting in May 1999, the national leadership raised the question, "Who owns ZCF [Zimbabwe Christian Fellowship]? Is the ownership of ZCF still under the missionaries or who?" (Reese 2005:105).

The missionaries, who did not attend that meeting, had already responded to this question in a letter, since a delegation from the National Committee had informed them of the agenda in advance. In this letter, the missionaries agreed that "lack of ownership at the grassroots is correct," indicating that local churches had lost confidence in the national leadership. They also sensed a loss of vision at the national level: "Vision cannot be delegated or owned by simply being placed in a position by others ... Vision comes to one man, but if it is to be successful, others must catch the vision and fulfill it" (Reese 2005:106).

In their May meeting, the National Committee responded to this letter as follows: "It was observed that vision cannot be delegated; however, the work of the vision can be delegated. Has the work been delegated? It is observed that the Father owns the vision but ownership of the work is not yet clarified" (Reese 2005:106). Here, the Zimbabwean leaders used the word "Father" to indicate the missionary who founded the work. They perceived the missionaries' letter to mean that the founder's vision was not being carried out satisfactorily by the Zimbabweans. They in turn complained that the missionaries were continuing to hamper their freedom of action in running the churches.

The founding missionary referred to himself as "Father" in the follow-up meeting in June, where he announced his intention "to work as a Father in the church and not a donor as previously done" (Reese 2005:106). He intended to reestablish a role for missionaries by changing the constitution to include them as spiritual fathers of the Zimbabwe Christian Fellowship. By describing his current role as a donor, he meant that he was becoming redundant in the national leadership apart from the funds he provided. Personally, I felt it was retrogressive at this stage to amend the constitution to reinsert missionary leadership over the Zimbabweans. Thus, the crisis of 1999 created divisions not only between the National Committee and the missionaries, but also between the missionaries, who now proposed differing plans .

My plan noted that "the national level of ZCF leadership is almost totally divorced from the district level of leadership." For me the cause was too much missionary subsidy: "Excessive missionary funding has deprived the districts of input at the national level, and hampered indigeneity." The solution was obviously that missionaries should "cease funding day-to-day, month-to-month expenses of ZCF ... [so that] only what the districts approve and fund will henceforth be operational" (Reese 2005:107). From my visits to rural churches, Zimbabwean leaders were telling me that money donated to the national leadership was not benefiting their churches as intended. Clearly something was wrong, yet the missionary money kept coming as usual. If foreign resources are terminated, then any possible corruption would cease and those interested in illicit gain would have no reason to continue in office.

The founding missionary responded to my proposals by saying that finances were only a "presenting problem" (a surface expression of a deeper problem) to the real issue of the leadership crisis at the national level. He complained that the current constitution placed missionary leaders outside normal channels of influence and relegated them to being donors. He admitted that the missionaries were partly to blame because of "excessive giving of money ... and inexperience with denominational structures and transitioning phases, [which] caused them not to lay the proper foundation for a truly indigenous church." His solution was to constitutionalize the role of missionaries as "Founding Fathers" who "will provide national initiative, strategy and spiritual authority within the Fellowship" (Reese 2005:107-8). He sensed the need to take back the reigns of control to hold the Zimbabwean leaders accountable.

This controversy was upstaged by the discovery of two men in the principal leadership roles of the National Committee who were systematically diverting funds intended for drought relief and other projects to their personal use. Ironically, these two were themselves being subsidized by missionary funds. They had been tasked with raising funds from member churches as well as with distributing subsidies. Since they had performed neither of these tasks, the local churches had lost confidence in the national leadership in general. Once this corruption was uncovered, both men were suspended from their positions at a meeting of all the ZCF churches in August 1999 (Reese 2005:108).

This revelation of financial fraud temporarily delayed any attempt to change the ZCF constitution, as Matthew Mpofu assumed the chairmanship of the Fellowship under the existing constitution for another twelve months. In a later interview, he acknowledged that the full revelation of the financial dealings between the missionaries and the two men accused of fraud became a turning point in his own desire to cooperate with the missionaries (Reese 2005:108-9). It thus proved difficult for the missionaries to work with the Fellowship effectively after the revelation of fraud.

After twelve months of Mpofu's leadership, the founding missionary decided to resume his quest to regain control of the leadership because of his frustration of trying to work under existing conditions. He won approval of the churches to become chairman and to rewrite the constitution as he had earlier proposed. Thus, almost nine years after the mission had "dissolved," missionary control of the Fellowship returned. The mission had not died after all!

The first result of renewed missionary control was a division in the Fellowship. Predictably, Mpofu withdrew the local church and two other urban churches with some rural churches they had planted followed his lead. To date, all of these churches remain outside ZCF. Meanwhile, the founding missionary was chairman of the Fellowship for only two years. Although he invited me to take an official position in the Fellowship, I declined and returned with my family to the United States in 2002. By 2004, all missionaries associated with the Fellowship had left Zimbabwe, and the association was under indigenous leadership.

In 2004, shortly after he left Zimbabwe, the founding missionary issued an assessment of the Fellowship: "They are functioning independently, making tough decisions on discipline, training, district help and revising the way they look at leadership. All these are signs of a fellowship that will go on without missionaries." Despite that progress, he acknowledged that the Fellowship remained dependent on outside funds, which he was donating regularly for travel to outlying districts and for leadership training seminars. He cited the harsh economic conditions in Zimbabwe as the main reason the local churches could not pay for these things (Reese 2005:110-1).

ZCF continues to emerge from a traumatic period that involved excessive missionary subsidies, financial fraud by its top leaders, reinstitution of missionary control, and division of the Fellowship. All of this weakened the young Fellowship, so that new church planting virtually ceased even as dependency on outside resources was fostered. The withdrawal of missionaries began to help the Fellowship to grow toward maturity, but it remains dependent at the time of this writing.

Such painful experiences are what prompted me to research and write about the dependency syndrome. One of my personal goals is to help ZCF move out of dependency, but I know only too well how easy it is to foster dependency unintentionally. The next case study from a very different part of the world also illustrates this point.

The Waodani Churches of Ecuador

The story of the five martyrs of Ecuador is so familiar that it need not be repeated in detail here, but can just be summarized briefly. In 1956 Waodani Indians (sometimes spelled "Huaorani" and formerly called "Auca," which means "savage") killed Jim Elliot, Nate Saint, Roger Youderian, Pete Fleming, and Ed McCully in the jungles of Ecuador when the North Americans landed their Piper airplane on a sandbar of a small river trying to make initial missionary contact with the Indians. Subsequently Elisabeth Elliot, wife of Jim, and Rachel Saint, sister of Nate, moved into Waodani territory with the help of Dayuma, a Waodani woman who befriended them (Wallis 1960). In this way they were able to share the gospel with those who had slain their husband and brother. Since the women were not as threatening as the men, and as they conveyed forgiveness for the killings instead of revenge, the gospel made a positive impact on the Waodani and churches were established from converts. Several of the killers of the five missionaries became Christians in what is now one of the most famous stories of modern missions.

Although Elisabeth Elliot returned to the United States after a few years, Rachel Saint continued to live with the Waodani, working on the translation of the Bible into Waodani under the Summer Institute of Linguistics (SIL). This coincided with efforts by oil companies to explore and drill for oil in parts of the Oriente Province where the Waodani lived. As nomadic hunter-gatherers, the Indians needed huge tracts of forest for survival if they were to retain their traditional means of living. The Ecuadorian government and oil companies constructed roads and moved in oil workers and other colonists, putting pressure on the Waodanis' habitat. The government gave SIL the right to create a reservation for the Waodanis, in part of their former territory in the late 1960s, to remove them from areas that would be subject to oil exploration, as well as from the possibility of violent confrontation with oil workers. Rachel Saint and Dayuma became, in essence, the guardians of the Waodani who chose to live on the reservation at Tiwaeno.

According to Rosemary Kingsland, the 160,000 hectare reservation was called "Dayuma's Auca [Waodani] Protectorate" (1980:121). Several major Waodani groups remained outside this protected zone, which was just a tiny fraction of their former territory. Continued pressure from oil exploration then opened the possibility of moving these non-Christian Waodani groups onto the reservation. Kingsland remarked, "The oil companies looked to the government, the government looked to the military, and the military looked to Rachel Saint" (1980:126). David Stoll said, "The companies, the government and the Summer

Institute found each other the solution to a shared problem" (1982:292). In other words, since the government desired revenues from oil, and the oil companies desired to explore for oil on land occupied by the fierce Waodani, the solution of letting the SIL take them to Saint's reservation seemed like a "win-win" situation for everyone. The question was how to attract non-Christian Waodani to the reservation peacefully.

Alvin Goffin said that techniques used to draw the scattered jungle Waodani to Tiwaeno included "flying over, dropping gifts, and talking over loudspeakers" (1994:69), somewhat similar to what Nate Saint had done to make the original contact with the Indians. Stoll put it bluntly: "Trade goods, kin ties and romance—bands seeking spouses from other bands—were the bait which drew the rest of the Huaorani into dependence" (1982:293). By 1971, about half of the Waodani population resided at Tiwaeno, with the majority being non-Christian (Goffin 1994:69).

When journalist Jerry Bledsoe visited Tiwaeno in 1971, he observed "once wild Aucas wearing oil company T-shirts and caps" (Goffin 1994:71). This indicated the financial backing of oil companies for the resettlement efforts, as well as attempts to change the nomadic ways of jungle Waodani to a more sedentary life. Since the state retained mineral rights even within the reservation, the continuous interaction between the oil companies and the Waodani tended to create dependency. Stoll reported, "Soon every house [in Tiwaeno] had a corrugated roof except for Rachel Saint's" (1982:300).

Saint's fellow missionary, Catherine Peeke, wrote regretfully about the reservation:

> What are a few machetes and kettles compared to the unrestricted game reserve they have always enjoyed? And we are offering them unknown territory for known, a foreign land instead of home, dependency for self-sufficiency, subjection to outside powers instead of resistance, and hunger where there had been plenty. (Stoll 1982:296)

The effort to maintain Christian influence on the reservation created understandable tensions. Kingsland reported that Christian girls were sometimes raped by non-Christians and became pregnant as a result; indeed, the whole concept of rape as evil was absent from traditional Waodani culture. She claimed that because of Rachel Saint's strict approach to morality, these young women were so afraid of becoming unwed mothers that some attempted to drown their babies and one committed suicide (1980:127).

In addition to moral clashes, a polio epidemic swept through the community which now lived more closely together and was thus more exposed to foreign diseases. The non-Christian Waodani blamed the crippling and deaths caused by polio on witchcraft and some fled the community back into the jungles (Stoll 1982:297). Efforts were made to bring them back to the reservation, along with the remaining Waodani still roaming the territory outside the Tiwaeno enclave.

Goffin reported that SIL began to be uncomfortable with Rachel Saint's leadership of the Waodani community. She "had become increasingly autocratic in her control of Tiwaeno, and the SIL's main governing body found this difficult to accept" (1994:72). The SIL was uneasy about the Waodani's dependency on Saint and on outsiders in general. For her part, Saint tried to keep others out of the reservation to avoid creating dependency, seeing herself as one of the Waodani. She maintained that it would be dangerous for any male colleague to reside with the Waodani at Tiwaeno, and the mission had begun to doubt this (Goffin 1994:72).

Consequently, the SIL sent an anthropologist, James Yost, to investigate the suspected missionary paternalism on the reservation in 1973. Goffin noted, "Saint did not welcome Yost; she feared that he was setting up her departure" (1994:72). While Yost noted many improvements in the quality of life for the Waodani, especially in the reduction of violent death, he was critical of Rachel Saint's supervision of the Indians. He found that life on the reservation under direct missionary control had caused extensive economic dependence. According to David Stoll, "Yost soon learned that Huao [Waodani] anxiety over outsiders vied with a consuming passion for trade goods" (1982:303). Bilingual Waodani, like Dayuma, had set up a "hacienda" system of patronage to distribute goods from outsiders with less sophisticated Waodani in return for labor (Stoll 1982:303).

When Yost determined that new arrivals in the colony were losing weight, he urged the cessation of flying in new Waodani to settle in Tiwaeno. Furthermore, he urged groups of Waodani to consider leaving the reservation, but none would because of the fear of losing trade goods (Stoll 1982:304). Finally, out of concern that the experiment at Tiwaeno might actually lead to the demise of Waodani culture, the SIL decided to terminate the venture, at least temporarily. Goffin noted, "[A]ll the SIL members were pulled out for a while as the first step in reducing Huaorani dependence on the organization" (Goffin 1994:73). The SIL forced Rachel Saint into retirement in 1976 "as she rejected the antidependency campaign of her fellow workers" (Goffin 1994:73), and withdrew its support for the reservation. Stoll noted, "The Huaorani would have to be left alone to figure out their problems by themselves" (1982:304).

Saint went to reside in Quito, refusing to leave Ecuador for long, despite being seriously ill. When Kingsland visited her there, she found her at an impasse with SIL over her role with the Waodani. Saint admitted, "Twenty years ago I started to translate the Bible into Auca. I've been sidetracked by helping the people. It seems I helped them too well, at the sacrifice of my prime work. My translations are way behind" (1980:162). She nevertheless yearned to return to the jungle where she felt she truly belonged with the Waodani.

Don Johnson, the Director of SIL in Ecuador, disapproved of Rachel's desire to go back to Tiwaeno: "Rachel Saint can't stay with these people for ever … They must be self-sufficient" (Kingsland 1980:162). According to Kingsland:

> The SIL say that the people of Tiwaeno must learn to get along without missionaries and outside help once the New Testament has been translated into their tongue. They must learn, once again, to look after themselves and to expect nothing from the outside world, not to be dependent on the Americans who have introduced cattle, new crops, fowl, clothes and medicine, and who made them dependent on those things in the first place. (1980:158)

When Kingsland visited Tiwaeno, she found Dayuma awaiting Rachel's return and wondering why the SIL refused to give the Waodani free medicine any more (1980:172, 183). Stoll added, "Dayuma and her confederates were incensed that Saint had been taken away and their main trade goods channel cut off" (1982:304). The SIL continued to wean the Waodani off their former privileges, however, and lack of food and support made life on the reservation increasingly difficult. Eventually the protectorate collapsed, dispersing the Waodani once again into the jungles. Rather than return to their traditional way of life, however, "contrary to the anthropologist's hopes, the Huaorani continued to relocate to maximize their contacts with the outside world" (Stoll 1982:305).

Ironically, it was the SIL who eventually lost this struggle rather than Rachel Saint. Goffin claimed that the ongoing rift between Saint and SIL, plus general Ecuadorian resentment over the granting of land for the Waodani in the first place, resulted in the temporary expulsion of SIL from the Oriente Province in 1981 (1994:74). Saint, however, decided to return to the area and continued her work

We don't know what would have happened if Rachel Saint had stood idly by.

with the Waodani. Maxus Energy Corporation of Dallas, Texas collaborated with Saint, since the directors were evangelical Christians. Maxus signed a "Friendship Agreement" with the Waodani in 1993 and began to provide many social services in exchange for the right to explore for oil on their land. Maxus supplied medical and dental care, educational materials, schools and clinics. In addition, they employed indigenous men and offered gifts to leaders. Joe Kane commented:

> As part of the deal that allowed the company to develop oil in the Huaorani territory, the Ecuadorian government had essentially put Maxus in charge of Huaorani health and education—much as it once had the Summer Institute of Linguistics. The government's bureaucrats had a dozen different ways to justify this, but the heart of the matter was that they were only too happy not to have to bother with the Huaorani. (1996:161)

When Rachel Saint died in 1994, the Waodani Christians asked Nate Saint's son, Steve, to come back to live with them in the jungle. Although Steve had spent time with the Waodani as a boy and had even been baptized by their Christian leaders, he had since become a businessman in the United States. Upon his return to Ecuador, he sensed the Waodani Christians had become dependent on outsiders to an extent that made him reluctant to live among them. By comparison with the vitality he remembered among them in the 1960s, by the 1990s they had now decided there was little they could do for themselves. Saint said:

> I was not surprised that the tribe felt threatened by oil companies, environmental groups, and the government. It was a major surprise to me, however, to find that they also felt threatened by all of the benevolence they were receiving from Christian missions and relief organizations. (2001:18)

Particularly in church leadership, Saint noticed the Waodani had changed from commitment to passivity. Saint remarked that the Waodani churches were "less able to govern themselves as believers when I went down in the mid-90s than they were in the early 60s when I was there. That's a travesty" (Wood 1998a:12). The reason was the intervention by well-meaning North American Christians on their behalf during short-term mission trips.

Two types of mission trips in particular had helped unwittingly to create dependency—Bible conferences and constructing church buildings. The North

Americans who conducted Bible conferences furnished rice and sugar to create "a big festive occasion." Since the Waodani could not duplicate this aspect, "they figured this is something that the outsiders do. So they never have a Bible conference of their own" (Wood 1998a:9). Short-term mission teams who built a church building for the Waodani likewise used material and methods beyond the capability of the local people. Saint noted that the result was that for almost two decades after the project, "The Huaorani, to my knowledge, have never built another building to be used for a place of worship" (Wood 1998a:9). They assumed that the style and materials they had traditionally used must be inadequate, so they simply waited for other North Americans to come along and do construction for them.

Saint and his family tried to be sensitive about creating dependency on themselves while they resided in the jungle with the Waodani. Then one day Ginny Saint, Steve's wife, noticed that they were not entirely succeeding despite their best efforts. Steve was in a meeting with the Waodani leaders but was intentionally remaining outside the discussion so that they would take the initiative. Ginny noticed that the Waodani were watching him so intently as they were making a decision that when he grimaced at a passing pig that had feathers in its mouth from eating chickens, they changed their decision to one that they hoped he would prefer! Steve was unaware of this dynamic until his wife pointed it out, but he could see the truth in what she said. As a result, Saint was determined to leave the jungle:

> The only way the [Waodani leaders] would really test their ability to make decisions was for me to get far enough away that they could not access me. I had to be distanced enough that I could not bail them out immediately if they made what seemed like a bad decision to me. (2005:224)

In an era of globalization that allows both greater freedom of travel and wider use of technology, it is not surprising that groups like the Waodani should feel overwhelmed by outsiders. This also means that dependency is common in such cases, even though outsiders have no intention of causing it. Dominant cultures may end up controlling those who seem more passive, and missionaries from dominant cultures may become paternalists without meaning to.

It is for these reasons that Steve Saint committed himself to helping the Waodani come out of dependency by helping them increase their self-confidence in facing the modern world. He understood that he would have to do this from a distance so that the Waodani would find their way into the twenty-first century by trial and error. Therefore he moved his family back to Florida where he established the Indigenous People's Technology and Education Center, or I-TEC. At the Waodani's request, he did research to enable them to have modern dental equipment that they could carry and use in the jungle, as well as a "powered parachute" to fly over the jungle (2001:105-118). This type of experiment was to establish a Waodani economy that could help them cope with the modern world on their own terms.

Without this, the Waodani would find themselves dependent on outsiders for all their needs. This in turn would sideline them in the mission of the church; they would remain recipients of the largesse of North Americans instead of contributors to the cause of Christ.

Multifaceted Dependency

These three cases indicate how multifaceted dependency has become. It results from the use of colonial mission methods, from financial subsidies by missionaries to local evangelists and pastors, from missionary paternalism, from short-term mission teams, and from partnerships between Christian organizations from various countries. It results from attitudes that Christians from dominant countries have towards peoples of other nations. It results from cultural differences and misunderstandings. Above all, it is a spiritual dilemma, indicating a shift of the gospel message from new life in Christ to dependence on materials and technology. It is a basic failure by modern missions to apply lessons on church planting from the New Testament.

In every case, the Christians who caused dependency had good intentions. Compassion often motivated missionaries to help their converts have material benefits along with the gospel. Missionaries wanted to cushion new converts from outside secular forces that might overwhelm them. Guilt over an abundance of possessions led missionaries to seek to shield converts even from the cost of discipleship. They sought to do things for local Christians that the local Christians could have done for themselves; but once the pattern of dependency set in, it was extremely difficult to eradicate.

By providing abundant resources from one central source, missionaries unwittingly fall into what economists call the "resource trap" (Collier 2007:38-52). Economists noted some time ago that countries rich in some valuable natural resource, such as oil, often develop undemocratic governments with weak economies. Paul Collier explains, "The heart of the resource curse is that resource rents [excess revenues] make democracy malfunction" (2007:42). Resource rents allow "the politics of patronage" as opposed to public service projects (2007:44). Two things tend to happen under a system of patronage: those who are corrupt are attracted to political office, and there is no need to tax citizens to support government activities (Collier 2007:46). Crooked politicians rely instead on slush funds from the resource rents to buy votes and influence others without the need to be accountable to their constituents.

In Christian missions, an analogous situation occurs. Abundant outside resources attract unscrupulous people to seek church leadership so that they may gain access to the resources. They then use these resources to set up a patronage system which ensures that they continue in leadership. Meanwhile, average church members are not asked to donate to the central leadership or to inspect what that leadership is doing. Actual dependency may then become strongest among leaders at the national level, while average members are ignored and discouraged from making any contribution.

The tragedy of dependency is that either converts become spiritually lethargic, content to be recipients of missionary compassion, or that they become antagonistic to the missionaries who brought them the gospel when those missionaries try to wean them off subsidies. Both responses, which are typical of the dependency syndrome, produce churches that cannot easily reproduce, since they require continued assistance from outside Christians. Therefore, dependent churches are often prevented from contributing to their God-given role in fulfilling the Great Commission.

We have now seen some of the historical roots of the dependency syndrome and how the syndrome happens in some specific cases. We are aware that various voices advocated methods that would avoid dependency, but they were overridden by historical forces that perpetuated the problem. As missions enter the twenty-first century, new waves of popular mission trends continue to create dependency to the extent that the problem is growing rather than diminishing. These trends include partnerships, short-term missions, and globalization.

6

RECENT ISSUES RELATED TO DEPENDENCY

IN THE TWENTY-FIRST CENTURY, THE GLOBAL CONTEXT for Christian missions has changed dramatically. Colonial empires died out in the twentieth century and have not been replaced. Old paradigms of doing mission are also dying, but new paradigms have not yet fully emerged. In the meantime, Christians from all parts of the globe debate the best postcolonial methods. After all, we are entering uncharted territory, since missions have operated out of a Christendom mentality since shortly after AD 300. By this, we mean that missions have been conducted from the powerful "Christian" nations to the weaker "non-Christian" ones for almost 1,700 years. That power was political, economic, and military. Now that Christendom is over, there is a unique opportunity to return to the type of missions conducted before AD 300, from the weaker Christians to the more powerful pagans.

What are the prominent new paradigms for postcolonial missions and how do they affect the dependency syndrome? This chapter investigates recent mission trends and evaluates them with regard to dependency. The first popular paradigm launched in the aftermath of colonialism is known as partnership.

Partnership and Interdependency

Now that missions have entered the postcolonial period, does this mean that dependency is less relevant? Some mission leaders think so, citing the era of increased interaction among the peoples of the globe as a signal that missions have entered a new phase of interdependency. For them, the postcolonial paradigm for missions is partnerships, and any discussion of dependency is neither necessary nor desirable. For example, Daniel Rickett said, "Let us be done with the debate over dependency. Rather, let us resolve to bathe our partnering relationships in prayer, and to reflect together on our standing in Christ" (2002:35). Paul Gupta, president of the Hindustan Bible Institute in India, agreed, "While colonialism often did lead to cultures of dependency, separation is not of God! The church is the Lord's, and the God of the Bible made the church interdependent, connected in all its parts" (2006:209).

On the other hand, some see the kinds of interaction occurring in the postcolonial period to be remarkably similar to those in the colonial era. From this point of view, partnership is another word for continued paternalism. For example, Ajith Fernando speaks of non-Christian Sri Lankans as believing "a new colonialism has dawned: 'First the Christians came with the Bible in one hand and the sword in the other. Now they come with the Bible in one hand and dollars in the other'" (1999:442). If this is true, then partnerships actually exacerbate the problem of dependency. Those who espouse partnerships not only want to overlook dependency, but also discard the Three-Self formula.

In postcolonial missions, debate lines are drawn between those who continue to advocate the independence inherent in the Three-Self formula and those who advocate partnership and interdependence. Luis Bush and Lorry Lutz said that the Three-Self formula hindered the development of partnership, isolated the indigenous church, and was an overreaction by Western churches: "They failed to apply the biblical principles of 'giving to those in need.' ... With the new era of partnership, the pendulum is swinging back, not to paternalism and dependency, but to helping each other fulfill the Great Commission" (1990:40).

For Bush and Lutz, partnership involved "an association of two or more autonomous bodies who have formed a trusting relationship and fulfill agreed-upon expectations by sharing complementary strengths and resources, to reach their mutual goal" (1990:46). For many, partnership is the new model for postcolonial missions to replace the outdated Three-Self formula. In fact, it is seen as the only model that can complete world evangelization in a short time. Bush and Lutz insisted, "Refusing to partner, particularly with Two-Thirds World churches or agencies, may mark the end of our own effectiveness in the world" (1990:45). This raises two important questions: Is the Three-Self formula no longer useful, and what kind of partnerships should Western Christians form with other Christians?

Is the Three-Self Formula Outdated?

Venn and Anderson used this formula in a colonial setting to set a standard for the emergence of a mature indigenous church that could contribute to missions through self-propagation. Self-support and self-government meant the indigenous church would not continue to need mission resources for its own ministry. Initially, however, it was not envisioned that indigenous church leaders would join the mission. Colin Reed said that between his 1851 and 1866 papers, Venn decided not to allow nationals to become missionaries, as this would remove "some of the most able pastors out of the indigenous church" (1997:7). Wilbert Shenk also noted that Venn and Anderson "redefined 'indigenous church' to be one in which indigenous peoples had become competent to lead an institution that met European standards" (1981:170). That is, they omitted from the Three-Self formula any reference to the local cultural context and called that indigeneity.

Primarily for this reason, some modern missiologists saw the formula as outdated and as a prisoner of its own historical period. William A. Smalley said that the Three-Self formula is a projection "of our American value systems into the idealization of the church ... based upon Western ideas of individualism and power" (1979:35). James Scherer was even more critical:

> The 'three-self' formula for church autonomy accurately mirrored Western Protestant, middle-class, democratic and capitalist values of self-government, self-support and local responsibility. However, it was silent about Jesus' love for the poor and his identification with the marginal and the oppressed. Such persons were viewed more as candidates for missionary charity than as potential members of local 'three-self' churches. (1993:84)

Alan Tippett noted the Three-Selfs should be integrated as principles or they would produce a monstrosity if used separately. He also added other "selfs" to the original formula to include cultural contextualization in the definition of an indigenous church: self-image, to mediate the ministry of Christ in the local environment; self-functioning, as all parts of the body of Christ were present and active in the life of the local church; and self-giving in service to the community with local funds (1979:60-4). He maintained that when all six of these principles were undertaken by a church "of its own volition, when they are spontaneously done, by indigenes and within their own pattern of life, ... then you have an indigenous Church" (1979:64). Paul G. Hiebert suggested a "Fourth Self"—self-theologizing, which is "the right to read and interpret the Scriptures for themselves" (1985:196). In this way, an indigenous church would answer its own questions that arose from its unique context through a process that Hiebert called "critical contextualization" (1985:186).

Beside the deficiencies of the Three-Self formula with respect to cultural indigeneity, Peter Beyerhaus attacked it as unbiblical. He concluded that the formula elevated the self, which the Scripture said should be crucified with Christ, thus possibly creating an evil autonomy within the body of Christ (1979:26-7). Beyerhaus was hinting at the interdependence that should exist among all churches, but which was nonexistent during the colonial period. The partnership that existed among churches in the New Testament was not envisioned by the Three-Self formula.

Harvie M. Conn was likewise troubled by the imbalance created by Western missions among churches worldwide. He cited the collection taken by Gentile converts for the benefit of Jewish believers in Jerusalem as a sign of interdependence and unity in the early church. With the current one-way flow of money from west to east and from north to south, Conn asked: "Has a cultural pattern made it impossible for brothers to love one another, to fellowship in the gospel? Could it be that, hidden behind mission's present methodology, still lurks an incipient paternalism that is not yet aware of the riches of 'Macedonia's' gifts?" (1978:238). Conn was hinting at the possibility of partnerships between East and West, but the obstacle was that the West could not yet perceive anything of value that the East had to offer.

While many modern missiologists have sought to revise the Three-Self formula because of its blind spots on issues like cultural contextualization and global interdependence, it was a sincere attempt during the colonial period to apply Pauline mission methods to modern missions. Melvin L. Hodges defended the formula, saying, "The promoters of indigenous methods really are calling for following New Testament church principles that will establish an on-going, thriving church—not dependent on foreign help" (1972:44). The question was how to apply Pauline methods to the current situation in world missions. Would it be better to stress indigenous principles, or to form partnerships, or some combination of both? Those who stressed indigenous principles, like Hodges, also stressed the need to avoid dependency so new churches could mature. Hodges insisted that concentrating on self-support alone was a faulty strategy, since self-propagation was the real goal:

A people trained in, and accustomed to, dependency do not overnight adjust to responsibility ... Money does not convert an indifferent group of Christians into an active soul-winning-evangelizing force. It takes the presence and power of the Holy Spirit to do this. (1972:44)

Those who stressed partnership as the new paradigm, like Bush and Lutz, also stressed the need to complete the Great Commission quickly and cheaply. They also could claim to be following Pauline methods, since Paul stressed interdependence among churches new and old. But what kinds of partnerships were actually being formed?

Partnerships: The Ideal versus the Actual

Partnerships in missions are desirable. As early as 1956, Max Warren described an ideal partnership that would consist of three essential components—involvement, responsibility, and liability: "The essence of partnership is that it is a relationship entered upon in freedom by free persons who remain free" (1956:13). Those who have emphasized partnership in missions have also used ideas from Stephen R. Covey about interdependence being a step up in maturity above dependence and independence (Fretz 2002:213). Covey stated:

On the maturity continuum, dependence is the paradigm of *you–you* take care of me ... I blame *you* for the results. Independence is the paradigm of *I–I* can do it; *I* am responsible; *I* am self-reliant ... Interdependence is the paradigm of *we–we* can do it; *we* can cooperate. (1989:49)

He added, "Interdependence is a choice only independent people can make. Dependent people cannot choose to become interdependent. They don't have the character to do it; they don't own enough of themselves" (1989:51).

Those who apply this thinking to missions agree that partnership should be among equals. Bush and Lutz stated:

Partners desire to be recognized as equal in selfhood and potential for maturity in Christ ... Partnership avoids dominance of one over the other ... Dominance encourages dependency ... Dependency robs people of opportunity to exercise their gifts and leads to apathy. (1990:50-1)

Daniel Rickett agreed that "it is important in a partnership to not only give but to receive … The seeds of unhealthy dependency are planted when the only deal struck in a missions relationship is the one-way flow of resources, whether that be money or personnel" (2000:17).

It was for this reason that Glenn Schwartz remained wary of partnerships as they were actually being practiced, despite the popularity of the idea:

Sometimes these terms [partnership and interdependence] are applied to situations … where the only thing that flows between the partners is money, and that flow is often in only one direction … Until partnerships reflect the gifts and abilities of all partners, they will continue to demean those who get more than they give. (Wood 1998b:37)

Schwartz understood that there is a temptation to use Western money as a shortcut to completing world evangelization and to label that as partnership. Robert L. Ramseyer wondered whether there could be real partnership between "rabbits and elephants" (1980:32). He added, "Obviously partnership and interdependence are not possible when it is assumed that one side is developed (has already arrived) and is now helping the other side to reach the same level" (1980:33).

Some, however, have bluntly advocated the one-way flow of money from west to east as the best current model for missions. Sherwood Lingenfelter proposed this simple plan:

The Western church has great resources, reflected in the mega-churches with multi-million dollar facilities and programs. While most middle-class families would not hesitate to spend four hundred dollars a month on a car payment, two or three hundred dollars on credit card purchases, and another two or three hundred on cell phone, cable television and internet access, they do not comprehend that they could fully support seven Indian missionaries or trainers of trainees with those same dollars … The Lord is waiting for the rich to partner with the poor to make disciples of the nations. (Gupta and Lingenfelter 2006:182)

Gary Schipper said, "The Western church has money, the non-Western missionary needs money. If there were ever a call for partnership, this is it." He claimed that "red flags" such as "the sacred 'three Self' principles, … have paralyzed us for too long. The time is ripe for creative experiments" (1988:199).

"Creative experiments" have abounded in the postcolonial period. Christopher Little noted a "burgeoning trend" of what he refers to as the "International Partnership Movement (IPM)." He found that there were over 140 agencies specifically supporting overseas ministries in partnerships, with the top four agencies disbursing over $53 million in 2004 to support approximately 22,000 individuals. Little concluded, "For the IPM, partnership clearly entails the one-way transfer of resources from the Western to the non-Western church" (2005:172).

K. P. Yohannan championed just such an experiment, touting it as a new postcolonial model for missions that could complete the task of world evangelization in a short time. He called on North American Christians to sponsor a native missionary evangelist for as little as $30 to $50 a month, citing this as "a wise investment of our resources because the native missionary works more economically than foreigners can" (1986:134). Furthermore, the native evangelists already understand the local languages and cultures, so can communicate more effectively than Westerners. Yohannan called for Western support of up to one million native missionaries at $600 million a year (1986:134). The support of an equal number of Western missionaries would amount to $35 billion by his estimate (1986:139). He maintained that besides completing world evangelization in the least time, this method would also prove to be "the quickest way to help Asian churches become self-supporting" (1986:193). Yohannan's proposal seemed to suggest, however, that Western nations should cease sending missionaries and send money only.

Such proposals alarmed Western missiologists for two reasons: they would continue to fuel dependency, and they would reduce Western missionary zeal. Yohannan's plan could become a double-edged sword that would not only cripple the newer churches' initiative in giving but also undercut Western involvement in world missions by eliminating Western missionaries. Far from speeding up world evangelization, this plan could dramatically delay it. Wade Coggins said:

> We can't substitute money for flesh and blood, ... [and any churches that did so] have lost their missionary vision ... Assistance that creates dependency, or that tempts to corruption, is counter-productive ... Our financial assistance can rob local believers of the blessing of sacrificial support for their own missionaries. We must not pour out so much money that they feel that their contributions are either not needed or are insignificant. (1988:204-5)

Robertson McQuilkin said that proposals like Yohannan's lead to churches becoming "mired in an ecclesiastical welfare state, because the send-money approach, rather than strengthening the souls of national churches, keeps congregations from becoming self-governing and self-supporting" (1999:57). He quoted Jerry Rankin, president of the International Mission Board of the Southern Baptist Convention:

> One thing inevitably occurs when North Americans subsidize the work of churches and pastors on the mission field: potential growth is stalled because of a mind-set that it can't be done unless an overseas benefactor provides the funds ... In the long-term, support breeds resentment, especially if the support is not sustained indefinitely, because it creates a patronizing dependency. (1999:57)

Glenn Schwartz attacked proposals like Yohannan's because the constant flow of American dollars to Christian agencies in the developing world that lured away Christian leaders from indigenous ministries to dependent ones. He called the dependency syndrome an addiction and accused plans like Yohannan's of enticing away the "best leaders with foreign money. This is what I call 'shepherd stealing.' The 'just support nationals' people are doing it shamelessly and on a very large scale" (Wood 1997:17). Some Africans criticized the idea of sending Western money only, because it would undermine African indigeneity. Solomon Aryeetey noted:

> Some have chosen a simple equation: Western missionary dollars + African availability and zeal = missionary enterprise ... [This model] has the potential of killing the very same African initiative it purports to bring about. For us, it is of the utmost importance that this enterprise be truly indigenous. (1997:34-5)

In essence, the "just support nationals" scheme was a proposal that would kill "the goose that laid the golden egg" (Covey 1989:52-4). By gutting the Western missionary movement of its personnel to get at its money and by severing Christians in the developing world from indigenous self-reliance to make them into employees of the West, the future of world missions would be in jeopardy. The proposal sounds simple and logical, but it overlooks the existing scale of dependency created by Western missions in the first place.

It is unlikely there is any quick fix to long-term dependency, so postcolonial models of mission will need to take this into consideration. Of course, there are other models than the "just support nationals" scheme for partnership, and partnership remains the ideal for the completion of world evangelization. True partnership in the gospel for Western and non-Western Christians will involve difficult choices that take into account the historical relationships and attitudes of both groups. Ramseyer wrote about this complex issue:

> The ideal for our relationships around the world would probably be a great pooling of all our resources in which all churches would be both contributors and recipients as they engage in mission. But such a pooling can only take place among responsible members, after debilitating dependency relationships have been permanently severed. To get from here to there will require radical surgery, a basic reorientation in the way that we think of each other in the worldwide church. (1980:39)

Partnership by itself cannot end dependency. Furthermore, modern missions are becoming more complex than ever in the postcolonial period. In areas where the local churches used to relate primarily to their founding mission alone, they now have many other potential "partners." With increased mobility, the mission field is now everywhere, and evangelists of all nationalities seek potential "donors." In addition, short-term missions have expanded so much that the interaction of Western Christians with those in other nations has increased dramatically.

The Impact of Short-Term Missions

Missiologists have debated the effects of this trend on world missions in general. Ralph Winter described short-term missions as "drive-by missions" and "amateurism in missions" (1998:4), reflecting a concern that the trend could divert attention and resources away from the serious effort of reaching the unreached peoples of the world through long-term commitments. Gary Corwin, on the other hand, took a pragmatic view that, since short-term missions are more than a passing fad, missiologists should find ways of working with the phenomenon rather than merely complaining about it. Douglas W. Terry even warned, "The academy must discover how to accept and incorporate this tsunami of fresh energy and personnel into its models of world mission, or it risks becoming irrelevant" (2004:174).

Corwin noted the motivation behind the growth of short-term missions: "The enormous popularity of short-term missions is a reflection of local churches' desire to be involved more directly in global missions" (2000:422). Local churches are simply trying to provide average church members with "hands-on" experiences in other cultures. Often these American churches use the facilities of mission agencies both for pre-field orientation and for guidance on the field. Sometimes the volunteers work under the direct supervision of a career missionary on the field. Many other such groups, however, follow their own agendas without assistance from mission agencies or missionaries.

According to Scott Moreau, United States mission agencies reported that a total of 97,272 short-term workers (defined as going from two weeks to one year) were sent out in 1998. By 2001, this official figure supplied by mission agencies jumped to 346,270 which represented a 256 percent increase in just three years (2004:14). Since an increasing number of volunteers form their own partnerships without assistance from mission agencies, the actual figure is several times higher. Robert Priest has estimated the total number of short-term volunteers recently, including those who go for less than two weeks: "It is almost certain that over 1.5 million U.S. Christians travel abroad every year on short-term mission trips" (2008:54). This "short-term avalanche" (Slimbach 2000:428) allowed direct contact between American Christians and their counterparts in other parts of the world.

Such direct links open new possibilities for partnerships that could in turn contribute to dependency. Don Parrott warned that short-term missions may reflect "an anti-long-term sentiment … [as] many churches are caught up in a craze for partnerships" (2004:357), sometimes leaving out career missionaries to connect with local Christians. Slimbach also warned that the "benevolent paternalism" of traditional Western missions continued to be perpetuated by short-term missions. He added that he had "rarely heard any serious reflection on the ways in which short-term missions activities … might actually do more harm than good." (2000:429-30). For example, he noted:

> [Short-term missionaries tended to identify with] the tourist group, [while locals] assessed commercial and political benefits of associating with these "outsiders" … Each party knows that the transactions will most likely be temporary and not repeated. This frees each from the constraints of a mutual, long-term relationship in order to act in terms of their own self-interest. (2000:431)

Where the scenario that Slimbach envisioned exists, the likelihood of dependency is real. It is also likely in situations where American activism encounters a slower way of life. Glenn Schwartz told of how American short-term missionaries created dependency in Guyana, South America, in a very short period of time. He reported that Americans built a church building in Guyana during a three-week stay. Two years later the Guyana Christians sent a message to the American builders to return because "the roof on your church building is leaking. Please come and fix it" (2007:239). This indicated that a significant factor in the issue of dependency is personal ownership of the project.

In the previous chapter, we noted that this was part of the reason for the dependency of the Waodani Indians of Ecuador. Short-term groups from the United States held Bible conferences and built church buildings for the Waodani. Since the Indians could not match the efforts of the North Americans, they decided not to try to hold their own conferences or build their own buildings (Wood 1998a:9). This illustrates how easy it is for well-meaning short-term volunteers to create dependency. Jo Ann van Engen says bluntly:

> Because short-term groups often want to solve problems quickly, they can make third-world Christians feel incapable of doing things on their own. Instead of working together with local Christians, many groups come with a let-the-North-Americans-do-it attitude that leaves nationals feeling frustrated and unappreciated. Since the groups are only around for about a week, the nationals end up having to pick up where they left off—but without the sense of continuity and competence they might have had if they were in charge from the beginning. (2000:22)

The essence of short-term missions is to accomplish something significant, preferably visible, in a short time. Rick Johnson said that this satisfies the American cultural value of "immediate gratification" (2000:41), but the short-term volunteers may not consider the impact that they have on the local people. In the name of partnership, American Christians link up with local Christians:

> Groups are sent to 'fix up' their buildings, do their evangelism, preach in their services, lead vacation Bible schools … Sadly, these churches find that their own efforts pale in comparison to the well-funded foreign campaigns. They can lose their initiative. Some become corrupted, seeking an inside track to foreign groups and the resources they bring. The church

may abandon its indigenous efforts and become dependent on the foreign support. (Johnson 2000:42)

Johnson noted that American materialism and a sense of pity toward citizens of developing nations often combine to produce dependency on short-term trips. Visible poverty can create a compassionate reaction in the short-term missionary that combines with a sense of guilt for having so much wealth. This, in turn, can cause rash decisions that produce dependency. This may be done through actual donations of money or materials, or simply through making promises that are soon forgotten when the trip is over and the scenes of poverty have faded from memory. Both Stan May and John M. Tucker warned short-term groups about the harm caused by unfulfilled promises (May 2000:445; Tucker 2001:437). Bruce R. Reichenbach commented, "Consistent with their guilt-complex, the Western churches continually search for new ways to infuse financial and material aid into the Third World churches," so creating "money greed" (1982:170).

Churches that emphasize autonomy are particularly susceptible to harm done by short-term missions, because local autonomy allows such groups to bypass long-term missionaries and mission agencies with ease. John Reese reported the testimony of a short-term worker who traveled to India:

The things that came to light during my second trip made me realize that all I had seen was a carefully staged charade aimed at separating Americans from their money. It seemed that what we had exported to India was not Christianity, but the same unholy worship of the Almighty Dollar that threatens to forever alienate our own nation from God. (2002:2)

Such abuses caused Slimbach to wonder, "Will short-terms be perceived as just one more of the many colonizing systems exported from America to the rest of the world?" (2000:435). Certainly, short-term missions present a challenge since it is not possible to "declare a moratorium on short-term missions" nor to "align ourselves with the new 'manifest destiny' of global Americanization" (Slimbach 2000:440). Instead, these issues indicate the great need for better training at the local church level for short-term workers and for more involvement of experienced missionaries in the training.

Since short-term missions will continue for the foreseeable future, what steps should be taken to ensure better results? Several steps are fairly obvious. We can classify them in three broad categories: better training, integration of short-term missions with long-term strategy, and a commitment to avoid creating dependency.

Better Training

Evaluation is a major tool for North Americans in most fields of endeavor, so it makes perfect sense to evaluate short-term missions too. As churches and Christian groups gain experience from multiple excursions abroad, we hope they will begin to have questions about those experiences. What impact has the short-term mission had, not solely on the volunteers who went, but especially on the people they visited? The impact on the people visited is clearly more difficult to assess, but this only makes the question more crucial, since mission by its very nature seeks to know its impact on those it ministers to. The answer to this question will indicate the direction training must take.

By emphasizing the host people, cultural issues become prominent. Cross-cultural sensitivity will be the most immediate training need, accompanied by studies of the cultural, linguistic, religious, and historical background of the people visited. What is their worldview and how does it compare to the typical North American worldview? For this important information there is an increasing number of help (Johnstone and Mandryk 2001; Livermore 2006; Burnett 2002).

Included in the need for better cross-cultural communication is the fundamental principle of putting human relationships ahead of tasks. Many North Americans tend to put tasks first. For short-term missions, this is especially true because of time constraints to complete some project that will preferably have visible results. Whereas a particular project may be in the forefront of the volunteers' minds, the people visited will probably rather be fascinated by the visitors themselves. This is because many cultures value relationships over tasks and the people visited probably feel little or no time pressure for the short-term mission project. Good training before going, therefore, will take the emphasis away from time and task, shifting the focus to building relationships with local people.

This is not just a cultural issue, because people must always take precedence in God's work. If the people visited are not Christians, then interaction with them is crucial for the testimony that the short-term missionaries will leave behind. If the local people are Christians, then fellowship with them in God's work is essential, as they must carry on with whatever work remains after the volunteers depart.

Integration with Long-Term Strategy

The need to be people-oriented leads logically to the need for long-term strategy. The best short-term missions will become so concerned with the impact that they are having that they will desire to integrate their own short-term goals with long-term planning. This leads naturally to more interaction with professional missionaries or local Christian leaders in the places the volunteers want to visit regularly. By asking field missionaries or indigenous leaders how the short-term mission might fit into long-term goals, the focus will again shift away from the volunteers' needs to the needs on the field.

By focusing on a specific people in one place for a longer period, the short-term mission will be taking a major step toward developing important relationships. When long-term goals take precedence, this increases the vision and purpose of each trip, which now becomes part of a larger plan. Training becomes more directed. Now the short-term missions can start to take advantage of all the wealth of mission history, writings, and field expertise. Even with this advantage, it may not be sufficient to overcome dependency since many long-term missions also created this problem, but at least it is an essential step.

Avoiding Dependency

When short-term missions continue to propagate colonial mission methods, they inadvertently conform to a long-established, but flawed mission model. Local people will automatically see the volunteers as an extension of colonialism when missionaries were expected to give and local people to receive. It becomes easy to slide back into comfortable but damaging codependent relationships. In codependency, local people are used to asking for and receiving material goods, while the donors receive a good feeling from helping people in need. Recipients even learn to place donors on a pedestal in return for favors granted.

For short-term missions, the proclivity to create dependency is even greater if long-term contact is not maintained. The short-term aspect creates a lack of accountability that colonial missions had, since the two sides stayed in contact with each other. In the case of short-term missions, neither side may really care about the ultimate outcome as long as the interaction feels good at the time.

The way to avoid dependency is to keep some simple rules like those of environmental clubs that insist that hikers in nature leave a minimum of physical traces of their passing presence. By traveling light and having an agenda of learning and sharing on a level of equality, short-term missions will avoid rushing in to help before understanding a situation. The goal is to create no dependency by keeping an eye on the future of the ministry in that place. Here are a few simple rules:

1. Do nothing for others that they can do for themselves. This eliminates most building projects, because most cultures have been building suitable structures with local materials for countless generations. The only way to justify a building project is if it fits into a long-term plan and can be done under the leadership of local people.

2. Let the local people determine your project. Assuming that there are responsible and mature local Christians, becoming their servant will be the most important exercise a short-term missionary could have.

3. Undertake no project that is not sustainable by local people. This eliminates most medical short-term missions. Whereas local people may be grateful for free medical care, there will always be some who fail to receive treatment or whose chronic illnesses will not be helped by short-term engagements. How much better would it be if western Christians actually improved health care year-round by training local people in their art? In other words, a better short-term project would empower the local people to deal with their own medical problems.

4. Do not create expectations that will burden future short-term missions in that place. By keeping an eye on the future, it will be easier to refuse to create dependency despite the temptations to do so. Most problems of poverty and disease are long-standing and have no simple solutions, so it is better to do the little that the short-term mission can do without making promises about what will be accomplished. Giving away free materials will not only create dependency but may also set a precedent that future groups will find hard to follow. Charging small fees for services, for example, can add dignity to the transaction and make the project more sustainable.

Beginning with just a few such simple steps may improve short-term missions from being a well-meaning but harmful exercise to one that contributes to world mission in a positive way. It may be helpful to ask how we would respond to swarms of short-term volunteers from other nations who came to do good in our neighborhood and then apply the Golden Rule. Certainly we would appreciate those who treated us and our culture with dignity and respect.

Globalization

The trend toward partnerships and short-term missions is part of the much wider phenomenon of globalization. Douglas Terry lists globalization as a contributing component of short-term missions, saying, "Globalization ... enables the short-term movement technically, informationally, and financially" (2004:174). Sociologist Robert Wuthnow states, "Increasing globalization is directly apparent in the growth of U.S. support for missionaries and churches in other countries and in the large number of American Christians who participate in short-term volunteer efforts abroad" (2009:viii). The link between short-term missions and economic globalization serves to cause many people in the developing world to see the phenomenon as a continuation of colonial missions. Westerners come bringing short-term solutions to long-term problems without asking local people what they know and are doing about these issues. Less scrupulous people in the developing world see the movement as a "gravy train" that they try to flag down so it will make a brief stop at their station. Globalization has made such processes much easier as the world continues to shrink into a "global village."

Declaring "The world is flat," Thomas Friedman indicates that technological innovations have enabled businesses to operate from anywhere with multinational work forces. He cites this as the newest wave of globalization (2005:5). Since Christian missions are also global, globalization is bound to have an impact on missions; globalization is, in fact, driving some mission methods. But what exactly is globalization?

Briefly, globalization is the current movement toward a single world economy. Characterizing the process of globalization as "McWorld," Tom Sine says, "We already have now a 'new one-world economic order'" (1999:50). This movement has greater significance since the collapse of the Soviet Union in 1991, leaving the United States as the sole superpower. There is now a widespread assumption that not only capitalism, but also American values will capture the entire world. Thus, globalization carries cultural and political overtones along with economic ones.

Jeffrey Sachs, an economist who advises the United Nations as well as many developing nations, points out that globalization is not a new phenomenon. The first wave of modern globalization was the European colonial era, "globalization under European domination ... [with] the infamous 'white man's burden,' the right and obligation of European and European-descended whites to rule the lives of others around the world." (2005:43). This raises an important question: Is globalization a period of neocolonialism with an American face instead of a

European one? Or is it a period of history that promises to end global poverty through increased international cooperation?

Sachs suggests that current globalization offers hope for fairness and justice to prevail, provided that Western wealth is used for positive gains in the developing world. He cites the Marshall Plan, which helped rebuild Europe after World War II, as a model for how the United States should now use its resources to improve conditions where poverty is entrenched (2005:341-2). Calling for "Enlightened Globalization" (2005:358), based on the ideals of human progress through the rationalism of the Enlightenment, Sachs believes that international globalization will even limit the United States' tendency toward establishing its own empire.

Despite hopes that globalization will end poverty, the issue that currently troubles both politicians and economists is why there is such growing disparity in wealth between the West and developing nations. Just when capitalism seems triumphant, the gap between rich and poor is widening. Peruvian economist Hernando De Soto says, "The hour of capitalism's greatest triumph is its hour of crisis." Since the fall of the Berlin Wall, "capitalism stands alone as the only feasible way to rationally organize a modern economy." Yet, De Soto concludes, the efforts of developing nations to adopt capitalism "have been repaid with bitter disappointment" (2000:1).

Sachs admits that whereas "all parts of the world had a roughly comparable starting point in 1820 (all very poor by current standards), today's vast inequalities reflect the fact that some parts of the world achieved modern economic growth while others did not" (2005:29). He classifies one billion people as "the 'extreme poor' of the planet, … all fighting for survival each day." An additional 1.5 billion are relatively poor, experiencing "chronic financial hardship and a lack of basic amenities" (2005:18). This combined sector of extremely and relatively poor people encompasses 40 percent of global population.

How does all this affect missions? A common assumption in mission circles today is that economic issues are the key to Christian mission. American Christian missions have long been known for pragmatism, so it is not surprising that mission strategists should seize on globalization as an opportunity for missions. Missionaries have reason to be more concerned than politicians and economists about global wealth disparity because of the Scriptures' abundant teaching on wealth, poverty, and because of their compassion. Relatively wealthy North American missionaries are increasingly uneasy about the contrast between their possessions and those of people they minister to (Bonk 2006).

Current Responses to Globalization

1. American Christians Should Fund Evangelists in the Developing World

This approach is the equivalent of Jeffrey Sachs's proposal of a Marshall Plan to end poverty, but this is a "Marshall Plan" for missions. John Rowell states, "[The] Marshall Plan offers a valuable model for modern missionary involvement. I am proposing that Western Christians should adopt the general format of this historical philanthropic milestone as a guide for giving today" (2006:142). In order to do this, he suggests that both dependency and sustainability must be redefined in order to promote generosity on a large scale. In this scenario, the United States becomes "the War Chest for World Missions" (2006:252) because it is the only nation that has that capability.

2. Globalization Fosters Healthy Interdependence

A slight variation of the first response, this approach calls for global partnerships in mission. For example, Chris Marantika, founder and president of the Evangelical Theological Seminary of Indonesia, insists that interdependence between eastern and Western Christians is essential for adequate church planting in Indonesia. He rejects the Three-Self formula because it focuses too much on self: "I came to the conclusion that self, self, self is not biblical. The concept of the body—the family of God—is togetherness. I believe togetherness or interdependence is the biblical ideal" (Mumper 1986:9). Interdependence without the Three-Self Formula, however, could easily be construed as Western funds financing non-Western church workers. *It didn't happen that way in Indonesia. Yet many churches were planted*

ETSI is in fact a good example of right sharing

3. Globalization Promotes Opportunities for "Kingdom Business"

Ken Eldred defines kingdom business as "for-profit commercial enterprises in the mission field of the developing world through which Christian business professionals are seeking to meet spiritual, social and economic needs" (2005:61). He understands this as superior to simple wealth redistribution by giving from rich Christians to the poor because it creates wealth in a sustainable way (2005:262). Steve Rundle and Tom Steffen agree with Eldred's position, stating, "We believe that globalization is a continuation of God's plan, first revealed to Abram, to bless all nations and peoples of the earth (see Gen. 12:3)" (2003:5). They see this happening through "Great Commission companies."

4. Globalization is a Mixed Blessing

Tom Sine warned, "The very greed that makes the free-market economy work so brilliantly in efficiently producing goods and services is what undermines its capacity to work justly on behalf of the poor and the marginalized" (1999:111). He noted that the economic benefits promised by globalization could mislead people: "The rapid movement of peoples into a new one world economic order is shaping their aspirations and values in ways that are often at counter-point to the aspirations and values of God's kingdom" (2003:354). Furthermore, the rapid increase of wealth in the West has not strengthened Western churches: "The rapid spread of this global culture of consumption could undermine the vitality of the church in the two-thirds world as it is doing in the church in the one third world" (2003:355).

5. Globalization Contains Much that is Evil

Some see globalization as a continuation and extension of colonialism. Jane Collier and Rafael Esteban call globalization part of the Western culture of economism, which "imposes the primacy of economic causes or factors as the main source of cultural meanings and values" (1998:11). This view claims that globalization is trying to reduce humans to mere economic beings. Collier and Esteban asserted, "Globalization is the visible manifestation of the obsessive drive for economic growth … to an extent unparalleled by any other imperial thrust" (1998:32). These authors see Christian missions as largely complicit in this drive for economic domination, since missionaries used colonialism in the same way. Justo Gonzalez likewise sees globalization as a period of neocolonialism extended up to the present (1999:9). Globalization is merely more of the same pattern of Western dominance now spread out over a few more nations that use their strong economies to control the destiny of humanity.

Analyzing Current Responses

The first three responses to globalization seek to cash in, literally, on America's dominant position, wealth, or brand of capitalism to aid world evangelization. At the same time, they desire to overcome the wealth disparity between the West and developing nations by putting American money to work—either by investing it in businesses or by simply giving it away. All three positions recognize the huge economic gap between industrialized nations like the United States and unreached peoples in nations where Christians are poor and evangelists underfunded. They assume that American Christians are in the best position to do something about diminishing this gap. Some cite scriptures that command rich Christians to help the poor and biblical examples of international aid from wealthier parts of the body of Christ to more needy parts of the body. Beyond the humanitarian aspect, however, these positions also seek to make American wealth the linchpin of strategies to complete world evangelization. What is wrong with these approaches?

First, American Christian wealth need not signify God's blessing or spiritual strength. From a Christian perspective, the vast disparity of wealth among churches can be seen as a sign that Western churches have capitulated to the prevailing culture of economism. This would signal, not the beginning of a new American-funded mission era, but the beginning of the end of American dominance in Christianity.

Second, the emphasis on Western funds could indicate a tacit acknowledgment that American Christians are no longer willing to put their lives on the line in Christian discipleship. While the people of the world may be impressed by American wealth, Jesus was unimpressed by the big donations made by the wealthy in the temple; rather he singled out one poor widow as the best example of giving (Luke 21:1-4). She alone gave in a way that showed she had committed her whole life to God.

Third, since the center of gravity of world Christianity is already shifting away from the West (Jenkins 2002), attempts to keep America as the central driving force for world mission amount to clinging to outdated Enlightenment mission paradigms. Sachs, as a secular economist, acknowledged that his dream of eradicating global poverty through American money rests on the ideals of the Enlightenment (2005:347-53). The Enlightenment embraced human progress through human ingenuity apart from the God of the Bible. Tom Sine warned, "The aspirations and values driving globalization are a product of the Enlightenment and modernity and are in many ways directly counter to the aspirations and values of God's new global order" (1999:20). Lamin Sanneh went so far as to say that what is now called "Global Christianity … is the faithful replication of Christian forms and patterns developed in Europe," whereas what he refers to as "World Christianity" (various indigenous responses to Christianity) is largely without any influence from the European Enlightenment (2003:22).

Fourth, advocates of American Christian wealth being the engine for world evangelization may unwittingly continue to promote dependency. How does this happen? By suggesting that the best postcolonial mission paradigm consists of

Western money combined with non-Western manpower, two problems occur: first, Westerners assume the role of paymasters as in colonialism; second, non-Westerners may assume that they need only receive and not give. American churches and Christian organizations bypass local indigenous churches to fund evangelists who are then not accountable to their own churches. In this scenario, the widow with two mites is not encouraged to give at the temple because the wealthy have everything covered. The problem arises because of the wealth disparity and the continued distinction from colonialism between the privileged and the underprivileged. In the church of Jesus Christ, however, there are no underprivileged members and wealth is not measured in money alone.

Fifth, in the event of a worldwide economic depression or recession, such as "The Great Crash" of 2008, described as the worst economic setback in over seventy-five years (Altman 2009), Christian projects that depend on American funding must downsize or collapse altogether with business projects. Those that are owned and operated on a more grassroots level will be less affected, just as first century Christian expansion did not depend much on the prevailing economic climate.

The "kingdom business" approach is more aware of the possibility of creating dependency and seeks to avoid it by creating sustainable businesses where Christians can earn money through the dignity of work:

By providing employment and enabling local Christians to improve their economic condition, Kingdom business efforts can help to break the dependence on foreign assistance. Christians in developing countries can learn the principles of giving … Instead of relying on Western funding, local churches can become economically self-sufficient and sustainable through their own members. (Eldred 2005:262)

On the other hand, global business itself may be a disguise for promoting Western values. Eldred betrays this bias when he cites kingdom business as an extension of David Livingstone's proposal in a speech at Cambridge University in 1857: "Those two pioneers of civilization—Christianity and commerce—should ever be inseparable" (2005:143). Eldred sees kingdom business as "an opportunity to bless a nation in the name of the Lord Jesus Christ, and a migration toward the basic living standards of the First World is the objective" (2005:160).

Much of what is today called interdependent partnership in missions is in reality a codependency. Luis Bush and Lorry Lutz described partnership in this way: "Western agencies need overseas ministries in order to justify and maintain their existence. And the non-Western agency or church needs the help of the Western agency to expand or reach out to new areas" (1990:62). Donors are placed on a pedestal by making donations that cost them very little, while receivers get to use money they have not sacrificed to give. This type of interaction maintains the status quo in international relations from colonialism with wealthy Western Christians in the driver's seat and poor, non-Western evangelists as their employees. No one should be surprised if such relationships turn into bitterness and resentment in the postcolonial world. True interdependence can only take place once steps are taken to eliminate dependency-producing, colonial-era mission methods.

While the world has moved to some degree into a post-Enlightenment, post-Christendom, and postcolonial era, Christian missions continue to operate with colonial models. They then link these outdated paradigms with globalization and call it a new paradigm. Economic globalization, however, operates under human power as much as any movement conceived by the human mind; therefore, it cannot fully embody the gospel message of the crucified Savior.

Supporters of Christian globalization may unwittingly continue with Christendom motifs from a time when the gospel was propagated through colonial systems of power. Westerners may feel good about themselves because they are economically developed and Christianized, while the mission field lies in those parts of the world where poverty is endemic. With humanitarianism as the new gospel, Bill Gates and Jeffrey Sachs then show us the way as our role models, yet these men have an agenda that arises from different motivations than those of biblical missions. With this scenario, mission continues from the developed world to the underdeveloped as it was in the colonial era.

Within many popular missionary paradigms that claim to be postcolonial, there is little recognition that many of the global poor are actually contributing more to world missions than the "Christianized" West. There is little recognition that many of the global poor are more "Christian" than affluent Western churches. There is little recognition that the gospel has enough power in itself not to need the wealth of the world's superpower.

The gospel has already taken root in many cultures and holds a hidden treasure that has nothing to do with economic globalization. If not overwhelmed by the desire of both Christian and non-Christian humanitarians to spread American wealth and values around the globe, people who are considered poor may prove to be rich in generosity and love so that they spread the Christian faith as the pre-Christendom church did. Christian mission cannot afford to tie its fate to globalization, which is a phase of world history linked to Enlightenment values that see no need for either God or Christianity. Even if Christians wish to take advantage of opportunities offered by globalization, they must exercise enough discernment not to propagate colonial methods and models. The poor widow must once again be permitted to give her two mites so that God, and not mammon, gains the glory.

Conclusion

The world has moved on from colonialism into a period of globalization that appears to many as an unprecedented time of opportunity and international cooperation. Partnership and interdependency are the key words along with images of unity and brotherhood, whether we are speaking of Christian mission or global politics. These are the ideal; the actual picture, however, is more complex because of colonial history, the division of cultures, and human nature. Samuel Huntington states, "Power is shifting from the long predominant West to non-Western civilizations. Global politics has become multipolar and multicivilizational" (2003:29). In fact, he lists nine current centers of world power: Western, Latin American, African, Islamic, Chinese, Hindu, Orthodox, Buddhist, and Japanese (2003:26-7). Recognizing that these centers of power are often based on competing religions and sometimes carry resentments toward other centers of power because of perceived historical injustices, we would have to be wary of rosy forecasts about global harmony.

In Christian mission, partnership and interdependency are desirable, but cannot be attained until the issue of dependency is solved. A dependent person or group cannot simply jump to being interdependent without first moving out of dependency. If we simply try to ignore the issues surrounding dependency and form "partnerships" between independent and dependent groups, we will only perpetuate dependency because some of the "partners" will have little to offer of any perceived value. Therefore, many arrangements now called "partnerships" are actually the continuation of dependency.

For those who see the Three-Self formula as an outdated colonial mantra that overemphasizes the self, we should not be so hasty to throw out a mission paradigm that has successfully stood the test of time. The issue of the "self" turns out to be nothing more than accepting personal responsibility for one's role in the body of Christ, so it is merely addressing the issue of maturity, which is perfectly biblical (Gal. 4:19; Heb. 5:12; 2 Pet. 3:18). While the Three-Self formula was certainly a product of its time, it was also ahead of its time, and it still adequately describes a Christian individual or group that can carry out basic functions of the body of Christ (Reese 2007b:25-7).

For those who feel that the time has come for American Christians to fund missions conducted by non-Western evangelists, we should note that this is a continuation of the same paradigm that characterized colonial missions. Western Christians were in control of resources and non-Western Christians were their employees. Furthermore, it would create only an indirect interest in world missions by Americans who would only rarely see or hear about unknown evangelists they support, since none of their own children would be directly involved. And finally, it would teach non-Western churches that they have no responsibility to contribute funds to world mission. Such a paradigm would not speed up the rate of world evangelization that its proponents expect, but would rather slow it down.

For those who feel that short-term missions are an adequate replacement for long-term involvement in mission, we should recognize that unreached peoples reside in cultures that are difficult to enter or to understand. Short-term missionaries cannot adequately take the time and effort needed to penetrate these final frontiers for the Great Commission; indeed they usually do not try to find the unreached, but work with existing churches (Priest 2008:65). Therefore, short-term mission can be described as "a form of collaborative partnership in witness and service with Christians who are already locally present" (Priest 2008:66).

Furthermore, short-term missionaries should rather be called volunteers because of their general lack of training in cross-cultural communication. Because of this, they may do more harm than good in the long run. Better training is certainly needed for most short-term groups if they are not to create dependency even where none existed previously. Oscar Muriu, pastor of Nairobi Chapel in Kenya, summarized:

> We don't call them "short-term missions" any more. We call them "short-term learning opportunities." The problem with calling it a mission is that it implies an agenda. There's something I need to come and do for you, or to you, to better your life. In reality that doesn't happen in two weeks. Life is far too complex for that. The greatest benefit is that you come and learn. (Crouch 2007a:100)

Finally, for those who sense that globalization is the wave that will bring the gospel to the nations through various opportunities like business, we should remind ourselves that we can be pragmatic without being naïve. Certainly we will take advantage of globalization for the cause of Christ, but we also remember that the gospel does not need such vehicles to succeed. And there may be a price to pay for hitching the gospel of Christ to a secular movement, as this often distorts its meaning. Unreached people may perceive the gospel as closely attached to Western values of global business and prosperity, rather than the cross of Christ. In any case, the aura of Western dominance in business has taken a severe bruising to the extent that Roger Altman predicted:

> Over the medium term, Washington and European governments will have neither the resources nor the economic credibility to play the role in global affairs that they otherwise would have played … [These economic weaknesses] will accelerate trends that are shifting the world's center of gravity away from the United States. (2009:2)

The postcolonial period begs for better mission models than these provide—models that will overcome dependency and are not a continuation of colonial mission methods.

extremely overstated.
Burdens partnership with the worst
possible outcomes!
Reese frequently uses
a strawman: sets up a weak
argument easily refuted.

7

The Roots of Dependency

F AR FROM ENDING WITH COLONIALISM, DEPENDENCY HAS become a more serious global problem in missions through the recent upsurge of amateur missions. With the rise of short-term missions, partnerships, and methods that link to economic globalization, current mission models are not moving toward eradication of dependency. To end dependency, missions need to understand its root causes. Just as hardy weeds resist halfhearted efforts at killing them, so the roots of dependency must be plucked out to eradicate the problem. From what we have said so far about dependency, we have a good idea of what these roots are.

Dependency Is a Relic of Colonialism

First, dependency stems from the colonial mentality when Europe ruled the world. In particular, it is a legacy of British imperialism with its benign concept of "the white man's burden." This implied both an obligation and a reward. The obligation came from the understanding that the British were heirs to a civilization unparalleled in history, built on Christian values that had also produced unprecedented prosperity and technology. With this high civilization came the obligation to extend it around the world to all other cultures and peoples. The expected reward was that these people would receive British supervision with grateful servitude.

In the United States, "the white man's burden" merged with the belief in Manifest Destiny and Social Darwinism. Americans absorbed the idea that their nation had a divine mission to the world, but this notion was tainted with feelings of racial superiority. Because of democratic ideals, egalitarianism, and the separation of church and state, American Christians assumed that they were immune to becoming like domineering colonialists who created dependency in mission churches. Americans still see themselves as fundamentally different from the classic colonialists because they have not sought to create a world empire.

Some would say, however, that the United States has been tending toward imperialism from the beginning. William Owen Carver, surveying mission history in 1932, said:

> While the United States is by its inner principles prohibited from seeking territorial expansion and while it consistently professes to desire the land of no other people, its history has been one of repeated and almost continuous expansions until it is surpassed in territorial growth in its century and a half of national history only by Great Britain. (1932:302)

More recently, British missions historian, Andrew F. Walls, concurred:

> The whole climate of American Christian thinking was conditioned by expansion. … Chronologically, America was the first modern imperial power, or perhaps second after Russia, the former expanding eastward as the latter expanded westward, until the two met. (1996:227-8)

Walls noted that, ironically, the United States "was also the first colonial independence movement" (1996:233). Therefore, the nation seemed to be on both sides of the imperialist-liberation movement equation. This fact tended to create in American missions a

> curious political naiveté, as though by constantly asserting that church and state were separate they have somehow stripped mission activity of political significance. Even the elementary political implication of their presence, let alone of patriotism, has not always been recognized. (Walls 1996:233)

Where the United States has intervened militarily, apart from some notable exceptions in World War II, the result has been to create a legacy of dependent nations. William Easterly, research economist with the World Bank for many years, analyzed the impact of military interventions during the Cold War. Tabulating thirteen nations (Vietnam, Cambodia, Afghanistan, Guatemala, Korea, Iran, Liberia, Ethiopia, Somalia, El Salvador, Nicaragua, Zaire, and Angola) where the United States intervened, Easterly found that "as of 2004, the typical nation described [in the tabulation] was in the bottom 15 percent on democracy, the bottom 18 percent on rule of law, the bottom 22 percent on economic freedom" (2006:316).

Accounting for the fact that some of these countries were already low in these categories before the intervention, Easterly is not arguing that American intervention caused them to be the way they are, just that intervention worsened the situation rather than improving it. He concludes, "The pre-cold war, cold war, and post-cold war record on intervening militarily to promote the more ambitious goals of political and economic development yields a cautionary lesson—don't" (2006:335).

As for the exceptions coming out of World War II, where American intervention boosted economic progress, Easterly emphasizes that countries like Germany and Japan already had a foundation of independent thinking and economic development to build on: "The Americans were at most reconstructing an economy that was already advanced" (2006:345). He adds that Germany and Japan were never colonized by Western nations, whereas the states that have proved to be economic disasters were all once dependent colonies (2006:347).

As representatives of the world's only current superpower, American missionaries should be aware that their very presence in developing nations may lead to dependency in their converts. As American power and global influence increase, the temptation will be strong to link the gospel to Americanism. In doing so, missionaries may inadvertently perpetuate the deep-seated mentality of dependency.

Most of the world is moving into a postcolonial frame of reference, but frequently American evangelicals continue to operate with a colonial mentality. In my experience in missions, we tend to be "take-charge" people, too impatient to let local Christians exercise initiative and leadership. After all, we have the resources to "make things happen," while local people seem passively helpless. We also have the ideas and analytical thinking that drive us toward "quick fixes" of complex problems, while overlooking local wisdom as out of date and irrelevant. Therefore, we perpetuate stereotypes from the colonial period that regard local people as inferior and in need of our guidance and resources, and often these local Christians seem quite willing for us to act this way; but this is all a deception born of a long history of Western domination over colonial peoples.

Missionaries may work hard to adjust their own thinking to fit the new political realities, but they also find that dependency has its own logic. Moreover, dependency is difficult to eradicate because it contains an element of codependency.

Not only do the converts become addicted to what they may receive from the missionaries, but also the missionaries come to enjoy the advantages of their superior position. Jonathan Bonk described this situation, saying that Western missionary affluence gained for the missionary "a degree of attention, influence, and power which could not have otherwise been achieved ... There is something about personal pecuniary advantage which inspires great self-confidence in treating with those who are poorer" (1991:40-1).

Besides having affluence, American missionaries also represent the world's greatest military power, so they are candidates for near star-like status among the poor of the developing nations. Thus, there is a great potential for a codependent relationship to develop with converts. While missionaries supply subsidies out of their prosperity, the converts feed the missionaries' self-esteem as they set them on a pedestal. Such a relationship is not only unhealthy but amounts to a perversion of the gospel. In the search for better postcolonial models of missions, it must be noted that dependency is in actuality a theological issue.

Dependency Is a Theological Issue

A simple comparison of modern missionary methods with those employed by Jesus and Paul reveals major discrepancies. The mission model used by Jesus and His disciples has been described as "incarnational." John R. W. Stott popularized this idea, basing the incarnational model of missions on the Great Commission as recorded in John 20:21. Stott saw this version as the most significant:

> The crucial form in which the Great Commission has been handed down
> to us (though it is the most neglected because is the most costly) is the
> Johannine ... Deliberately and precisely he [Jesus] made his mission the
> model of ours, saying "as the Father sent me, so I send you." (1975:23)

Stott added, "Our mission, like his, is to be one of service ... He sends us 'into the world,' to identify with others as he identified with us" (1975:25). Therefore, Stott saw the Johannine Great Commission as a call to incarnational missions. Since he was one of the framers of the Lausanne Covenant in 1974, this terminology has been widely adopted by evangelicals.

Andreas J. Köstenberger, however, challenged Stott's application of the word "incarnational" to missionary methods, on the grounds that the incarnation was unique to Jesus' mission and can never be repeated (1998:212-7). Certainly, missionaries can never "be Jesus" in any situation, as there is only one Savior of the world, but they can identify with people and serve them as Jesus did. Perhaps the terminology of "identificational" mission might help us avoid thinking of ourselves as the people's Savior, but only as Christ's ambassadors, and flawed ones at that. We cannot, after all, even identify with people of other cultures to the extent that Jesus identified with the Jews, since he was born into that culture.

Jesus and Paul engaged in missions by proclaiming the arrival of the kingdom or reign of God in Christ. This demanded a radical repentance and conversion away from Satan's realm into God's. They avoided the possibility of money perverting the gospel by living a simple lifestyle and by working with their own hands. Christian missionaries today are called to identify with these aspects of biblical missions. George W. Peters captured this meaning from his study of John 20:21, saying, "The mission implies a spiritual identification of the disciples with the Lord in a work which is delegated to Him by the Father ... We are not doing mission work for Christ but rather with Christ" (1972:193, 195). This emphasis recovers what Rufus Anderson called "a purely spiritual character to mission" (Beaver 1967:73) without the necessity of adding the propagation of any civilization. Rather, "the sole object [of missions] is the reconciling of rebellious men ... to God" (Beaver 1967:81).

Missionaries today can repeat neither the incarnation nor the crucifixion of Jesus, but they can proclaim them and live in the light of them. Bonk stated, "At the very least, the Incarnation means giving up the power, privilege, and social position which are our natural due. Christ's mission in Christ's way must always begin, proceed, and end with the great renunciation" (1991:117). In John 12:20-26, Jesus explained the necessity of His death for the sake of the harvest. He then invited His disciples to follow Him in "hating" their lives in this world, so that "where I am, there shall My servant also be" (12:26b). Since the dependency syndrome is the fruit of self-centeredness both on the part of missionaries and their converts, dying to self is essential for its cure.

The history of Christian missions in Africa reveals that missionaries failed to heed the indigenous principles advocated by Anderson and Venn, and this resulted in their work having a secularizing influence more than a spiritual one. Missionary institutions such as schools and hospitals were intended to be spiritual forces to combat ignorance and disease, but they were perceived as tools of Western civilization. Non-Pentecostal missionaries tended not to believe in miracles, so they explained healing in Western scientific terms to Africans who understood healing to be primarily spiritual. In schools, the Bible or "Religious

Knowledge" was one subject among many, most of which were secular. When these missionaries preached the gospel, their converts often entered a "split-level Christianity" (Hiebert, Shaw, and Tiénou 1999:90). Paul Hiebert, Daniel Shaw and Tite Tiénou explained that Western missionaries

> built churches to focus on religious matters, and schools and hospitals in which they explained nature and disease in naturalistic terms. When people spoke of the fear of evil spirits, the missionaries often denied the existence of these spirits rather than claim the power of Christ over them. The result was that in many parts of the world Western Christian missions became a major secularizing force. (1999:90)

Under these conditions, it was not surprising that many converts were converted to something in addition to Jesus Christ. If a convert was attracted by material benefits such as health care, education, or employment, then it is quite possible that the spiritual component of the conversion was minimal. Glenn Schwartz noted this as a frequent motivation for conversion in Africa: "Again and again decisions to become believers have something to do with the attraction to the benefits from employment by expatriates or, more commonly, assurance of enrollment in a much coveted school program" (1989b:4). Schwartz added that another key reason for marginal conversion to Christ is that "the gospel is presented as 'free salvation' with little or no cost to discipleship" (1989b:3). Those who were converted for the personal benefits only could hardly be expected to give of themselves or their resources for the cause of Christ.

If such marginal converts became church leaders, it was natural that they should seek such positions for the perceived benefits and not for service to Christ. Where there was subsidy of local pastors, the wrong types of people were often attracted to the position.

Many of the problems associated with dependency, then, can be traced to a flawed presentation of the gospel that led to a nominal conversion. In Africa, such marginal conversions left the predominant spiritistic worldview unchanged by Christianity. The "Christian" side of such a "convert" related to an orientation toward the Western world in secular matters, while the spiritual side remained at the mercy of the spirit world as before. In this way, dependency in Africa also has its roots in the African context.

Dependency Is a Contextual Issue

Glenn Schwartz asserts that dependency in African mission churches has stemmed from "untrained missionaries" (2004) caught up in the colonial mentality of white supremacy. By "untrained," he means that early missionaries did not receive cross-cultural training and therefore had little idea how a spiritist thinks. Spiritism is the view that life is dominated by the activity of spirits, good and bad. A person who holds this belief must try to discern which spirit is causing events and then try to appease that spirit to secure the outcome the person desires. Such belief systems are common not only in Africa, but also in many parts of the world.

Schwartz maintains that a spiritistic worldview lends itself to fatalism and dependency, and a nominal conversion leaves this worldview unchanged. Uninformed missionaries may present the gospel from a Western frame of reference, emphasizing individual guilt for sins, while the spiritistic worldview focuses neither on the individual nor on personal guilt.

According to Hiebert, Shaw, and Tiénou, spiritists "live in a world surrounded by spirits, ancestors, witchcraft, curses, magic, and other supernatural beings and forces, many of which are hostile to human beings" (1999:81).Therefore, there is "near constant fear and the need for security" (1999:87). The spiritist, then, does not primarily seek forgiveness, but rather power over spiritual forces: "In folk religions the focus is on power—the ability to make things happen" (1999:84). Spiritists may "become Christians to acquire more power" (1999:85). They may perceive Western missionaries as possessing great power because of their abundant resources, and they may wish to manipulate this power magically for their own benefit. Schwartz says that in such cases, "the center of the [worldview] is still African spiritism and not the Lordship of Jesus Christ" (1989b:5).

The cure for dependency in such a situation is conversion on a deeper level, so the worldview changes from spiritistic to biblical, with the Lord Jesus Christ in control. Hiebert, Shaw, and Tiénou summarized, "Folk religions are human efforts to control life ... The desire for control also leads to magical approach to problems ... The gospel rejects an ego-centered religion and a magical mentality" (1999:371). Certainly, when missionaries from the affluent West preach the gospel to spiritistic Africans, there is a strong possibility of misunderstanding.

Besides shallow conversion, another contextual issue was raised by John Cheyne, a Southern Baptist missionary to Zimbabwe. Cheyne noticed that the foreignness of Western mission stations, institutions, and organizations created new problems. He stated:

The very process of planting churches, developing the supporting institutions, providing training facilities, and opening up new media has further entrenched the missionary. The effect has been the elaborate structuring of denominational organizations on huge compounds set up in the midst of primitive societies. This has tended to reproduce a Western model of the church amidst ethnic groups whose cultural patterns and concepts are oft times antithetically orientated. (1972:1)

With this discussion, Cheyne opened two important and related issues: the existing rural African social structure had no category in which to place Western concepts of organization, and this in turn made the Africans dependent on Western missionaries to operate those foreign institutions. Cheyne expressed the dilemma presented to Africans by missionary organizations: "Mission-sponsored institutions present one of the greatest paradoxes to the indigenous society" because they are useful "ministries of mercy, training, and welfare," but they also can be seen as "disguised bribery" (1972:206). By this, he meant that Africans might perceive organized Christian services as enticements to conversion.

Such mission structures interfered with the formation of indigenous churches in the Baptist Mission in Zimbabwe. The Baptist Publishing House in Bulawayo became a source of dispute between the Mission and the Convention. At the dedication of a new building some years ago, a pastor who spoke on behalf of the convention stated that they should be given the publishing house. Henry Mugabe, the current principal of the Baptist Theological Seminary of Zimbabwe, confirmed that the Convention initially desired to take over all mission institutions, but later realized that it could not successfully operate those like the publishing house (2004).

The Convention then concentrated on nationalizing the seminary, and Mugabe stated that this institution remains a source of dispute between the Convention and the Mission to this day. Isaac Mwase, a graduate of the seminary and now a professor in the United States, explained that the shift in priorities of the International Mission Board away from supporting such institutions "seems to reflect a fear that mission-founded Baptist churches are overly dependent on the IMB" (2005:73).

Considering the real aim of the Baptist Mission to plant indigenous churches, it seems clear that it would have achieved this goal better by using the original models of Baptist churches on the American frontier. In those churches, the leadership and organization were as flexible as life on the frontier, and there were no cumbersome institutions. Such a model would suit the cultural context in Zimbabwe. Instead, the Baptist Mission brought in its structures after they had evolved in the United States and tried to make them fit into a situation more akin to an earlier era in America. On the frontier, few pastors were ever subsidized or trained in seminaries, but the Baptist Mission imposed both subsidies and formal training on rural Zimbabwean churches.

Winston Crawley admitted that "the expectation of a seminary-trained full-time pastor for each congregation" was a product of "Western cultural overhang" (1985:208). He added:

> Many persons, without knowing it, have a colonial concept of what we do in missions. They think that we are creating outposts or branches of our own churches and our own Convention ... The opposite principle from the colonial, and the one that fits Baptist beliefs, is the indigenous principle. Instead of thinking in terms of "Southern Baptist churches," we seek to plant New Testament churches. (1985:196)

The irony of dependency is that even those who know better often create dependent churches and institutions. Even if missionaries have better training so that they understand contextual issues, seek deeper level conversions, and avoid encumbering converts with programs that they will have trouble managing, they may still not avoid dependency. They may pursue strategies that inadvertently cause the problem.

Dependency Is a Strategic Issue

American missionaries avoid creating dependency only by implementing a specific strategy. The case study of the Baptist Mission in Zimbabwe in Chapter Five clearly indicates that missionaries should neither subsidize local pastors nor use gradual reduction of subsidy to terminate support. Schwartz emphasized:

> A church does not simply slide into indigenization bit by bit. The matching funds system of reducing subsidy ten percent each year does not indigenize a church. To state it more clearly, a church does not become indigenous ten percent at a time ... A church can no more become indigenous gradually

than a person can become a believer little by little. There must be a definite time of decision. (1989a:12-3)

Even with its inadequacies, the Three-Self formula has proved to be a better strategy than current models of partnership which continue to promote dependency.

Surprisingly, Winston Crawley criticized the Three-Self formula, stating that self-government did not "fit Baptist ecclesiology (Anderson and Venn were not Baptists). We would say that a church is by nature self-governing, under Christ, from the time it comes into being" (1985:201). By subsidizing local pastors, however, the Baptist Mission ensured that local churches would not be self-governing, since pastors were employees of the Mission. Crawley added, "Self-support ... should not be taken as a goal in missions. If taken as a goal, it is one of the easiest in to the world to achieve. All that is necessary is that there be no church building, no pastor, no literature, no program of training or outreach" (1985:333). He confirmed that the core principles guiding Southern Baptist mission strategy at that time "do not rule out the use of money to help overseas churches" (1985:333).

Crawley cited T. P. Crawford, an early missionary to China, as someone who "insisted that the Foreign Mission Board should rule out any use of funds for aid to churches anywhere in the world, but the Board refused to adopt that arbitrary position" (1985:334). These views, expressed by Crawley in the 1980s, indicate how far Southern Baptist mission strategy had moved from the Three-Self formula.

In more recent years, Keith Eitel took the International Mission Board to task for what he considered its outdated paradigms of mission strategy. Ironically, it was the views of T. P. Crawford that Eitel championed as a suitable postmodern paradigm for missions (2000). He cited these principles in Crawford's own words:

First—the gospel of Christ as the power of God unto salvation, in every mission field unaccompanied by any kind of pecuniary inducement to the people ... Second—the churches of Christ should, as organized bodies, singly or in cooperating groups, do their own mission work without the intervention of any outside convention, association or Board. Third—self-denying laborers for Christ's sake, both by the churches at home and by the missionaries abroad. (2000:46-7)

These views reflect both a close adherence to the Three-Self formula and distinctly frontier values that might have served the Baptists well if they had been implemented in Zimbabwe from the beginning.

Clearly, the best way to plant indigenous churches is to start that way. In the Baptist Mission, the missionaries used nonindigenous methods that produced dependency. The number of missionaries was disproportionate to the number of churches planted. *The Commission* of December 1965 reported forty-eight missionaries for thirty-three churches (1965:15). The sheer size of the missionary force would tend to create dependency because it would be well-organized and well-funded compared with the local churches.

Roland Allen stated a memorable principle: "No sound missionary policy can be based upon multiplication of missionaries and mission stations. A thousand thousand would not suffice; a dozen might be too many" (1962b:19). He meant that sheer numbers of missionaries could not achieve the evangelization of the world as well as a few who, in a movement of the Holy Spirit, become catalysts for "the free spontaneous activity" (1962b:19) of local converts. Even if the missionary force is so small that it will inevitably disengage, the advantage can be squandered by the unwise use of money, which hinders the possibility of a people movement to Christ similar to Roland Allen's "spontaneous expansion."

A key element that was missing in the strategy of the Baptist Mission was a clear exit policy (Steffen 1993). For the Baptists, the denial of work permits in the 1990s significantly reduced the size of the missionary force, but since then there has not been much further disengagement. From the beginning, mission institutions interfered with orderly withdrawal, and this continues to be the case in ongoing discussions about the ownership of the seminary.

Even now, over thirty years later, Davis Saunders' comments are relevant: "This study pinpoints the area of greatest uncertainty as being the organizational relationship between mission and convention in the transitional period" (1973:302). Lack of an exit policy is an indication that missionaries did not prepare themselves or their converts mentally for the time of disengagement. Missionary attitudes are a key factor in encouraging or preventing dependency.

Dependency Is an Attitudinal Issue

Zimbabwean Pastor Levy Moyo describes some fictional missionaries who represent real characters he interacted with in colonial Zimbabwe. A British couple, David and Jezee Voner, arrive in Bulawayo, Zimbabwe with great expectations of mixing with Africans in order to build strong churches. Upon arrival, however, they first encounter other missionaries already in the country. This diverts them from their original intention of living in an African suburb to living in an upper class white neighborhood. When Jezee tells the other missionary wives that she and David had not planned to employ servants:

> Jezee was advised that she could pay the garden boys anything, even the change from the grocery shopping. Kath explained to Jezee how it works. She said, "If you buy a 20 kg maize meal for the workers and also give them leftovers, that would be sufficient. Even expired food such as meat and tinned food would satisfy them; they know nothing." (2006:23)

Soon the Voners are transformed into thoroughgoing colonialists like the society around them. They are afraid even to go to the African suburbs their fellow whites deem unsafe. They adopt a lifestyle far above the African Christians they came to serve. Although this disappointed some African church leaders, it also served to make the missionaries seem like superstars to many impoverished Africans: "A white missionary was just like a light at night; all the insects would fly to it" (2006:33). This elevated the Voners to the status of mission directors, even though African leaders had more experience:

> The real missionaries were the locals, who saw David and Jezee as their directors. Many local pastors worked hard to get [David's] approval. [The] result was that some were giving false reports about themselves and about the number of souls saved, just to be seen as "good boys." ... White missionaries were highly esteemed to the level of gods. (2006:35)

The evolution of such relationships is highly conducive to creating dependency:

> The missionary's spending was uncontrollable and not subject to accountability ... Rev. David Voner could use his money to divide and rule the locals. He starved and harshly disciplined those who argued with him. Those who accepted him as the boss got everything they wanted (2006:73).

Is Moyo's scenario far-fetched? Having grown up around missionaries in Zimbabwe during colonialism, I can recognize some of Moyo's characters. The tragedy today is that many postcolonial missionaries and humanitarians continue to have similar attitudes. Indeed, if the full truth is told, we, ourselves, are guilty of some of the attitudes that Moyo describes among white Christians who seek to serve God in Africa.

Fundamentally, dependency is a frame of mind. Schwartz emphasized, "The problem of true indigenization is related to a mental process locked up in a space about eight inches square sitting on the shoulders of missionaries, former missionaries, mission executives, and national church leaders" (1989a:11). Psychological ownership by Africans of their churches, structures, and institutions is a key to eliminating dependency.

8

REMEDIES FOR DEPENDENCY

I N THE FORMER SOVIET UNION, A MISSIONARY wanted to avoid dependency from the beginning, yet he saw that it was happening despite his best intentions. He described how this came about:

> We knew theoretically that dependency is not good, but then we realized that every organization working in the city (including ours) was creating, sustaining, and encouraging a permanent dependent culture. It was scary because it was obvious that a strong indigenous group would not develop and we were the reason. The prevailing mode of operation was "get them started" by providing start-up funding for everything. What we didn't realize was the "getting-them-started" model was laying the foundation for dependency clear and simple. (World Mission Associates 2006:1)

While the obvious solution to dependency is to avoid it by all means from the start, good intentions of missionaries and the obvious needs of converts make it difficult to avoid. Eradicating dependency once it has set in requires difficult decisions and determination on the part of all stakeholders. And since there are more stakeholders in the postcolonial period, including missionaries, partners, short-term volunteers, and local Christians, solutions are often complex.

Understanding the roots of dependency supplies an outline for suggested remedies. Since theology rooted in colonial mentalities is one of the main roots of dependency, the first place to start thinking about how to overcome dependency is with the Bible.

Biblical Remedies

One of the most important themes to notice from the Bible is that mission is God's idea from the start, and not ours. Whatever the term *Missio Dei* is taken to mean in modern missiology, it surely indicates that all mission originated from God's heart and purposes. David Bosch wrote:

> In attempting to flesh out the *Missio Dei* concept, the following could be said: ... There is a church because there is mission, not vice versa. To participate in mission is to participate in the movement of God's love toward people, since God is a fountain of sending love. (1991:390)

Discovering the heart of God requires fresh Bible study from Genesis to Revelation. However, since that is beyond the scope of this book, let us concentrate on the section of the Bible most relevant for missions today. Starting with a study of Jesus' missionary methods from the Gospels, we should also pay close attention to the precedents set by the early churches in Acts and the epistles. Of immense practical significance are Paul's missionary practices. What Roland Allen did for Christian missions in 1912 (1962a) has recently been investigated by others, since Paul's methods continue to be relevant (Gilliland 1983; Little 2005; Schnabel 2008).

It must suffice for this study to summarize a few issues that would arise from such Bible studies. First, none of the biblical mission methods fostered or created dependency because missions did not flow from the "powerful" to the "weak" in worldly terms. The power in missions was the power of the Spirit of God, not the power of military might or financial resources. Current missionary methods need to recover the biblical concept of the kingdom of God as the clash of God's reign with the reign of Satan, not as the clash of superior governmental or technological systems with inferior ones. Jesus saw the arrival of God's kingdom in His Person as the casting out of demons and the binding of the strong man, Satan (Matt. 12:28-29). If Western missionaries would preach the gospel of the kingdom of God in this way, spiritists would understand it better and be more likely to be converted to Jesus rather than to something else.

Second, Jesus and Paul preached the kingdom of God primarily for the salvation of men and women out of Satan's power, which in turn could transform their culture and society from the inside. Christianity has usually brought social improvement, and Jesus defined God's kingdom as God's will being done "on earth as it is in heaven" (Matt. 6:10). The social improvement that occurred in the New Testament came as indigenous churches let their understanding of the Bible interact with their culture and environment. This implied both a deep conversion at the worldview level and an ability to think biblically. When foreign missions or humanitarian organizations export systems of social improvement or political action, it tends to create dependency because it does not arise from within the hearts of the local converts themselves. It is rather what outsiders think is best for them. The Jerusalem Conference of Acts 15 decided that the Holy Spirit's leading was not to engage in cultural imperialism, even if the culture in question was that of God's chosen people, the Jews. That profound decision defined Christian mission primarily as planting seeds of the kingdom that would produce strong contextualized expressions of Christian community able to interact with and change their own society.

Third, a study of biblical mission methods would indicate that missionaries need to be mobile, travel light, and have flexible structures. American tourists often have heavy baggage and American missionaries are tempted to do likewise, but so many possessions and resources usually prove to be a distraction for local converts. Davis Saunders commented:

Southern Baptist missionaries often appeared to take casually their seemingly unlimited resources and to act with a lack of tactful concern for the sensitivities of others less able to muster any kind of adequacy in resources and appeared blithely unaware of the impression which they gave. (1973:313)

In the interviews that I conducted with African pastors, this was the issue that irritated them the most about American missionaries. In response to a question about whether missionaries treated them as equals, a common reply was that in some respects, like eating and sleeping together on mission trips, they could name missionaries who treated them with equality. Financially, however, they expressed resentment over their inferior position. For example, the missionaries had access to vehicles while they did not.

The methods used by Jesus showed to what extent He emptied Himself of overt privilege in order to preach to the poor. Paul, too, worked with his own hands in order to make it clear that Christians should work hard for a living and not expect easy financial gain. Today's American missionaries need to recover a simpler lifestyle. They also need to cease imposing institutions or foreign forms of church organization and leadership. The minimalist approach that Paul used would serve well in Africa, Asia, or Latin America, as local churches do not need buildings or paid pastors in the early stages to thrive and plant new churches. Even a small missionary force may be a catalyst for a people movement to Christ armed only with the Bible and the Holy Spirit.

Paul successfully planted indigenous churches wherever he went, without experiencing the kinds of problems seen now. Here we highlight those of Paul's methods that seem most helpful in coming to grips with self-government, self-propagation, self-support, contextualization, and mission theology as they pertain to indigeneity. In the words of Christopher Little, "There is just as much one can learn from Paul's orthopraxy as his orthodoxy" (2005:2).

With Regard to Self-Government: Freedom with Unity

Paul clearly understood his primary mission as the multiplication of local churches, "for it is only as visible congregations that the church can be indigenous" (Wagner 1972:36). One might think that he had no long history of denominational structures and traditions to carry around with him. Paul, however, always thought of himself as a Jew and in several instances subjected himself to Jewish law (Acts 16:3; 21:26). Thus, he had a much longer history of tradition behind him than any modern missionary, and this compelled him in every city where there was a synagogue to preach there first. Yet for the sake of the gospel he was not willing that his own traditions should hamper the free spread of Christianity among Gentiles. When it came to church government, no one could accuse Paul of imposing unwieldy foreign ideas. He gave formal structure to local churches only; structures above the local level were usually ad hoc and informal. There was no official link back to Jerusalem or Antioch, and mission churches were not considered inferior to these older churches. Whether new or old, all churches were equal "parts of a still incomplete whole" (Allen 1962a:131).

It could thus be said that Paul's prime consideration with regard to church government was freedom with unity. It is remarkable that "a Hebrew of Hebrews" (Phil. 3:5) would permit such local autonomy, and allow unity to be maintained apart from formal structures. The only reason can be that he fervently desired the gospel to take root in each local soil unencumbered by foreign (even Jewish) elements. Of course this would mean a nonuniform practice, and indeed this triggered the Jerusalem Conference of Acts 15.

At that conference, even the Jerusalem leaders vindicated the validity of Paul's indigenous approach, and Christianity was released from its Jewish straitjacket to spread like wildfire in innumerable local cultures. Furthermore, it is remarkable that Paul so seldom referred to the decisions made by the Jerusalem council. He was not interested in imposing rules from outside, but rather that each local assembly should take full responsibility to think for itself what obedience to the gospel required. In this, he did not leave them without guidance.

Above all, Paul and his team always empowered local leaders to take responsibility for pastoring, teaching, equipping, and serving in local churches. David Shenk and Ervin Stutzman noted, "Paul never left his congregations with a lack of clarity as to whom was in charge" (1988:172). At the end of the first missionary journey, "Paul and Barnabas appointed elders for them in each church and, with prayer and fasting, committed them to the Lord, in whom they had put their trust" (Acts 14:23). The Greek word *cheirotoneo*—translated as "appointed"— means "to stretch forth the hands" as in voting (Vine 1940:69). This seems to indicate congregational participation in selecting church elders. According to Vine, the Greek word *kathistemi*—translated as "appoint" in Titus 1:5—has a similar meaning and does not indicate a formal ecclesiastical ordination (1940:67).

Thus elders were simply men chosen to lead because they had already shown themselves capable and willing. The office of elder, overseer, or pastor was a functional position, tasked with leadership of the local church especially in the areas of teaching, shepherding, and guarding against error (Acts 20:28-31). They were also "to prepare God's people for works of service, so that the body of Christ may be built up" (Eph. 4:12). Beyond the office of elder the only other office in the local church Paul mentioned is that of deacon, indicating a person whose service to the church frees the elders to give more attention to "prayer and the ministry of the word" (Acts 6:4). There is no indication that Paul felt it necessary that he appoint deacons, perhaps leaving this to the church itself, or perhaps to the elders.

Before very long in every case, Paul moved on and left this local leadership in full control of the church. Some think he stayed only three weeks in Thessalonica (Hodges 1953:4) before being forced to leave. Yet even when he was not chased out so soon, twenty-seven months was the longest continuous stay in one place during Paul's years of church planting, as recorded by Luke (Acts 19:8-10). This is in stark contrast to modern missions practice: "The traditional mission pattern has been for the missionary to stay, often for years, in one place, in a culture not his own, and to form the church by his own theological convictions, rather than showing the church how to think for itself" (Gilliland 1983:33).

In doctrinal issues Paul taught the essentials. The first letter written to the Thessalonians, with whom Paul's time was so short, lays out "an extraordinarily clear and coherent scheme of simple mission-preaching," which Roland Allen summarized in just nine points (1962a:68). Paul's aim was not to impart a foreign system even of doctrine, but to leave behind a good basic foundation with easily reproducible concepts along with the Old Testament for deeper study. The foundation would consist of "a simple system of Gospel teaching, two sacraments [baptism and communion], a tradition of the main facts of the death and resurrection" (Allen 1962a:90). Even in matters of doctrine Paul's mission churches were soon self-governing.

As could be expected, this approach led to abuses and many local variations of practice and emphasis. Even here Paul was undaunted, writing letters, sending emissaries, and using powers of persuasion, preferring that his converts "should make many mistakes, and fall into many errors, and commit many offences, than that their sense of responsibility should be undermined" (Allen 1962a:145). When it came to matters of discipline, he preferred to put the onus squarely on the church's shoulders to work out the solution for itself. Even if the church failed to take action, as in the case of 1 Corinthians 5:1-5, Paul was as much concerned about the church's lack of action as he was about the sin committed. Whether 2 Corinthians 1:23-2:11 refers to this case of discipline or to another, clearly Paul was willing to delay personal visits to a church in order to give it time to rectify its own disciplinary matters.

In all matters, Paul showed respect for local leaders, never bypassing them, but rather trusting that they had the Holy Spirit and the Scriptures just as well as he did. Paul's practice of giving mission churches self-government was meant to empower the local church to be the church in its locale from the very beginning, with all the responsibility that involved. Because Paul was mobile and set up no central administrative authority, his mission churches had to learn through struggle what being an authentic Christian community meant in their corner of the world. Self-government meant learning to think for themselves, and it naturally produced vigorous indigenous churches with great diversity, unified through self-respect. Only in this way could they impact their communities and the world for Christ as mature agents of God's kingdom.

With Regard to Self-Propagation: Every Christian a Worker

Paul intuitively grasped that only indigenous churches can carry out the Great Commission effectively. As his own life was dedicated to establishing churches in many Gentile cultures, so he in turn expected these churches to extend that mission. He encouraged mission churches to participate in several ways: by contributing financially to the sending of mission teams (Rom. 15:24; Phil. 4:15-16), by supplying workers to be trained in missions (Acts 16:1-3), by prayer (Eph. 6:19-20), and by being self-propagating in their own area (1 Thess. 1:8).

Paul personally targeted cities and towns for his mission work. He chose urban areas because they contained Jewish communities where he could begin to preach (Schnabel 2008:282) and because he "did not expect people to come to him: he went to the places where people lived" (Schnabel 2008:257). His strategy seems to have been to start a church in an urban area from where he expected the gospel to spread into the province through self-propagation. For instance, we are told that after daily discussions in Tyrannus's lecture hall in Ephesus for two years, "all the Jews and Greeks who lived in the province of Asia heard the word of the Lord" (Acts 19:10). It is very likely that in Tyrannus's lecture hall Paul was busy converting people, and then training them as evangelists to go into the province of Asia.

One such convert was possibly Epaphras who went on to plant the church in Colosse (Hunter 1959:111; Schnabel 2008:254), his own hometown (Col. 1:7; 4:13). Significantly, Paul seems to indicate in Colossians 2:1 and 4:13 that churches had been planted also at Laodicea and Hierapolis, but not by himself. Paul operated in mission according to his own dictum to Timothy: "And the things you have heard me say in the presence of many witnesses entrust to reliable men who will also be qualified to teach others" (2 Tim. 2:2).

Through this kind of discipleship chain, every Christian would be put to work using his or her spiritual gift. Self-propagation involved multiplication of local evangelists, and full utilization of every Christian's gifts. Paul's use of the body as an illustration of how the church is to function is given to emphasize the fact that "each one is to consider himself to be as much in ministry as anyone else … There is no Christian who is not enabled in some way to perform a service (1 Cor. 12:7)" (Gilliland 1983:139).

Paul was careful not to stifle spiritual gifts in others by staying too long, or by becoming a local pastor himself, since his own main gift was that of apostle and church planter. He expected the churches he planted to "shine like stars in the universe as you hold out the word of life, in order that I may boast on the day of Christ that I did not run or labor for nothing" (Phil. 2:15-16). For Paul, self-propagation was not an end in itself, but a vital necessity if the Great Commission was to be fulfilled. Just as a championship soccer team has players who know their position and play it well, so Paul knew that evangelizing a lost world would require every Christian being mobilized to use his or her gifts through diverse self-propagating churches, expressing biblical Christianity in their own provincial flavor.

With Regard to Self-Support: Responsibility and Equality

Paul was acutely aware that "[m]oney can hurt and cripple, but it can also build and bless" (Gilliland 1983:256). Therefore he always exercised caution in this area. Regarding his personal finances, he was careful not to give an impression that he was working for money, as this would have subverted the gospel message into a kind of prosperity gospel. While he did accept gifts from mission churches on occasion (Phil. 4:15-18), and he did expect these churches to give towards mission, he refused to supervise the financial operations of local churches. With finances as with church government Paul "traveled light."

Because finances could so easily create misunderstanding between the missionary and mission churches, Paul took pains to avoid such problems. He never raised large sums of money before setting out on his mission journeys, and therefore he often ran out of funds (Acts 20:34; 1 Thess. 2:9). He knew that as an apostle he had a right to raise funds from his converts, but he refused to exercise these rights: "On the contrary, we put up with anything rather than hinder the gospel of Christ" (1 Cor. 9:12). He was conscious that his attitude toward money would either help or hinder the gospel, so he was careful to make himself "a model for you to follow" (2 Thess. 3:9), and offer the gospel free of charge wherever he went.

The model Paul was eager to set in place was that of self-support and the wise use of funds. Since "dependence does not train for independence [and] slavery does not educate men for freedom" (Allen 1962a:125), Paul never created any financial dependence on himself. Of course, he had no funds to dispense, but neither did he seek any. He hired no employees, built no buildings or institutions, and created no financial obligations to himself. As a result, the obligations people felt towards him were much stronger and more lasting than could be created by monetary obligations. He successfully stayed out of the financial traps that so many modern missionaries fall into by never introducing this complication between him and his mission churches. His personal lifestyle was on a par with that of his converts, and he never interfered in their management of church funds.

This is not to say, however, that he avoided church money issues altogether. The main way he used church funds was to promote church unity, and he did that by organizing a collection of money from mission churches to take to the mother church in Jerusalem. Most of Paul's teaching on giving comes from this collection, where again Paul was careful to avoid impropriety (2 Cor. 8:20). Since there was no over-arching ecclesiastical structure, Paul desired to cement ties between diverse churches through this offering. Shenk and Stutzman observed, "The European Gentile congregations and the Asian Jewish churches had almost nothing in common except their commitment to Jesus Christ. Division and schism were a real possibility" (1988:183). No doubt Paul used this occasion to teach indigenous churches to be aware of a wider obligation in their giving, including world missions, as implied in 2 Corinthians 8:9.

Beyond that, Paul was raising the stature of mission churches by even asking them to give to the mother church, much as John Gatu's churches in East Africa could claim to have come of age by donating to orphans in Scotland where their mother churches were located (Schwartz 1989a:12). By treating his mission churches as self-supporting bodies equal in every way to the original Jerusalem church, Paul went a long way in ensuring that they would always give and be self-supporting. They would also expect that if they fell into financial hardship, other churches would assist them "that there might be equality" (2 Cor. 8:13).

For those who understand Paul's collection "for the poor among the saints in Jerusalem" (Rom. 15:26) as a model for modern subsidies to flow from west to east or from north to south, closer inspection reveals that the modern equivalent would actually be a donation in the reverse direction. Paul's major effort to help the poor in Jerusalem was far more than humanitarian aid, and the resources went from recently planted churches to the original Christian church. Keith F. Nickle argued that Paul had three goals with the collection: "(1) the realization of Christian charity, (2) the expression of Christian unity, (3) the anticipation of Christian eschatology" (1966:100). Nickle understood the collection primarily in terms of Paul's attempt to cement unity between Jewish and Gentile churches, and the collection underscored Paul's confidence that the new Gentile churches were equal to the original Jewish ones.

After a thorough study of the reasons for the collection, Christopher Little did not see the humanitarian motive as central. Rather, he concluded, "Given the circumstances surrounding Paul's collection project, it is inherently problematic to use it as a model for the missional task of the church in any age. This is because it was pursued with the hope of saving Israel by way of demonstrating the Gentiles' gratitude" (2005:169). Eckhard Schnabel concurs:

> The collection which Paul organized in the churches he had established can hardly constitute the biblical precedent for modern partnerships between missions organizations and national churches. Paul's main concern was the promotion of unity between the churches he had established as an apostle to the Gentiles and the Jewish believers in Jerusalem, perhaps linked with the hope that this project may prompt skeptical Jews to come to faith in Jesus the Messiah when they see "the nations" come to Zion. (2008:443-4)

Thus, the collection in no way serves as a model for modern Christian humanitarian efforts that may see "receiving" churches as inferior because they are needy.

To sum up, self-support, along with self-government and self-propagation, was an aspect of being a mature and equal part of Christ's church, with responsibility to missions both locally and worldwide. Sacrificial giving and living were as essential for mission churches as for Paul and Jesus, so that mission could continue unhindered.

With Regard to Contextualization: Ownership and Relevance

Charles Taber emphasized that contextualization goes far beyond traditional understandings of indigenization because 1) it includes not only local cultural factors, but social, economic, and political factors as well; 2) it considers the rapid changes taking place in all societies and cultures; 3) it touches both the culture being evangelized and the missionary's culture; and 4) it seeks complete and true indigenization, rather than leaving outsiders in control of some institutions, or handing over westernized institutions to local control (1979:144-6).

A fairly simple test of contextualization is to ask, "Who owns the work?" That is, who feels and takes responsibility for the care of the church members, upkeep of the facilities, running of programs or institutions, and funding of local outreach? If it is a foreign missionary, then it would be difficult to say the work has been indigenized. For a work to be contextualized there must first be ownership.

For Paul, ownership was never a problem, since in this respect his mission churches were in control as soon as they had been organized. Paul would no doubt have agreed with Alan Tippett's words, "If you ever face the problem of changing over from the mission to the national church, there must have been a problem somewhere. It should have been the national church from the beginning" (Schwartz 1989a:11).

Paul gave over ownership from the beginning so that he would soon be free to move on, but also so that these churches would be contextualized. That is, so that they would be able to work out an expression of Christianity appropriate to their local situation, and so be effective in local outreach. While Paul was concerned that the absolutes of the gospel not be violated (for then there would be no Christianity), he was also unwilling to introduce unnecessary foreign elements even from the Mosaic Law.

Inadequate contextualization can easily become syncretism, that is, a combination of Christian elements with ideas from other religions. This apparently happened in the Colossian church, where Paul warned Christians against becoming captive to human philosophies and elementary principles of the world (Col. 2:8). He specifically mentioned rules about what food and drink to consume, keeping special holy days, worship of angels, promotion of personal visions, religiosity that centered on a list of prohibitions, and harsh treatment of the body (Col. 2:16-23). This sort of syncretism arose through poor contextualization of the Christian message, leading to an incomplete understanding of the gospel's implications.

That Paul took contextualization seriously is apparent from his thorough teaching on eating food sacrificed to idols in 1 Corinthians 8 and 10. Although the Jerusalem Council in Acts 15 had apparently settled that question by a flat prohibition, when it came to Corinth, Paul allowed eating such food in some circumstances (1 Cor. 10:25-27). The Corinthians, however, were drifting into syncretism because they misunderstood Paul's teaching on freedom in Christ (a key to Paul's teaching and the basis of contextualization). But whereas Paul had a golden opportunity to reiterate a rule as decreed in Jerusalem, he chose contextualization instead. While carefully avoiding syncretism, he used a significant section of 1 Corinthians to explain the limits of Christian freedom and to detail circumstances where eating food sacrificed to idols was permissible, giving full explanations and reasons.

Rather than impose an apostolic rule, he appealed to the Corinthians to think through the dimensions of this issue with him, and then for themselves. Particularly he was aware of the Corinthian context where questionable food would often be placed before a believer, and his desire seems to have been to avoid damaging the believer's witness by automatic unthinking rejection. Paul highly valued contextualization as a means of appropriate mission because local believers had to take responsible ownership of local issues.

Paul's Mission Theology: The Church on Mission

Paul lived and breathed mission: "Woe to me if I do not preach the gospel!" (1 Cor. 9:16). As already noted, his reasons for insisting on contextualization were so as not to hinder the gospel. Only indigenous churches could spread the gospel endlessly. Because he was on mission, Paul developed a high view of the church (Eph. 3:10; 1 Tim. 3:15). The many and varied images he used for the church indicate a depth of thinking on the subject. Referring to the church as the body of Christ indicates the church's function and unity even with tremendous variations among its members. As a body it is obedient to the Head, Jesus Christ, and in turn Christ uses the church to continue His ministry and mission today.

Therefore the church is Christ's agent on earth, with the task of seeing His work to completion as Christ works in and through it. The church as bride of Christ (Eph. 5:25-27) indicates respect and intimacy. This shows that the church is the people of God since the same imagery was used in the Old Testament for God's relationship to Israel (for example, Ezek. 16). Since husband and wife are one, this image also indicates that Christ's work and the church's share the same goal. Ephesians 2:19-22 uses images of the church as God's household and as a building or temple where God's Spirit dwells. These dynamic pictures, relating back to the Israel of the Old Testament, prove that the church is far more than a collection of people. Clearly the mission of God in Christ continues in and through the church, as God Himself empowers and indwells it.

Paul saw his primary mission as the establishment of the church in each province, and expected the churches to multiply the effort. While one can agree with Virgil Gerber that, "in the course of history, churches produced missions. Missions produced churches. Their success produced tensions" (Wagner 1972:9), at the same time it does not sound much like Paul to separate church and mission. Certainly Protestant missions have spread very rapidly throughout the world in the past 200 years through the use of missionary societies. Quite possibly Christianity would not have advanced very much without their use. However, it is also true that these societies have created the church/mission dichotomy and tensions that were addressed at Green Lake in 1971. Missionary societies by now have taken on a life of their own, very often apart from any church oversight. Indicative of this kind of thinking coming out of Green Lake was Ralph Winter, who spoke of planting both new churches and new missions (Wagner 1972:129).

While Winter was ahead of his time in foreseeing the emergence of mission agencies in developing countries, and was motivated by a desire to see mission churches go into mission themselves, he also left the impression that "Missionary societies ought not only to plant churches but younger missions" (Costas 1974:170). One then gets the feeling that parachurch structures could theoretically work and perpetuate themselves altogether outside the church. Others, however, have objected to such a sharp cleavage between church and mission, usually on theological grounds. Orlando Costas noted, "There is no ground in the New Testament for a concept of mission apart from the church, just as there is no concept of the church apart from mission" (1974:168).

Paul's model is not one of planting churches and missions, but of planting churches that were on mission. Indigeneity would have been impossible if all efforts at mission were because of foreign missionaries. Of course if Christianity is not present in a culture, a foreigner must bring it in, as Paul did. But from there, Paul planted indigenous churches and moved on, expecting his mission to be multiplied through his converts. Paul is the model of a highly mobile missionary, untrammeled by heavy mission structures, yet intent on church planting in every culture. His focus was always the church; his aim was the planting of churches; and his desire was to see the church on mission both locally and worldwide.

Those who are alarmed at the prospect of American missionaries evangelizing in Africa in the postcolonial period accuse them of being "a rather neo-colonial type of mission which seems to be anachronistic in the post-independence era of Africa" (Verstraelen 1995:194). This viewpoint understands American evangelical missionaries to be the continuation of the colonial mentality. This alarm should be real if the charge that Steve Brouwer, Paul Gifford, and Susan Rose made is true:

> Under the twin covenants of Americanism and their churches, the new fundamentalists are having a profound effect in promoting both an acceptance of American (U.S.) cultural norms and the kind of civic and psychic orderliness that does not question the role of the powerful. (1996:271)

If it is true that Manifest Destiny still drives American missions, then it should be made clear that that is an unbiblical method of missions.

If American missionaries preach the gospel of Christ as the only Lord and Savior, however, without the element of Americanism, one suspects that these same critics might still be alarmed at the arrogance of this method. In response to that, Lesslie Newbigin said; "To affirm the unique decisiveness of God's action in Jesus Christ is not arrogance; it is the enduring bulwark against the arrogance of every culture to be itself the criterion by which others are judged" (1989:166).

It is not imperialism to let the gospel take deep root in a culture and then work its way out from inside. This was the method used by Jesus, Paul, and others in the New Testament. By it, Christianity conquered the Roman Empire in 300 years with nothing but spiritual weapons. Whereas Paul refused to champion his own Jewish culture as superior, later missionaries often acted as agents of a foreign way of life, adding this to their preaching. In order not to propagate cultural imperialism along with the benefits of the gospel, it is necessary to respect local cultures.

Contextual Remedies

American missionaries have often tacitly assumed that their culture is superior because it was shaped by Christian values, while that of Africans is inferior because it was shaped by spiritism. While missionary anthropologists used to affirm that cultures are relatively neutral and all are suitable vessels in which to receive the gospel (Mayers 1974:70; Kraft 1979:113), some have more recently challenged this view. Sherwood Lingenfelter stated, "Culture is created and contaminated by human beings; culture is the pen of disobedience from which freedom is possible only through the gospel" (1998:17). Just as individuals are fallen, so are their cultures. Just as the Jewish culture into which Jesus was born was corrupt, so is the current American culture. Eddie Gibbs said, "Given the fact that Western societies are rapidly transitioning from Constantinian to secular, neo-pagan, and pluralistic cultural contexts, the Church must recognize that all evangelism has become a cross-cultural activity" (2004:20).

Indeed, syncretism is not unique to spiritists; it is rampant in the United States among Christians. Gailyn Van Rheenen stated, "While Westerners are syncretistic on the secular side of the continuum, peoples from the Third World are frequently syncretistic on the animistic side. Both extremes are dangerous" (1991:96). Since Western missionaries have been raised in a secular society, they too absorb many values that are unbiblical. For example, "Western theologians have ignored the concept of spiritual powers in biblical writings" (Van Rheenen 1991:96). Such missionaries going into spiritistic societies convey the idea that secularism is superior to spiritism, when in fact the gospel condemns both. Moreover, it is this excessive secularism among many missionaries that tends to create dependency in Africa.

What ought to be done instead? The remedy is to allow the gospel to judge all cultures, making Christians neither superior Americans nor inferior Africans, but sinners saved equally by grace from equally corrupt societies. This frees Western missionaries to learn about the reality of the spirit world from Africans and from the Bible, while Africans can learn about the sovereignty of God over spirits from the traditions of Western theology and from the Bible.

Andrew Walls described the two opposing tendencies inherent in the gospel that he called the "pilgrim principle" and the "indigenizing principle" (1996:7-9). The indigenizing principle stems from the God-given desire "to live as a Christian and yet as a member of one's own society" (1996:7). The pilgrim principle, on the other hand, makes a Christian feel somewhat out of place in the society. Walls summarized, "Along with the indigenizing principle which makes his faith a place to feel at home, the Christian inherits the pilgrim principle, which whispers to him that he has no abiding city" (1996:8). Sherwood Lingenfelter applied the pilgrim principle as "a necessary counterbalance" to indigenous church principles (1998:15). He understood that an indigenous church isolated by the Three-Self formula for too long becomes contaminated by its own fallen culture: "The indigenous church without connection to the universal church and the Word dies. Entrenched in its own private vision of righteousness, it ceases to contextualize its message to needy people and loses vision and outreach" (1998:15).

Lingenfelter emphasized the need for continuous interaction between churches from all parts of the globe, but this is beneficial only if Christians see each other as fellow pilgrims who are citizens of a heavenly kingdom and not primarily as representatives of superpowers or of nations that are "basket cases." Even though he came from a highly ethnocentric nation, Paul was able to regard fellow Christians from all races as "neither Jew nor Greek, ... neither slave nor free, ... neither male nor female; for you are all one in Christ Jesus" (Gal. 3:28). For Paul, these words were not idle theory, as they translated into his actual relationships; therefore, he avoided creating dependency. He did not seek to convert people to the worldview of a particular culture, but to a radically biblical worldview that could stand in judgment of any culture, including his own. Yet we are all prisoners of our own worldviews if these are not biblical.

From my own experience in leading short-term teams from the United States to Africa since 2003, I have found that contextual misunderstandings that often cause dependency come about because of the clash of Western secularism with African spiritism. American Christians have usually adopted secularism from the indigenizing of their faith in a culture heavily influenced by the Enlightenment. This provides them with a "can-do" spirit that believes in action and achievement using human resources and reason. African Christians, on the other hand, have usually absorbed spiritism from the indigenizing of their faith in the milieu of African beliefs in an active spirit world. The clash of assumptions of these two worldviews sets up the possibility of creating dependency in four major areas (Reese 2008b).

Use of Time

Secular thinking sees time as a commodity to save, spend, or waste. Since short-term missions by definition have only a little time to spend in the new culture, they naturally want to make the most of that time. Often, they expect supplies and equipment to be in place ahead of time, with schedules worked out well in advance, so that the volunteers can hit the ground running. Here is a situation tailor-made for secular problem solving, but it may also run counter to the lifestyle of the local people.

The local people are not nearly so worried about saving time, especially if they have collective thinking. Rather, they may desire to use time for building relationships instead of completing tasks. This calls for careful thinking by the short-term volunteers: Is the top priority the given task or relationships with local people? Who is the task for anyway? The temptation will be strong to override local concerns to complete a given task, but this might leave the hosts wondering if the project is really theirs, thus setting up dependency. Sharing who we are in Christ is far more important than completing some visible task; submitting to and serving one another is the way to build the body of Christ.

Problem Solving

It would be a rare short-term mission that faced no unexpected problems. The question is: How do the short-term volunteers react to these problems? A secular-thinking person will naturally come up with a materialistic solution, while a spiritual person will seek a spiritual solution. North American Christians are compassionate, but tend to think in secular categories first in response to problems. For instance, when faced with sickness, is the first response to pray or to take a pill? When faced with poor technology, is the first response to see how local people have worked through this issue, or to propose American solutions? When faced with poverty, is the first response to raise money or to seek to grasp the spiritual causes for it?

North Americans tend to judge other cultures based on their technology or lack of it. We compare their infrastructure, health care system, transportation, economy, and military with our own and generally find them lacking. At the same time, we may omit to compare their social systems and family structures with ours, as we value hardware perhaps more than relationships.

People from a spiritist background, however, tend to focus on spiritual solutions to technical problems. For them, sickness or poverty may have a spiritual cause more than a material cause. Even if we show them a scientific explanation, they may persist in seeing a spiritual explanation behind the science. If the short-term volunteers insist on solving problems materialistically, what message do they convey to the local people? They would tend to secularize the people rather than make them more spiritual. They would be promoting American solutions rather than biblical ones. Foreign secular solutions to common problems are at the root of the dependency syndrome.

Decision Making

North American thinking emphasizes individualism and tolerance of the beliefs of others. This may mean that if I don't like the decision the group makes, I am free to reject it and do my own thing. North Americans have a long tradition of individualism, but it doesn't communicate well with people in other cultures who see the benefits of togetherness more. While Westerners will often opt out of group decisions, collectivists seldom do that because their survival depends on unity. While Westerners like to stand out in a crowd by looking or acting differently, collectivists value conformity. Which is more biblical? The gospel certainly teaches our individual worth, but that is in order to build a united body of Christ of which the individual is a part. So if the short-term volunteers convey excessive individualism, it may undermine the unity God desires in Christ's body.

Consider the local people where the short-term ministry takes place: some of them may also be part of the body of Christ. They are brothers and sisters in Christ who may be directly affected by the project. What input do they have in the project? What contributions do they make and what part do they have in deciding? If the North Americans leave them out of decisions, then the question arises again: Who is the project for? Submitting to the wishes of others is an important step in reducing the possibility of dependence.

The Source of Power

Ultimately the short-term mission will uphold its source of power as a standard for others, so it is crucial that it understands what the source of power is. If it is the power of the cross, then the mission will preach the good news of the gospel in unmistakable terms. If it is the power of money or technology, that will come across clearly. The power of materialism makes us activists as long as our resources allow, but the power of the cross is limitless because it does not depend on human knowledge or skill. The power of the cross does not depend on our resources but on God's. It does not depend on our actions but on our dependence on God. How much then do we take time to pray before acting in our missions? This may show us whether we think secularly or spiritually.

If the first reaction of short-term volunteers to situations they encounter is to pray and depend on God for answers, then true success of the project is much more likely, because this shows that they value God's agenda more than their own. This means something to people of less secular cultures, who struggle daily with problems for which they have no solution. If they can see that even North Americans must depend on God for answers, then the likelihood of dependency will be greatly reduced.

No party alone can resolve the problems of dependency, especially since the influx of short-term missionaries and overseas partners has further complicated the situation. Both Western and non-Western Christians need to evaluate how they see each other: as rich versus poor, powerful versus weak, white versus black, superior versus inferior, or as fellow pilgrims in Christ? Such an evaluation should produce specific strategies to eradicate the debilitating dependency that now exists, so that non-Western churches can become effective in global missions.

Strategic Remedies

While the Three-Self formula has been heavily criticized, it has perhaps been overlooked as a necessary first step to selfhood for any church with the simple addition of the "Fourth Self," or self-theologizing (Hiebert 1985:193-224). That is, any dependent church or association of churches would still do well to evaluate itself by the criteria of the Four Selfs. Can they make their own decisions? Can they carry out those decisions with their own funds? Can they contribute workers to the task of mission? And can they interpret the Scriptures in their own context? In most cases, only local leaders who see dependency as a spiritual dead-end can do such an evaluation. This, therefore, requires leaders of integrity who desire spiritual renewal for themselves and their flocks.

Glenn Schwartz cited examples of dependent churches that experienced such renewal when spiritual leaders challenged their people "to become the Body of Christ on earth, doing what Jesus would do if He walked among the people today. In addition, these leaders will make self-reliance thinking the topics of their sermons, Bible studies and administrative meetings" (1993:1). Schwartz suggested setting aside times of prayer and discussion, because the move away from dependency is essentially a spiritual decision. Any attempt at such renewal will invite Satan's opposition, so that makes it all the more necessary for leaders to understand that overcoming dependency is a spiritual battle.

What might this mean in practical terms? First, local leaders would review the role of any institutions that they inherited from the missionaries. Do these institutions contribute to Christ's work on earth or do they feed dependency? If they distract from the main work of the church as revealed in the Bible, then they can be sold, set up as private trusts, or handed over to other agencies. If the institutions are deemed essential for the churches, then they should be fully funded by the churches; otherwise they will remain a cause of dependency.

Second, these leaders would review their own church structures, especially at the national level, to determine if the structures themselves invite dependency. Assuming that local churches have achieved the Four Selfs, which may not be the case for all of them, they should fully fund any associations or conventions that they desire to have. If they cannot fund such associations, then they should look for ways to restructure that are affordable for them. Such an evaluation should include the funding of traveling evangelists, of planting new churches, of trips by national leaders, and of church meetings. If the local churches cannot fund any of these, they should restructure them to make them affordable.

Third, these leaders would review their relationship with their founding mission. Does this relationship empower for Christ's work or add to dependency? It would be helpful to the missions if the local leaders announced that they were seeking to end dependency and become fully self-reliant. Together, they should seek to terminate any sources of contention that still exist between them. The indigenous churches, with the stated goal of self-reliance, should then be free to have frank discussions about what they desire in the relationship with their founding missionaries. Such discussions would bear much more fruit if the relationship is not poisoned by dependency.

Fourth, these leaders would review their relationship with short-term volunteers and overseas partners, since these new relationships have often contributed to dependency. As these may not be long-term relationships, the local leaders may desire to make policies about any such relationships that would let existing and potential partners know their desire to avoid the abuses of the past. All such partners would probably welcome such formal policies, as they would indicate the maturity of the indigenous churches.

Fifth, missionaries would develop a "release mentality" (Schwartz 1993:4) toward their work in order to let the local Christians assume full control as part of their self-hood. This would include releasing institutions that self-reliant churches say are essential for them to operate. Other institutions that the mission intends to keep and that local churches do not want should have their status clarified to all parties. It is a mistake to indigenize local churches only and leave out of any discussion the institutions that affect those churches. The goal of indigenization is to allow the local churches full responsibility for their own life and ministry, and this means full ownership of the existing structures and institutions vital to them.

Sixth, missionaries would review the relationship of the mission to the local churches in all areas. While some missionaries have the option of the "euthanasia" of the mission, this does not seem to be the case with certain missions. Winston Crawley did not envisage the dissolution of the mission in a place, saying:

> The [Southern Baptist] Foreign Mission Board has continued to believe in the validity and the value of a mission organization ... The main danger for the mission organization is that it will become an end in itself, concerned to maintain itself, to strengthen itself, to increase its authority and powers and functions. (1985:223)

Saunders affirmed:

> Seeking to amalgamate the two [the Mission and the Baptist Convention of Zimbabwe] ... was not possible under the limitations of the Southern Baptist Foreign Mission Board's policy. However, this type of solution was utilized by the Seventh Day Baptists, who had only a few missionaries and modest external financial support. (1973:302)

Saunders hinted that the "euthanasia" option might remove the chronic uncertainty in the organizational relationship between the mission and its daughter churches.

The dissolution of the mission is the strategy that will end dependency sooner. For the local churches to meet the criteria of the Four Selfs, they will have to be responsible for all the functions that the mission does. The ultimate goal is that all the local churches become sending churches, participating fully as initiators of world missions. They cannot reach this goal if other "partners" continue to do the things for them that they should be doing for themselves. Remaining dependent cannot train them for independence or interdependence. The indefinite presence of the mission will certainly delay achieving these important goals.

It has been difficult for American missionaries to release the churches that they planted. Dependency and resentment have marred the relationship even as the world has evolved from the colonial to the postcolonial period. Eradication of dependency requires changes of attitudes on all sides.

Attitudinal Remedies

A truly secular mindset tends to ignore feelings in its pursuit of solutions for difficult problems; yet feelings play a large part in the success of any venture. First of all, we Americans often have preconceived notions about the rest of the world. News broadcasts and appeals for donations by charitable agencies build a picture of the developing nations as needy and ripe for rescue. This predisposes us to approach people of those nations as victims whom we can help, seeing ourselves as resourceful and innovative.

The people we wish to help also have feelings and will react to how we treat them. Our treatment of people we deem to be poor often degrades them without our knowledge. Robert Lupton describes a case of a woman who came to help at a clothes closet for the needy in inner-city America. She was mistaken by the people in charge of the clothes closet as being someone in need of clothes herself. Lupton commented about the impact of this incident on the volunteer: "Her face reflected the hurt that loss of self-esteem can inflict. Receiving ... is a humbling thing" (2007:21). This embarrassing episode that the woman experienced could be the common lot of the needy on a regular basis.

Bryant Myers has considerable experience working with the poor of developing countries through his work at World Vision. He says that viewing the poor as helpless allows us to "give ourselves permission to play god in the lives of the poor"

(1999:57). We may see the poor as passive and in need of the wholeness we can supply. Myers says this wrong attitude has two negative consequences:

> First, this attitude demeans and devalues the poor. Our view of them, which quickly becomes their view of themselves, is that they are defective and inadequate. We do not treat them as human beings made in the image of God. We act as if God's gifts were given to us and none to the poor. This attitude increases their poverty and tempts us to play god in the lives of the poor. Second, our attitude about ourselves can become messianic. We are tempted to believe that we are the deliverers of the poor, that we can make their lives complete. (1999:66)

In other words, attitudes can damage both the recipients of our generosity and ourselves. Lupton states, "Perhaps the deepest poverty of all is to have nothing of value to offer in exchange. Charity that fosters such poverty must be challenged" (2007:26).

Jayakumar Christian, who works for World Vision in India, echoes the language used by Myers:

> My assumption is that the poor are poor because someone else is trying to play God in their lives. Human beings were designed to submit their spirit only to the Creator. Any attempt to take the place of the Creator leads to poverty … For the agent of transformation to refuse to play God requires great strength of character. (Crouch 2007b:42)

But how can we view the world's poor as anything but helpless? We can begin by realizing that the poor must have discovered some principles of survival because they are still there. "Even the poorest community already has some level of sustainability. If the community were not sustainable before the development agency came, it could not exist" (Myers 1999:128). Second, those deemed the poor of the world may be rich in faith and heirs of God's kingdom, according to James 2:5. That is, wealth and poverty in God's sight is measured differently and the poor may be able to teach us something. Third, we can realize that poverty is not only an absence of goods but also a state of mind. There are not only physical dimensions to poverty, but also social, mental, and spiritual dimensions (Myers 1999:129). This is why attitudes are so important when trying to alleviate poverty.

In essence, the key to poverty alleviation is the poor themselves. They may need outside help, but first they need to speak for themselves. Instead of our asking them first what they need, we can let them tell us how God is already working in their lives. Myers stated, "Asking the community to locate God in its history is a way of helping its members to discover that they are not god-forsaken" (Myers 1999:139). Faith in God's provision can easily wipe out any trace of dependency.

In our own mission work, we often tried to find ways to stimulate some type of low-grade local economy for rural Zimbabwean Christians to make a living without relocating to urban areas. While the vast majority of our schemes failed in the long-term, the ones that succeeded were taken up by the least dependent Christians. In 1987, a Tonga Christian announced that he was going to resign from his job as a farmworker to return home to preach to his own Tonga people in the distant Zambezi River valley. He didn't ask for any help, even though he had no particular way to make a living. In open discussions with him, he said he could use some cattle to start a herd that might sustain his family. Through the generosity of a church in California, we were able to help him with just two cattle, enough to begin a herd that has helped in part to sustain his growing ministry among the Tonga people for over twenty years.

Faith in God and dependency do not go together; people need to know that with God their situation is never hopeless and they do have valuable contributions to make when God energizes them. From the context of his work in inner city Atlanta, Robert Lupton summarizes, "Dependency is not for the healthy. How then have we created systems of dependency for those in need and thought it good?" (2007:44). Our attitudes can either sink people into dependency or help free them from it.

Conclusion

Turning the tide against the dependency syndrome requires more than mere self-criticism. Keith R. Bridston said:

> Radical self-criticism has a largely negative function. It must be supplemented by a positive principle for action and policy in the present and the future. Old paternalistic demons cast out, however clean the room is swept, will be replaced by others—less barbaric but no less demonic. (1965:79)

The end of colonialism failed to terminate dependency despite widespread condemnation of colonial attitudes. Old harmful attitudes persist into the present, delaying real reform and innovation. Positive steps still need to be taken in order to move to a productive postcolonial mission model.

First and foremost, biblical remedies are essential. Scripture is full of positive models of mission and these cry out for contemporary exposition in light of twenty-first century contexts. Thankfully, many are undertaking new missional studies of Jesus, Paul, and the Old Testament (Wright 2006). Jesus' mission provides us with the inspiration to empty ourselves of Western privilege to walk with people of any nation in dignity. Paul's practice of mission stands out for us as the goal of our own mission: the establishment of healthy churches that can impact societies for God. After all, it was these churches stemming from the Jesus Movement that transformed the Roman Empire in a mere 300 years.

From biblical remedies should come spiritual renewal—the *sine qua non* of overcoming dependency. As Jesus told the Pharisees, reading the Scripture alone may not lead a person to know Christ as the true source of life (John 5:39). The Holy Spirit must become active in the person's life to supply "streams of living water" (John 7:38) that will stamp out dependency on what only humans can supply. Having the mind of Christ enables far more than human wisdom alone can accomplish, as this opens the promises of Christ:

> I tell you the truth, anyone who has faith in me will do what I have been doing. He will do even greater things than these, because I am going to the Father. And I will do whatever you ask in my name, so that the Son may bring glory to the Father. You may ask anything in my name, and I will do it. (John 14:12-14)

Armed with such assurances, Christians of any nation may develop churches that are self-governing, self-propagating, self-supporting, and self-theologizing, despite any seeming lack of normal resources. Self-government allows the freedom inherent in Christ to provide innovative leadership suited to local situations, while maintaining the overall unity of the worldwide body of Christ. Self-propagation arises from the average members of local churches employing their God-given talents and spiritual gifts. Self-support comes from each member contributing whatever God has supplied, however meager it appears to wealthy outsiders. Self-theologizing arises from having the Spirit of God to help with interpretation of Scripture for local situations.

All of these "selfs" come from the confidence that God is not limited by our background or resources. The churches belong to him and he has entrusted them to us for now. This allows our churches and institutions to be contextualized and relevant to local needs, so they need not look like churches elsewhere. They are primarily for God's own mission in our area and beyond; they bear the marks of our culture but they also challenge local beliefs because they also bear the marks of the one who bought them with his own blood.

Accepting this means that no segment of Christ's body is better or more indispensable than any other (1 Cor. 12:12-31). This is because Christ is the single head and all the rest are parts of his body at his disposal. This makes the various worldviews that we may have grown up with myopic because they may not reflect the Lord's viewpoint. We operate within human worldviews such as secularism or spiritism, but these are flawed. Secularism in particular propagates dependency, especially when it comes into contact with spiritism. Yet neither of these worldviews is biblical. Part of our self-theologizing is to form a more biblical worldview to see the world as God does.

Only with biblical worldviews and spiritual renewal are we enabled to tackle strategic and attitudinal remedies for dependency with success. We can more accurately see mistakes of the past and how to correct them. Then the house swept clean of old demons may be filled with the Spirit for productive missions.

9

ISSUES FOR POSTCOLONIAL
MISSIONS

———————

WITH THE END OF THE COLD WAR and the emergence of globalization, the world today is vastly different from the days of colonial rule. By its very nature, colonialism trapped nations in unhealthy dependent relationships, but now that we live in a postcolonial era, we have a fresh opportunity to realize mission methods that are more biblical, and thus more suitable. Paul Hiebert noticed a trend: "There is a growing sensitivity in modern missions to national and cultural pluralism and a concurrent search for postcolonial models for mission ministry" (1985:294-5). David Bosch, in his treatment of the various mission models throughout the centuries, suggested that we are now between an old and a new paradigm:

> New paradigms do not establish themselves overnight. They take decades, sometimes even centuries, to develop distinctive contours. The new paradigm is therefore still emerging and it is, as yet, not clear which shape it will eventually adopt. For the most part we are, at the moment, thinking and working in terms of two paradigms. (1991:349)

He called the old paradigm "modern," based on the Enlightenment, and thus the new paradigm is "postmodern." As we noted earlier, the Enlightenment produced mission models that instilled dependency in converts through its doctrines of Western superiority and emphasis on natural solutions to common problems through science and technology. Enlightenment thinking led to the utopian ideal of inevitable human progress in everything from rocket science to the conversion of the nations to Christ, with the West leading the way. Such an ideal was strongly linked to the concept of Christendom, which was defined as the part of the world where Christianity had already had such a decisive impact that all segments of society were deemed enlightened or at least significantly improved.

Noting that "the spirit of Christendom has persisted across the centuries" (2003:3), David Smith emphasized, "Nonetheless, it is quite clear by now that this particular model of the Christian mission has lost its credibility and cannot survive" (2003:4). This is because of the growth of the churches planted by missionaries in the global South and East and because of the end of Christendom itself. It is no longer adequate to think in terms of Christian territories or Christian sending nations for world missions. With increasing secularization and pluralism, the Western nations are shifting from being the traditional sending nations to becoming a mission field. With the migrations of peoples under globalization, the mission field is now literally everywhere; with the conversion of multitudes of peoples, the sending churches are now also everywhere. In this emerging context, what are the essential ingredients for healthy postcolonial mission models?

Independence before Interdependence:
The Surprising Relevance of the Three-Self Formula

Despite the heavy criticism of the Three-Self formula that we have noted, there is still a surprising case to be made in its favor in postcolonial missions. Certainly, Venn and Anderson were men of their own time; it would be surprising if they were not. Yet, they were also beyond their own time, and this is what gives them continued relevance.

Wilbert Shenk discussed three stages of Protestant mission practice: replication of Western models in other cultures, indigenization with Christendom still the basis, and contextualization where control lies in the context itself (1999:50-8). Shenk noted:

> Most proponents of indigenization assumed Christendom continued to furnish the norm by which they were to judge their work. The goal of indigenization was to see that norm reproduced, albeit in indigenous clothes. (1999:55)

Shenk noted further that some of the statements that Venn made would logically lead beyond the indigenization model: "Venn's statement of 1868, if pushed to its logical conclusion, would have stretched the concept of indigenization to the breaking point" (1999:55). In his 1868 statement, Venn urged both "the utmost respect for national peculiarities" (1999:54), and the early leadership of converts in their own churches with the prerogative to "supersede the denominational distinctions which are now introduced by foreign missionary societies" (1999:55). Shenk remarked that such an approach would "allow the new church greater freedom in expressing its faith in its own cultural idiom" (1999:55). Thus, in some ways, the proponents of the Three-Self formula anticipated the movement toward contextualization, despite holding onto the Christendom concept.

Many current critics of the Three-Self formula wish to abandon it because they favor interdependence in the postcolonial world. For example, Isaac Mwase calls for a "reappraisal of the 'three-self' philosophy of missions" in the area of self-support (2005:63). Citing the inability of Zimbabwean Baptists to support their seminary because of "economies of poverty that prevail in Zimbabwe," he calls on Southern Baptists in the United States "to acknowledge that we now live in a world where interdependence is a fact of life" (2005:72-4). In essence, he urges the International Mission Board to resume funding the Baptist Theological Seminary of Zimbabwe in order to restore interdependence.

As already noted, interdependence is the ideal in missions, but it is often inhibited by unresolved dependence. If one party is a victim of the dependency syndrome, then attempts at interdependence are doomed to fail. In these situations, "interdependence" has been used to camouflage continued Christendom approaches, with donors on one side of the world funding Christians on the other. This was standard procedure during colonialism, because new churches were not seen as capable of succeeding without continuous help and supervision. Vincent Donovan said:

> It is one thing for generous American Christians to offer food, medicine, or other supplies to the poor people of the world, whether those people be Christian or not. It is quite another for the American church to take over the running expenses of the young churches of the third world. Leaving aside what this practice does to the independence and maturity of those churches, it is, in itself, a thought and an ideal which would have seemed incredible to the people of St. Paul's time. (1982:130)

The distinctions drawn by Donovan clarify that much of what is called world missions by those who champion partnership is really the support of weak churches and institutions rather than missions. Since this support will apparently be perpetual, it really accomplishes nothing of lasting significance, certainly not any outreach to non-Christians. Churches mired in the dependency syndrome have not yet attained maturity, nor will they until they cease being dependent. True interdependence implies that maturity already exists.

Few evangelical mission leaders today seem to appreciate the stance taken by John Gatu in his call for a moratorium on missionary personnel and funding. At the heart of his 1971 appeal laid a desperate cry for enough space to achieve authentic self-hood for the Presbyterian Church of East Africa. Gatu explained the sad effects of the dependency syndrome on his churches:

> As long as money came when we requested it [from Western missions], there was no reason to ask (a) whether the structures we inherited [from missionaries] were still relevant, (b) whether it would be possible for us to maintain a differently restructured edifice, or (c) whether or not we could find local people to manage those structures. Just as African governments did not feel embarrassed to keep begging year in and year out, the dependence syndrome became something to live with. (1996:1)

The continuation of colonial models meant acceptance of dependency as normal. There was a general failure to indigenize foreign structures and institutions, since no evaluations of these inherited projects were ever undertaken. In short, Gatu reacted against the colonial system being extended into the postcolonial period. Foreign funding and oversight prevented young churches from attaining mature self-hood with their own more workable structures. Much of what is now called "partnership" and "interdependence" is a projection into the postcolonial period of earlier flawed methods that prevent young churches from making their own decisions. Foreign partners continue to do the funding as well as the thinking for new churches long past the time when these churches should be doing both of these things for themselves.

The insistence that self-reliance is a wrong emphasis because it elevates the "self" misses the point. Although Peter Beyerhaus was critical of using words like "self" or "autonomy" when speaking of Christian missions or churches, he and Henry Lefever admitted that when Venn and Anderson used words like "self-government," "self-support," and "self-propagation," "they assumed the rule of Christ before they spoke of self-rule. Without Christ's Lordship, there was no theological significance in either dependence or autonomy" (1964:16).

With the rule of Christ in the hearts and actions of His people, dependence comes to be seen for what it is: unhealthy weakness bordering on idolatry, because it places some other source of blessings in the place of Christ. Independence does not mean trusting in self or an evil autonomy, but rather it is the opposite of dependence, that is, trusting in Christ to provide resources. Independence in this context is the biblical equivalent of maturity, reliance on God's wisdom and provision above all else, taking responsibility for one's actions and decisions, and correcting wrong decisions. Interdependence then is the interaction of individuals or churches that are independent to start with. It is cooperation of those who are independent (mature) in Christ that produces the needed synergy in the body of Christ. Independence must therefore precede interdependence.

Given that the Three-Self formula has been so strongly criticized for its outdated setting and assumptions, what makes it still relevant? Simply this: it remains a basic criterion for defining a church or institution that is not dependent. This explains why various Christian organizations that fail this simple test also claim the Three-Self formula is outdated. For example, the Hindustan Bible Institute (HBI) has operated since its founding with external support. Paul Gupta and Sherwood Lingenfelter described the church planting movements associated with HBI, insisting that this could not have been done without foreign funding:

> The American and European churches that partnered with HBI provided much of the financial support (80 percent) that enabled these men and women to follow the Lord in this ministry. Without these partners, the people God called to the movement would have staggered under such a heavy work load, they could not have planted these churches. (2006:214)

Working with these assumptions preempts the Three-Self formula, but are the assumptions valid?

India has seen numerous church planting movements over a long period of time, and most did not depend on foreign funding. In fact, there were so many "mass movements" to Christ in the early twentieth century that the National Christian Council of India, Burma, and Ceylon became alarmed, since it was assumed that salvation is valid for individuals only. The Council appointed J. Waskom Pickett to investigate ten such mass movements; his findings are in his classic book, *Christian Mass Movements in India*, published in 1933. Pickett discovered that these movements occurred away from missionary presence among the lowest castes who preferred to make communal decisions. Although the new converts were extremely poor, they were not dependent on outside funding at first. Significantly, all ten movements became dependent on mission aid once the missionaries began to reach them (1933:219).

Pickett noted that those movements that succeeded in supporting their own pastors became significantly stronger: "When these mass-movement groups support their pastors, great benefits accrue to them. The result is most stimulating. Their self-respect gains, and they value the ministry of their pastor more highly. This is not mere theory" (1933:221). Pickett estimated that 80 percent of all Indian Christians were the product of such mass movements at that time (1933:314), and concluded that these movements were "the most natural way of approach to Christ" (1933:330). He cautioned, however, that these movements could easily be retarded by rapid economic rise or by social shifts that broke the converts' connections with their groups (1933:337). He urged missions to cease activities that created dependency: "Missions should take special care to discontinue or revise all of their processes of work that have interfered with the development of initiative" (1933:352).

Much later in that century, J. P. Masih characterized Indian church history as "the history of 'people movements,'" but noted that three current people movements were halted by "a silent game of money bargaining" by new converts with the heads of different denominations in a quest to receive relief aid (1986:300-1). It is clear that foreign funds can derail promising movements to Christ.

Despite insisting on foreign funds, Gupta and Lingenfelter also acknowledged the danger of money in partnerships: "Caution: the partner with the money will be tempted to use the control of money to dominate the partner who does not have money. The most common quarrels in partnership focus upon the control, use, and accountability of money" (2006:200). Although they recognized the problems of foreign money, Gupta and Lingenfelter rejected the Three-Self formula because it would undermine their current mission methods.

While we can agree that the Three-Self formula is not completely current with regard to cultural indigeneity, it remains relevant for assessing dependency. That is, we cannot say that churches and institutions that abide by the formula are necessarily indigenous, since the formula says nothing about the indigenous culture, but we can say that they are not dependent. Conversely, we can affirm that those that do not meet the formula's criteria are dependent on outside help—and being dependent they cannot really be interdependent. Those that remain dependent long after the time when they should be mature are in need of spiritual renewal.

Spiritual Renewal versus Human Ingenuity

A number of models claiming to be the best options for postcolonial missions actually depend on human ingenuity, whereas overcoming dependency from colonialism requires nothing more or less than spiritual renewal. The apostle Paul warned, "See to it that no one takes you captive through hollow and deceptive philosophy, which depends on human tradition and the basic principles of this world rather than on Christ" (Col. 2:8). Mission methods can also be based on human tradition and the basic principles of this world rather than on Christ. Just as colonial methods were based on ideas of Western superiority, current methods may also derive from so-called human ingenuity.

For example, globalization invites Christian mission to join its bandwagon. Dana L. Robert notes, "With its internal logic of universalism, or catholicity, Christian mission of necessity finds itself in dialogue with the secular globalizing tendency of the historical moment—whether European expansion, Western capitalism, or the World Wide Web" (2002:50). Lamin Sanneh also observes, "'Global Christianity' as an expression also carries connotations of parallels with economic globalization, with the same forces of global trade and the Internet revolution fueling the spread of a seamless environment of information and exchange without borders" (2003:23). Missionaries have certainly taken advantage of all these historical movements and will continue to do so, but there is a hidden cost for attaching the propagation of Christianity to secular forces. Secular movements operate from a worldview other than a biblical one; that is, basic assumptions about reality are profoundly different from—and often antagonistic to—biblical values.

Globalization often operates from an Enlightenment worldview, with similar assumptions to those that drove colonialism. Jeffrey Sachs explained that his thinking on how to eradicate poverty derived from Enlightenment social philosophies:

> Bold and brilliant Enlightenment thinkers throughout Europe and the emerging United States began to envision the possibility of sustained social progress in which science and technology could be harnessed to

achieve sustained improvements in the organization of social, political, and economic life. (2005:347)

Sachs adopts four key ideas from Enlightenment thinkers: (1) democracy as conceived by the American and French Revolutions, (2) economic policies as conceived by Adam Smith, (3) a global system of governance to create world peace as conceived by Immanuel Kant, and (4) social improvement through science and technology as proposed by Francis Bacon and Marie-Jean-Antoine Condorcet (2005:348-9). In particular, he believes human reason can lead to a reduction of warfare, and social progress can become universal through economic globalization. He concludes, "It is our breathtaking opportunity to be able to advance the Enlightenment vision of Jefferson, Smith, Kant, and Condorcet" (2005:351).

Where Sachs differs from these thinkers is that he has learned from history that progress is not inevitable and cannot be forced through compulsion or violence (2005:353). This stance causes him to be critical of current American foreign policy for its negative impact on universal social improvement and to favor the United Nations as the best vehicle of his ideas.

Sachs represents contemporary Enlightenment thinking at its best. The fact that he has stated his worldview so clearly allows us to see where his thinking comes from and where it may take us. Just as Christian missionaries can claim to have learned from past mistakes to improve on old methods by shifting from colonial models to "partnership" and "interdependence," Sachs seeks to improve on former Enlightenment thinking by taking a lesson from history. The problem with this approach is clear: the underlying flawed paradigm is still in operation. The powerful in worldly terms are still in charge of deciding what is best for the "weak". The West is joined by westernized leaders of other nations to plan social improvement (or general mission strategy) for others. The same kinds of people who ruled during colonialism continue to rule by making decisions for the marginalized without accountability for their decisions. Just as in the colonial period, the methods advocated continue to create debilitating dependency.

Even in the secular world of those who have taken charge of poverty eradication, there are some voices that realize that the predominant trends, as expressed so forcefully by people like Sachs, are operating from a failed paradigm. William Easterly, who spent sixteen years as a research economist at the World Bank, describes approaches such as Sachs's to poverty eradication as a form of neo-imperialism: "It is at least ironic that some offer a new White Man's Burden to clean up the mess left behind by the old White Man's Burden" (2006:272). Easterly concludes, "Like today's donors and postmodern imperialists, the colonizers were outside Planners who could never know the reality on the ground" (2006:276). Current mission models based on globalization may likewise be neoimperialistic despite denials. They insist that the key to mission success is economic just as secular globalists do. This automatically places the centers of former colonial power, which are also the centers of the world's wealth, in charge of deciding how to fund missions. With Western churches as the bankers of world mission, the rest of the world takes the role of negotiating for those funds through "partnerships." World mission becomes the relentless search for donors to finance the workers of other nations on the frontlines. This is exactly how the secular aid system works and it is clearly an extension of colonial methods. Easterly sums up:

> Even with the best of motives, colonial officials suffered from all the same problems that characterize today's White Man's Burden: excessive self-confidence of bureaucrats, coercive top-down planning, desultory knowledge of local conditions, and little feedback from the locals on what worked. Under the theory that "whites know best," colonialists forced development schemes on the locals rather than respecting their economic choices. (2006:281)

This is about the best that can be expected from human ingenuity, since the desire to dominate through wealth and power with the best of intentions is the best that unaided human reason has to offer. Human ingenuity in this form is what produced the culture of dependency.

Africans themselves are beginning to revolt against the common view that their continent should subsist on perpetual aid. Noting that foreign aid to developing countries is based on the Marshall Plan that helped rebuild Europe and Japan after World War II, Humphrey Orjiako, a Nigerian, recognized that behind the largesse of Western nations was the political desire to contain communism and promote capitalism (2001:1-2). Yet aid to sub-Saharan Africa did not alleviate poverty at all because it did not create economic growth. Orjiako stated, "Foreign aid has failed in Africa because it was never conceived as a growth performance policy or freedom-creating strategy. Such a strategy would focus primarily at promoting self-confidence and self-reliance and not dependency of its recipients" (2001:68).

In a recent book, Dambisa Moyo, a Zambian economist who has worked with the World Bank, issues a blistering indictment of the way aid has rendered Africa dependent on foreign donations. Stating that Africa has received "over US$1 trillion in development-related aid" from rich nations during the past five decades (2009:xiii), she asserts, "Millions in Africa are poorer today because of aid ... Aid has been, and continues to be, an unmitigated political, economic, and humanitarian disaster, ... the single worst decision of modern developmental politics" (2009:xix). The amount of aid already given to Africa far exceeds the original Marshall Plan on which the postwar concept of aid is based (Moyo 2009:35-7), but it has not achieved the expected results. Moyo summarizes, "The trouble with the aid-dependency model is, of course, that Africa is fundamentally kept in its perpetual childlike state" (2009:32). Since few in the developed world apparently expect Africans to act maturely, people like Moyo have actually found it difficult to remain at home to try to solve Africa's problems (2009:xiv).

Given the poor track record of aid to Africa and the developing world, why should Christian mission attach its hopes to such systems? Spiritual renewal, on the other hand, depends neither on human ingenuity nor on the current historical movement. It is the best way out of dependency. Wilbert Shenk writes:

> Authentic revival is never a program; it is a movement of the Holy Spirit. It emerges in situations where faith has grown cold and spiritual vitality is at a low ebb ... We cannot predict when such a fresh stirring of God's Spirit will take place; we can only step into the stream of God's movement and transformation. (MacMaster 2006:9)

Since "faith is being sure of what we hope for and certain of what we do not see" (Heb. 11:1), those who live in dependency often show a lack of faith in God to provide what they need. Spiritual renewal of those who are dependent can reverse the situation, enabling the revived to find sources of blessing close at hand that they had previously neglected.

Describing the effects of the East African Revival that started in 1929 and continues to have an impact around the world, Richard K. MacMaster and Donald R. Jacobs stated:

> The East African Revival had been financially self-reliant. When "the saved ones" felt that God was calling them to do something locally or on a broader scale, they simply announced the need and received the funds from

the local fellowships. What they could not afford they did not undertake. When they commenced huge projects, like the stratified evangelization of an entire town or city, they did so with their own finances. (2006:257)

Not by coincidence, John Gatu, general secretary of the Presbyterian Church of East Africa from 1964-1979, was influenced by the East African Revival. He realized that his denomination was dependent on foreign resources, and he saw that the revival fellowships provided an alternative paradigm. Thus, his call for a moratorium on foreign funds and personnel was based on the knowledge of what spiritual renewal can do for dependent churches. MacMaster and Jacobs report that within twenty years, Gatu's moratorium steered his denomination from receiving 85 percent of church funds from abroad to receiving 85 percent locally (2006:258).

MacMaster and Jacobs make it clear that behind the call for a moratorium lay the assurance that spiritual renewal allows funding to arise from local sources. Despite the consternation of those who thought that Gatu might be calling for the end of missions, or that he might wish to terminate Western missionaries in order to receive Western money:

Gatu defended the idea [of the moratorium] as consistent with the ethos of the revival fellowships, which knew the freedom that comes from raising and using their own money ... The revival fellowships loved their friends overseas, but they never wanted to be beholden to them for financial support. They had to believe that God would supply the money to do the things he wanted them to do. (MacMaster 2006:259)

This system is much more in line with biblical emphases. In Scripture, God has a habit of turning down what looks like the best option humanly speaking to promote a surprising option based on human weakness. To take just a few examples, barren women become the means by which God blesses the chosen people. Moses, after growing up in the household of Pharaoh, must learn to be a shepherd in the desert before he can lead God's people out of Egypt. Gideon, the unlikely hero, must tell thousands of his soldiers to go home before God approves the battle plan against Midian. God told Gideon to send home all but 300 men "in order that Israel may not boast against me that her own strength has saved her" (Judges 7:2). King Saul with all his armor is no match for the giant Goliath, but the boy David kills him with one stone and a slingshot. With the restoration of Jerusalem after the Babylonian exile, the rebuilding effort of the temple seems tiny and insignificant. God sends a prophet who says, "'Not by might nor by power, but by my Spirit,' says the Lord" (Zechariah 4:6) and "Who despises the day of small things?" (Zechariah 4:10). The Prince of Peace comes not on a warhorse, but on a humble donkey, seeking to conquer by self-sacrifice rather than violent rebellion. A boy with a few loaves and fish becomes the source of food for five thousand. Andrew asked Jesus, "How far will they [the loaves and fish] go among so many?" (John 6:9). In the Master's hands, however, they are more than enough.

The ultimate repudiation of human ingenuity is the cross of Christ. Before the cross, we all must bow in recognition of our inability to bring anything of use to our quest for salvation, but we must recognize that God has provided it all through the unlikely instrument of torture and death, the cross. God will continue to provide all that his mission needs. He does not search for our wealth and power, but rather seeks to show his own power through his choice of the weakest of people who give themselves to him. It would be strange indeed if God were to change tactics because of the success of globalization and begin to rely on what human ingenuity can do. No, we can count on the fact that God will continue to surprise us with unlikely people to fund and carry out his mission, probably even those people whom we would consider least capable of fulfilling this task.

Local Initiative versus Globalization

Bafundi Mpofu was the headmaster of a Christian primary school in Bulawayo, Zimbabwe. In addition, he is an elder in his local church in Bulawayo, and president of his local association of churches. He has a remarkable story of a personal awakening to the need for greater self-reliance (and God-reliance) on the part of Zimbabwean churches in light of the Great Commission.

Mpofu became a key fundraiser for Zimbabwean churches, frequently traveling overseas for that purpose. He received an invitation to visit Australia in June 2003 in order to raise funds to purchase motorcycles for evangelists. He was trying to help his association overcome a period of stagnation by promoting organized evangelism. His association had targeted an area for intensive church planting where people were receptive to the gospel. This area was situated between existing congregations. Mpofu initially asked his overseas brothers and sisters for three motorcycles, but the response to his messages in Australia was so positive that he decided to go for nine!

During a month of fundraising, Mpofu visited a small church in Melbourne. Noting that this congregation had only thirty members, he asked a former missionary to Zimbabwe—his host at the church—how they could afford to support two pastors with such a small congregation. The prompt reply was that all members tithed, which led to further discussions. The missionary wanted to know about the situation at Mpofu's home church. Mpofu confessed that his local church only partially supported one pastor, with an American missionary supplying half his salary, despite there being 280 members in the church. The missionary asked many questions over the next few days about the type of jobs and salaries that members had and the weekly offerings. Mpofu answered that there were teachers, headmasters, nurses, business managers, and even a magistrate in the church, but the offerings were small. This was the trend throughout his association where 300 congregations supported only nine full-time pastors.

The Australian missionary was trying to decide how Mpofu would respond to what he had to say, praying that he would receive it well. Finally, the two of them were on a boat leaving Tasmania for the mainland, when the missionary revealed his heart. He began by saying that members of the body of Christ ought to be able to challenge and educate one another. He saw Mpofu as a motivator who could influence the Zimbabwean churches to change the way they operated. Then he prayed that God would anoint the Zimbabwean leader to carry an important message to his people. After that promising start, he surprised Mpofu by saying, "You have been stealing from God!" He had seen by his calculations based on Mpofu's answers that neither Mpofu nor the Zimbabwean Christians were tithing, and he stressed that the command to tithe had never been removed, since Christians are told to give as they have been prospered. He urged Mpofu to encourage his people to begin tithing and to support missions, as they had been recipients of mission efforts for a hundred years.

Mpofu had never heard the matter of tithing put quite like this, so he resolved to tithe himself. Furthermore, he preached on tithing at his local church in August 2003 upon his return to Zimbabwe. He presented the message that the missionary had pressed on his heart to the Board of Elders at the end of that month, and all the leaders agreed to start tithing as an example for the rest of the congregation. He then began to spread the message to other churches. The results amazed him and the other elders. First, his church asked the American missionary to stop his contributions to their pastor, as they were prepared to carry his full salary. In fact, they now support two full-time pastors. Beyond that, they support evangelism in their target area where they have planted ten new churches, sending two evangelists to each new church once every two weeks. They plan for one of their pastors to spend several days a week training new preachers and leaders at the new churches. They are praying that the example of increased giving that they have set will catch on with other congregations of their association.

This amazing transition from a posture of feeling they could do little on their own to generating funds they can use for church planting has left the church with a new sense of purpose—and this at a time when the country of Zimbabwe is facing near total economic collapse. What is the moral of the story? In vivid terms, Mpofu admitted that his own assumptions about the limitations of what Zimbabwean Christians could do were mistaken. Furthermore, the realization that he and others could tithe even in harsh economic conditions came as a spiritual awakening—an awakening that has spread to his whole church and beyond. His church is now experiencing the joy of giving to promote the gospel in their own region, with their own evangelists. The fact that they no longer have to ask outsiders to fund their work gives them a new sense of purpose, which in turn makes them better evangelists in a situation where few have hope. The church has become a beacon of light in dark times, as faith has produced fruit in giving and outreach (Reese 2006:72-4).

How did this transformation from dependence on outside resources to learning the joy of tithing come about? The key was that the former missionary to Zimbabwe knew enough about local conditions in that country to challenge the status quo in fundraising. Despite general assumptions that Zimbabweans can do little for themselves, he was able not only to help Mpofu see new possibilities at home, but also to create the right conditions for spiritual renewal as Zimbabweans began to move away from the typical modes of behavior encouraged by globalization to promoting local initiative.

Those who advocate attaching mission models to globalization because it is the current successful trend overlook some key issues. The main problems that arise through the use of short-term missions and partnerships come from the fact that these ventures seek to have an impact over a long distance without spending enough time learning about conditions in the places they wish to impact. This is a frequent issue with globalization: it emphasizes global solutions for local problems, regardless of the fact that local people may know better how to solve their own problems.

Glenn Schwartz calls this "the principle of geographic proximity" (2007:145). By this, he means that as far as possible there should be local solutions to local problems. Long-distance benefactors carry the danger of creating dependency because they have faint knowledge of local issues. For example, suppose a country experiences drought and famine in one part of the nation, but crops are produced in another part of the same country. Under normal conditions, farmers who reaped crops would be able to sell to those who did not, so redistributing the available food. However, foreign donors may decide to help the situation by shipping tons of free food to the affected areas, bypassing the food that is locally available. The normal assumption is that free food is always better than having to buy food, especially if the people in need of food are poor. This approach, however, fails to consider how free foreign food may harm local farmers who could have made a living selling food to those who needed it. The chances are that the next time there is a drought, farmers nearby who could have helped will no longer be in business, making foreign aid the only option. This process of neglecting local solutions introduces dependency on a large scale.

Dambisa Moyo calls this "the micro-macro paradox" (2009:44). She gives an example of an African mosquito net manufacturer who makes 500 nets per week and employs ten people. In the Western drive to fight malaria, such small-scale net production will never cover the needs:

> Enter vociferous Hollywood movie star who rallies the masses, and goads Western governments to collect and send 100,000 mosquito nets to the afflicted region, at a cost of a million dollars ... With the market flooded with foreign nets, however, our mosquito net maker is promptly put out of business. His ten workers can no longer support their 150 dependents (who are now forced to depend on handouts), and one mustn't forget that in a maximum of five years the majority of the imported nets will be torn, damaged and of no further use. (2009:44)

In his first book on understanding globalization, journalist Thomas Friedman recognizes the tension between local values and globalized values. The book's title, *The Lexus and the Olive Tree*, gives a picture of the struggle between the global and the local. The Lexus is a luxury car, the symbol of globalized technology that everyone wants; the olive tree stands for local customs and values that produce local flavor and color. Friedman wonders if the rush to economic globalization would erase local flavor altogether: "Globalization can be deeply disorienting. To have your own cultural olive trees uprooted or homogenized into some global pulp is to lose your bearings in the world" (2000:293).

For this reason, Friedman advocates "glocalization." This is an attempt to enjoy the benefits of globalization while maintaining your own local values as much as possible. He writes, "The whole purpose of glocalizing is to be able to assimilate aspects of globalization into your country and culture in a way that adds to your growth and diversity, without overwhelming it" (2000:295). He warns, however, that "glocalism alone, … even in its most healthy form, is not sufficient to protect cultures from globalization" (2000:297). Clearly, Friedman views globalization as the stronger movement that can easily overwhelm local values. Indeed, by the time he wrote his updated book, *The World Is Flat*, he saw globalization as survival of the fittest, with nations either glocalizing successfully or failing to cope in the modern world (2005:324-9). This evaluation sidelines vast areas of the world as hopeless: "Africa, sadly, is that part of [the global] town where the businesses are boarded up, life expectancy is declining, and the only new buildings are health-care clinics" (2005:317).

Such a global economic perspective may write off Africa as a basket case, even while local initiative in Africa is far from dead. The globalizing tendency is to measure every nation by one criterion, that of the economically developed countries, and then to apply aid to those nations that fail to measure up. Friedman says:

> Let's stop here for a moment and imagine how beneficial it would be for the world, and for America, if rural China, India, and Africa were to grow into little Americas or European Unions in economic and opportunity terms. But the chances of their getting into such a virtuous cycle is tiny without a real humanitarian push by flat-world businesses, philanthropists, and governments to devote more resources to their problems. (2005:380)

William Easterly challenges these popular assumptions, saying that Western donors spent $2.3 trillion in foreign aid in the past five decades without solving such simple problems as providing children with malaria medicines or bed nets (2006:4). He analyzes the reason as being the difference in thinking between a "Planner" and a "Searcher." He explains:

> Planners apply global blueprints; Searchers adapt to local conditions. Planners at the top lack knowledge of the bottom; Searchers find out what the reality is at the bottom … A Planner thinks he already knows the answers; he thinks of poverty as a technical engineering problem that his answers will solve. A Searcher admits he doesn't know the answers in

advance; he believes that poverty is a complicated tangle of political, social, historical, institutional, and technological factors … A Planner believes outsiders know enough to find solutions. A Searcher believes only insiders have enough knowledge to find solutions, and that most solutions must be homegrown. (2006:6)

In a nutshell, experience is showing that local initiative is more important in the long run than globalized solutions. This applies in economics as well as in missions. Just as there are a majority of "Planners" in economics today, so world mission has a majority of advocates for linking mission methods to globalization. These methods overwhelm local initiative and create dependency in the recipients of aid. Healthy postcolonial mission methods will return to an emphasis on local initiative over globalized solutions. Mark Noll states:

It is increasingly clear that all true expressions of Christianity, like politics in the famous American saying, are local. When the Christian faith takes real root, it takes real root in particular places and works in and through the cultural values of those places to restore fellowship with God, undergird functioning churches, and do the work of Christ in the world. Agents from outside that culture may play important roles in assisting, or hindering, Christian maturation, but Christianity has to be local or it can barely be called Christianity. (2009:197)

It is important to note that globalization is a historical movement that may even be short-lived. Paul Gupta warns that "tribal resurgence" threatens to undermine the peace and unity carved out by globalization (2006:217). He believes we should prepare for increased fragmentation in the postcolonial world. Thomas Friedman agrees that global terrorists use global networks to melt the glue holding globalization together. For example, he says that al-Qaeda is a "mutant global supply chain" that uses the flat world for "destruction, not profit" (2005:429). Jeffrey Sachs fights poverty in hopes of eradicating terrorism, noting, "[Terrorists'] bases of operation are unstable societies beset by poverty, unemployment, rapid population growth, hunger, and lack of hope" (2005:330-1).

For these reasons, even if it lasts for centuries, globalized planning for the world's future will not be able to compete with local initiative—either in economics or in Christian mission. In either case, then, Christian mission needs to emphasize local resources and solutions for local Christian issues. This applies especially to Christian humanitarianism.

Christian Humanitarianism Revisited

Almost a century ago, conservative Christians in America disavowed the Social Gospel and opted for the primacy of evangelism instead. Advocates of the Social Gospel, supported by theories of Social Darwinism and theologies of postmillennialism, thought that Christians could build the kingdom of God on earth through improving society. World War I, however, gave the lie to steady human improvement and proved that society was adrift. Fundamentalists rejected the glowing optimism of postmillennialism and opted for the more pessimistic premillennialism as they sought to return to biblical moorings. George Marsden explained that by the 1920s, "Modernism and the theory of evolution, they [fundamentalists] were convinced, had caused the catastrophe by undermining the Biblical foundations of American civilization" (1980:3). In reaction, fundamentalists stressed biblical inerrancy and shied away from reforming society. This approach tended to leave socio-political activism largely in the hands of less conservative Christians. The result of the "fundamentalist-modernist controversy" was cultural isolation for conservatives, especially after the infamous Scopes trial in 1925 where the teaching of evolution was put on trial in Dayton, Tennessee (Marsden 1980:184-88). Although John Scopes was convicted of teaching evolution, fundamentalism became a synonym for backwardness.

By mid-century, some evangelicals felt that conservatives had thrown out the baby of social concern with the bath water of the Social Gospel. In 1947, Carl F. H. Henry rekindled an interest in social involvement with his book *The Uneasy Conscience of Modern Fundamentalism.* He sought to overcome the impression of many Americans that with fundamentalism "the humanitarianism has evaporated from Christianity" (2003:11). Even so, he cautioned that the liberals' interest in social improvement was not identical with the evangelicals': "The revitalization of modern evangelicalism will not come by a discard of its doctrinal convictions and a movement in the direction of liberalism. For current history has decisively unmasked liberal unrealism" (2003:59). His desire was that evangelicals should seek to reenter the mainstream of American cultural life to try to penetrate all facets of it with the gospel.

Slowly but surely this began to happen. As evangelicals emerged from cultural isolation, they once again voiced concern over social issues even as they began to join forces in world missions. By the time of the Lausanne Congress in 1974, the social agenda was restored to Christian missions. That meeting assembled 2,700 delegates from 150 nations and from a broad spectrum of Protestant denominations to discuss the task of world evangelization (Stott 1996:xi). Organized by Billy Graham, the Congress issued a statement called the Lausanne Covenant that continues to influence evangelical missions. Part of the covenant states:

> We express penitence both for our neglect and for having sometimes regarded evangelism and social concern as mutually exclusive ... We affirm that evangelism and socio-political involvement are both part of our Christian duty. For both are necessary expressions of our doctrines of God and man, our love for our neighbor and our obedience to Jesus Christ. (Stott 1996:24)

John Stott was influential in this emphasis. He states that "social action is a partner of evangelism ... Neither is a means to the other, or even a manifestation of the other. For each is an end in itself" (1975:27). His linking of the Great Commission and the Great Commandment to love God and love one's neighbor (1975:22-30) became a common understanding of the two sides of mission. Yet Stott maintained that the congress was correct in insisting on the primacy of evangelism (1975:35).

In the early twenty-first century, evangelical churches not only relish their newfound significance in American politics, but also have increasingly seen their wealth and influence as a key to solving global problems of many kinds. In this, they have joined the bandwagon of globalization to tackle major problems with American money. Some advocate copying the Marshall Plan, only now it will be wealthy American churches that pay for social improvement in the developing world by eradicating poverty and disease (Rowell 2006:141-5).

For example, Rick Warren, author of *The Purpose-Driven Church* and *The Purpose-Driven Life* created this slogan which became the motto of the Saddleback Church that he founded: "A Great Commitment to the Great Commandment and the Great Commission will grow a Great Church" (1995:103). More recently, he embarked on world missions with the PEACE Plan. Warren identified five global giants as obstacles to be tackled in world missions: spiritual emptiness, egocentric leadership, poverty, disease, and illiteracy. In response to each of these giants he proposed the acronym PEACE to represent the following strategy for world missions: "Plant new churches, or partner with existing ones; Equip leaders;

Assist the poor; Care for the sick; Educate the next generation" (Morgan 2005:35). Later, Warren changed the first strategy of planting churches to "Promoting Reconciliation" (Morgan 2008:43). He explained:

> We are still doing church planting, but now we put it under partnership with the local church. We don't expect government and business, the other two legs of the stool [of the PEACE Plan 2.0], to do church planting. But there are biblical principles of reconciliation that apply to everybody. (Morgan 2008:43)

Warren's overall strategy with the revised PEACE Plan is to incorporate the three powerful legs of private, public, and church partnerships in order to defeat global giants successfully.

Such global strategies for Christian humanitarianism could easily be a return to outsiders dictating the social agenda for local people as it was under colonialism and the "white man's burden." Christian social activists from wealthy countries may believe that they have a clear idea of what poor people in developing countries need and how to deliver it. Any person who have worked in relief and development, however, know that what outsiders suggest may not ultimately meet local needs if there is no local ownership of the projects from the start. That is, the colonial approach to social action among poor people has actually produced little improvement in the long run for the amount of time and money spent. Humanitarians can also be imperialists.

The humanitarian emphasis often places the cart before the horse. Christian humanitarians may slip back into an Enlightenment mentality that believes that human reason is all that is necessary to overcome social ills. A more biblical basis for mission, however, sees social ills as symptomatic of spiritual problems. For example, alleviating poverty is a complex issue not easily solved by mere bureaucrats; If it were that easy, then fifty years of bureaucratic efforts should have produced better results (Easterly 2006:4). The missing ingredient in those efforts is the spiritual issue. The apostle Paul said, "The man without the Spirit does not accept the things that come from the Spirit of God, for they are foolishness to him, and he cannot understand them, because they are spiritually discerned" (1 Cor. 2:14). People need to be spiritually reborn before they can see life from God's perspective and reorient their lives in more productive ways.

To put the horse back in front of the cart requires that people be awakened spiritually to see themselves as God sees them in His image. As such people are renewed, they are able to study Scripture for themselves and start to provide homegrown solutions for their problems in redeemed communities. Vincent Donovan said it precisely:

The incarnation of the gospel, the flesh and blood which must grow on the gospel is up to the people of a culture. The way people might celebrate the central truths of Christianity; the way they would distribute the goods of the earth and live out their daily lives; their spiritual, ascetical expression of Christianity if they should accept it; their way of working out the Christian responsibility of the social implications of the gospel—all these things, that is, liturgy, morality, dogmatic theology, spirituality, and social action would be a cultural response to a central unchanging, supracultural, uninterpreted gospel. (1982:30-1)

Donovan's approach to missions expects and allows people to take the gospel and interpret it themselves in all areas of life, especially including social action. Although modern missionaries have seldom practiced missions like this, it is a good description of how the gospel was propagated in the early church across the Roman Empire. Outsiders did not need to peer over the shoulders of converts to direct their steps and social agenda. The gospel itself taught them how to act in community.

From my own experience in missions, I found it remarkable how often my point of view on social issues was at odds with that of local people. What was to me the clear solution for any number of issues like unemployment, benevolence, famine relief, women's issues, education, agricultural methods, and so on, was not that clear to the local people. They had alternative ideas as they had lived with these problems their whole lives and I was still new on the scene even after two decades. When they are energized by the gospel, they are in the best position to solve their own problems if outsiders give them that chance and do not overshadow their efforts. The best social action is what arises from local people living under the gospel.

Mission from Every Continent without Dependency

The postcolonial era signals the end of long-standing paradigms for mission. The Constantinian era combined state power with the missionary enterprise from the fourth to the twentieth century. With the close of colonial empires, that era of mission is ending. Despite methods that created dependency through the use of worldly power, even military might, instead of the power of the cross, Christianity became truly a world religion by the end of that period. Often, the number of members of denominations that originated in Europe or North America is now more in the global South than in the North.

Philip Jenkins notes, "Over the past century, ... the center of gravity in the Christian world has shifted inexorably southward, to Africa, Asia and Latin America" (2002:2). Furthermore, as Christianity takes hold in these diverse cultures, the global North is witnessing a decline in the strength of Christian churches even as its church members grow in wealth. Jenkins adds, "Christianity is flourishing wonderfully among the poor and persecuted, while it atrophies among the rich and secure ... Christianity demonstrates a breathtaking ability to transform weakness into strength" (2002:220).

It is exactly this ability to transform weakness into strength that makes it possible now to speak of missions from every continent to every continent. On the one hand, people from every faith and culture now find their home in the North; on the other hand, Christians in the North find they have much to learn from Christians of other cultures. Pluralism changes the landscape so much that no one can easily tell the sending nation from the receiving nation in missions. For example, in the American Episcopal Church, some parishioners are no longer satisfied with their own indigenous leaders because of what they see as the leadership accommodating Scripture to fit current American culture. As a result, numerous Episcopal churches in the United States have opted to come under African Anglican bishops. Mindy Belz reports that several dozen Episcopal churches in the United States have asked for oversight from Ugandan Archbishop Henry Luke Orombi and Nigerian Archbishop Peter Jasper Akinola (2006:16-21). Mark Noll comments, "As the worldwide Anglican Communion has experienced in its conflicts over the ordination of practicing homosexuals, the moral voice of the newer Christian regions of the world can be a strong voice indeed" (2009:32-3).

This is just one example of how Christians from the global South are impacting the nations formerly regarded as mission senders. Southern Christians are generally more conservative in interpreting Scripture and more active in evangelism, so it is natural that their brand of the faith should spread more rapidly. They also sense that the gospel brought to them by Northern Christians is not the same gospel that the North now preaches. If the North fumbles the message of salvation by confusing the gospel with its own cultural values, then the South is eager to pick it up and run with it, even returning it to the North if necessary.

A key question is whether the Christianity of the South will ultimately fit the mold of the Christianity received from colonial missions, or will it produce something different? Philip Jenkins assumes that "the next Christendom" will result from the alliance of Christians in the global South with their politicians to form replicas of the earlier Christendom of the North and even foresees the possibility of Southern Christians demanding wealth redistribution from the North to the South (2002:160). If this scenario is accurate, then we can also predict the continuation of the dependency syndrome with some certainty, because the underlying mission paradigm will not have changed. Only the exterior would change, but the heart would remain the same as in colonialism, as long as the emphasis lies on worldly power.

Kwame Bediako, a Ghanaian Christian scholar, however, believes that Africans approach Christianity from a different frame of reference. He insists, "Africa has not produced and is not likely to produce, a new Christendom" (1995:249). Instead, he regards Christianity as native to Africa and as simply making a comeback in modern times, as evident from his book title, *Christianity in Africa: The Renewal of a Non-Western Religion*. In other words, Christianity was non-Western to start with and it belongs naturally in the non-Western world without all that went with colonialism. Even Jenkins agrees, "As Christianity moves South, it is in many ways returning to its roots" (2002:15). If this scenario is accurate, then we may see healthier mission models in the postcolonial era that avoid dependency. Although our current missions are conditioned by seventeen centuries of Western domination, there is urgent need for a change that circumvents the use of worldly forms of power and reverts to the power of the cross.

Patrick Johnstone is fairly ecstatic about the end of Christendom because of the opportunities it brings for new mission paradigms:

> The era of Constantinian Christendom is ending. A Church deprived of political power is freed from the burden of trying to use human power to dominate and influence the world … Christendom is doomed, but the future of biblical Christianity is bright. (1998:263)

From his European perspective, Johnstone sees the end of Christendom as the liberating end of seventeen centuries of spiritual bondage. Now a revived biblical Christianity will be able to reevangelize a secularized Europe without pretending that nominal Christians are reached with the gospel. The mission field is now everywhere and missionaries originate from everywhere; Christianity is finally a world faith.

Certainly the opportunity afforded by the postcolonial era is unique for missions. The first three centuries of mission history did not produce the crippling dependency that the Constantinian paradigm caused by using incentives and punishments as evangelistic tactics. Although we cannot return to that early time, we can learn from it in the postcolonial age by adopting methods that avoid and overcome dependency. Postcolonial mission methods cry out for an end to paradigms that contribute to dependency. The time is ripe for adoption of methods that regard every Christian as an equal in a church that lives a pilgrim life subject to persecution and misunderstanding because it lives out the cross of Jesus in its ministry. May God hasten the day that this becomes a reality.

10

BEST MISSION PRACTICES FOR THE TWENTY-FIRST CENTURY

YOU PROBABLY REMEMBER THAT WE APPROACHED THE end of the last millennium with some trepidation, not sure if all computers on earth would crash, ending civilization as we know it. Then we crossed that invisible barrier separating the millennia and landed safely on the other side, which does not seem all that bad. As a nation, we are getting used to change, and even crave it. During our election seasons, the popular slogan is for change, and one of the worst things you can say about candidates is that they represent the political status quo. As consumers, we look for the latest gadgets. Last year's technology is so outdated now that it must be replaced. We want things to improve and be brand new over and over again.

What can we say about change in Christian missions? How can we improve on recent practices? Should we merely throw up our hands and accept that the day of Western missions is over? Or is there a way to move into new paradigms that are actually the original paradigms of mission? This final chapter offers some ideas about how to spend our time and money in God's mission in ways that are as productive as mission in the first three centuries. The key for current mission is to duplicate both the actions and spirit of early Christian mission. Mission is not over until God declares it so by calling for the return of Jesus.

A simple way to divide the history of Christian missions is to look at it in three stages:

1. The Early Church from the Book of Acts to AD 300
2. The Time of Christendom from AD 300 to 1950
3. The Postcolonial Era from 1950 to the present

What Was so Good about Early Church Missions?

One thing we know for sure about the mission of the early church is that it was dynamic, with remarkably little indication of the dependency syndrome among new churches. Christianity spread not only throughout the Roman Empire in 300 years, but also far beyond into Asia and Africa. We read how ordinary Christians went everywhere preaching the gospel in the Book of Acts. We see how they gladly withstood persecution as a misunderstood minority. This persecution became more marked once Roman authorities discovered that Christians were different from Jews, who had official protection for their beliefs. From the pages of the New Testament and from the writings of early church leaders and other historians of the first three centuries, we find the following reasons for the rapid spread of Christianity.

The rank and file of church members spread the gospel. For example, Acts 8:4 tells us that those Christians from Jerusalem who were scattered by the persecution that followed Stephen's martyrdom went everywhere preaching the gospel. Even though the apostles set the example at this stage, this passage makes it clear that other disciples, apart from the apostles, carried out this evangelism. Cross-cultural mission was thus launched into Samaria for the first time. The Holy Spirit used persecution to scatter believers beyond Jerusalem, knowing that ordinary Christians had a story to tell. This pattern continued for three centuries.

Evangelism rested on historical events in the life of Jesus. His astounding teaching, atoning death, and miraculous resurrection inspired his followers to tell people about these events far and wide. Paul, the apostle, went so far as to say in 1 Corinthians 15:14 that if Christ has not been raised then our preaching is in vain and our faith is of no use. Early Christians believed so strongly in the resurrection that they preferred to die rather than to renounce their faith. The reason was that the resurrection proved that Jesus was more than a mere man, and that therefore there is more to come for every believer than this life alone. His resurrection signaled that the countdown had started for the end of time; his death provided the possibility of reconciliation with God before Judgment Day.

Christians believed and taught that Jesus is Lord. Among the myriad pagan religions that filled the Roman Empire, Christianity alone proclaimed that Jesus must have control of one's life. Other religions taught people to manipulate the gods and spirits for their own advantage, but Jesus could not be manipulated. This set Christians on a collision course with Roman authorities, who insisted that despite what a person believed everyone must confess that Caesar is Lord.

Christians upheld one Lord, Jesus Christ, and therefore refused to accept Caesar as a god. Accepting Jesus as Lord automatically set Christians apart from the rest of society, making them subjects of criticism, ostracism, and persecution (Shelley 1982:54-60).

Christians upheld high moral standards. By accepting Jesus as Lord and in light of the coming Judgment Day, Christians maintained strict behavioral standards and church discipline (see 1 Corinthians 5, for example). In sexual conduct, Christians were a distinct counterculture resembling the Jews only among all the peoples of the Roman Empire. Adultery and homosexuality were common in the society (Ferguson 1993:64, 69), but Christians insisted on faithfulness to one spouse of the opposite sex for life. They refused to take part in ritual prostitution and disciplined their members who fell into such practices. Known also for fairness and honesty, Christians' conduct set them apart in Roman society.

High standards led Christians to care for the neglected and defenseless people of society. For example, it was common to leave unwanted babies, especially girls, out in the elements to die or be eaten alive by animals (Ferguson 1993:73). But Christians would take these abandoned babies in and raise them. Similarly, slaves were considered as property that could be disposed of in any way (Ferguson 1993:56-7). But in Christian worship services, slaves could become respected leaders (Chadwick 1993:60). Greco-Roman husbands also often treated their wives with disrespect, and divorce was common in Roman society (Ferguson 1993:69). But Christians honored women and gave them opportunities to serve the church (Chadwick 1993:59; Stark 1996:108-9). In particular, churches took care of their widows and orphans. In this way, Christians became known as people who cared for the less fortunate and championed the defenseless. One of Christianity's fiercest critics, Celsus, saw this as weakness: "Their aim is to convince only worthless and contemptible people, idiots, slaves, poor women, and children" (Shelley 1982:47), but such actions won the hearts and minds of the dispossessed.

Christians became known for charitable acts. Henry Chadwick asserted, "The practical application of charity was probably the most potent single cause of Christian success" in the early churches (1993:56). For example, they would help those who suffered loss or illness. Whether natural disasters like earthquakes or floods struck people or economic downturns put people out of work or lowered their income, Christians organized themselves in their groups to show kindness to those in need. When others would shun the ill, Christians tended to them. While others treated the deformed or mentally ill as outcastes, Christians nursed them.

Sociologist Rodney Stark goes so far to call early Christianity "a revitalization movement that arose in response to the misery, chaos, fear, and brutality of life in the urban Greco-Roman world" (1996:161). He elaborates:

> To cities filled with the homeless and impoverished, Christianity offered charity as well as hope. To cities filled with newcomers and strangers, Christianity offered an immediate basis for attachments. To cities filled with orphans and widows, Christianity provided a new and expanded sense of family. To cities torn by violent ethnic strife, Christianity offered a new basis for social solidarity. To cities faced with epidemics, fires, and earthquakes, Christianity offered effective nursing services. (1996:161)

Christians treated people as equals in a hierarchical society. In Roman culture, certain people were regarded as inherently superior, while others were looked down on. In churches, however, people found a place to belong regardless of their social standing. In fact the churches were the only places where people of widely differing social classes could mingle freely without recrimination. It could even happen that the local church leader might be from a lower class than some of the members, so that a lower class individual taught the higher-class people. In the intimacy of house churches, people from all levels of society found acceptance. Stark summarizes, "In my judgment, a major way in which Christianity served as a revitalization movement within the [Roman] empire was in offering a coherent culture that was entirely stripped of ethnicity. All were welcome without need to dispense with ethnic ties" (1996:213).

Apologists explained why Christians were so different from other people, yet were model citizens. In this sense, apology has nothing to do with regret, but it means defending one's beliefs and practices. Christian apologists wrote in reaction to misunderstandings and persecution. Christians were so different from the rest of society that many assumed them to be dangerous to the well-being of Roman civilization. Men like Justin Martyr wrote extensively to defend Christianity against its critics. Far from being a threat to society, they said, Christians were actually the best Roman citizens and had good reasons for not going along with some of the Roman customs (Maier 1999:144, 165).

When persecuted, Christians showed their faith in the face of intimidation and even death. Some, of course, did not withstand the pressure to recant their faith, but when they wanted to be reinstated as church members in good standing, there was a process of church discipline. Yet there are many reports of how

Christians, including young women, withstood threats, beatings, and torture even to the point of death. From their witness (the word "martyr" originally meant "witness") came many new converts to Christ (Maier 1999; Shelley 1982:50-60). Far from exterminating Christianity, persecution caused it to grow and spread, as happened with both the original martyrdoms of Jesus and Stephen.

Through such means, Christianity developed an empire-wide network that provided homes to stay in when traveling, safety nets for those in distress or privation, and fellowship with those who shared their faith. Behind the network remained the Lord Jesus who was understood to be very much alive and ready to return for judgment, to right every wrong in a cruel society. Roman emperors began to notice this social and religious phenomenon and either feared it or tried to make it work in their favor. Those who feared it, such as Diocletian (Maier 1999:289-305), resented the fact that their own deteriorating empire could not match the cohesion evident among Christians. They also viewed Christians as disloyal to the state, which used emperor worship to hold things together. Eventually emperors like Constantine realized that they needed Christianity on their side and they issued edicts of toleration allowing Christianity to be practiced freely (Maier 1999:343), even with some state support.

Missions during Christendom

That brings us to the long period of Christendom, stretching from just after 300 AD to modern times. By Christendom, we mean the linking of church and state as happened first with the reign of Emperor Constantine. Constantine went further than just tolerating Christianity; he positively supported it through such policies as tax breaks, state funding, and declaring Sunday a public holiday for the first time (Maier 1999:360-6). This had some notable advantages; it often helps if powerful people endorse Christianity because this allows others to look at the faith more seriously. It allows Christians to come out in the open about their beliefs and practices and not be afraid of being ridiculed or attacked. Furthermore, the addition of state funds was a welcome source of income for Christian projects, which included some ornate church buildings during the reign of Constantine. Bishops were now respected community and regional leaders. The church historian, Eusebius, thought the millennium had come because things seemed too good to be true, especially after all the decades of persecution (Maier 1999:373-5). Christianity had arrived.

But what about missions? Here, a huge problem occurred. By declaring Christianity the religion that the state favored, Constantine opened the door for two major events: unconverted people flocked to become church members for the perceived benefits and politicians now felt free to interfere in church matters. By 380 AD, Emperor Theodosius outlawed all other faiths except Christianity (Shelley 1982:110-1), effectively declaring all Roman citizens to be Christians. This falsely implied that mission work inside the Roman Empire had finished. Henceforth professional missionary monks did missions outside the empire among the barbarians that threatened Roman civilization (Shelley 1982:170-8).

State funding of churches meant mixing political and spiritual objectives. For instance, the strategy for missions to neighboring kingdoms was to convince a chieftain or king that conversion to Christ was good and then he would persuade or coerce all his subjects to be converted. For many monarchs, becoming a Christian was more of a political decision than a spiritual one, as it meant sharing in the legacy of Rome (Shelley 1982:175-6). In addition, some monarchs only knew one way to spread Christianity to new realms, through military intervention. In this way Christendom extended to all of Europe eventually, but a price was paid.

Now Christians were not known so much for charity as for forcefulness. Parts of the world that were political enemies of Christian nations remained resistant to the gospel, which was now associated with a type of civilization. The epitome of this new mission method was the Crusades against Islam. Western Christians tried to win back the Holy Land from Muslims at the point of a sword, but to no avail (Shelley 1982:204-10). Muslims came to associate the cross of Christ, prominent on the shields of the crusaders, with violence against them instead of with the grace of God. The legacy of this ill-advised adventure is that bitter enmity remains between people of these two faiths. Fortunately, most Christians have realized that coercion is not the best way to spread the faith.

The overall difference between the two time periods in the way missions were conducted is that the early church operated of necessity from a position of weakness, while the missions of Christendom operated from a position of perceived strength. The problem with the kinds of strength shown is that acceptance of the gospel was often for the perceived benefits that came with it, such as access to markets, political power, or social acceptance. This became particularly marked during the period of European colonialism, when impoverished people of the developing world often accepted Christianity for the commodities that this might bring. This was fundamentally different from the methods of the early church, because Christians then were outsiders in society who offered what little they had.

If anything, early Christians were of a lower class than the majority in Roman society, but by acquiring political power this was reversed.

Political power changed the way that non-Christians viewed Christianity. Perhaps the most bizarre example of this came from Papua New Guinea and neighboring islands during World War II. Spiritistic people there noticed the power of Allied Forces and took it as potent magic. Spiritists believe in the activity of spirits in everyday life and assumed that Western Christians had discovered how to tap into the spirits' power. They developed cargo cults to try to emulate the results they witnessed.

New Guineans had seen that the Allied forces built airstrips and control towers where they spoke into radio microphones to call large cargo planes. When these planes landed they were inevitably loaded with all sorts of amazing goods. The New Guineans reasoned that if they could build airstrips and control towers they too could gain magical access to such precious "cargo." Hence the term "cargo cult" indicates that these spiritists made a pathetic attempt to access the goods that Christian nations had. Yet their attempts to speak into handmade microphones were doomed to fail as no one was listening. They were not praying to the Christian God whom they had not heard of, but they assumed that Christians had stolen goods that New Guinea's gods had intended for them (Worsley 1959:117-28).

Perhaps such confusion was unavoidable when formerly isolated cultures came into contact with developed nations. The differences in technology were bound to startle and disorient these cultures. But from a missiological point of view, the issue is the difference between the way Jesus conducted missions and the way Christians conducted missions during the period of Christendom. Jesus emptied himself of his heavenly prerogatives and advantages, while Christians began to use their power and wealth to overwhelm people perceived as primitive and inferior. This was not always deliberate, of course, but assuming racial superiority was a distinct tendency in Christian missions of the Christendom period. The end result was prolonged dependency on the West.

Postcolonial Missions

This brings us to the current period of mission history, which we designated as starting around 1950. That date was chosen because it represents the time shortly after World War II when the European colonial powers started to lose their empires. Two world wars had sapped their ability to rule such far-flung places. Furthermore, colonized peoples were clamoring for more say in their own affairs. Perhaps the best-known example is Mahatma Gandhi, who insisted that Great Britain release India from colonial rule. That goal was achieved in 1947 after intense struggle that culminated in the formation of both India and Pakistan (Neill 1966:109-15). Following that, many other new nations formed and the postcolonial era began.

Looking back over history, we can see that mission work was done most effectively with the fewest resources in the first 300 years, including the missions described in the New Testament. As usual, our template for missions, as for any Christian practice, must remain firmly attached to the early church. Our own time period has numerous fads that affect missions, but these must not overshadow the basics described in the mission work of the apostle Paul. For example, it is assumed that the United States is in the driver's seat economically and hence should fund world missions, but the recent downturn of global economics shows the danger of such assumptions. Those ministries that rely heavily on American funding are the quickest to collapse in a global economic downturn, while those that rise up with grassroots support will still thrive. The early church proves over and over that anything backed by the Holy Spirit can succeed despite economic depressions.

What, then, are the best mission practices for the twenty-first century? Our discussion so far suggests the following ten points:

1. Sharing the gospel remains the top priority.

Missions today often begin with social problems that are so deep that they consume all the missionaries' time and energy. Mission work from the "haves" to the "have-nots" comes from the Christendom period. The reason the gospel spread so rapidly in the first three hundred years had to do with deep conviction about the life, death, and resurrection of Jesus. Once people are converted to Christ then they are in a position to tackle their own social problems with much better hope of success. Christian insiders have a much better chance of solving long-standing social issues than foreign missionaries. Still, these foreign missionaries are in a good position to train their converts to tackle such issues.

Viv Grigg, a missionary from New Zealand to the slums of Manila, Philippines, describes his task:

> This is our mandate: to bring these slum communities under the authority of the kingdom of God. Our methodology is that of preaching the good

[handwritten marginal note: Many have been converted and are now addressing (— Their neighbors and criting help. human needs]

news of Jesus, teaching the whole counsel of God and establishing disciples in worshipping, economically stable fellowships" (1984:22-3).

While "economic transformation is an immediate pastoral concern," and "evangelism cannot be done outside of compassion" (1984:23), Grigg adds, "Those choosing simplicity to reach the poor need to continue to put priority on proclaiming the kingdom and teaching the scriptures rather than getting locked into the social and economic programs they generate" (1984:24).

2. We must view non-Western Christians as our equals.

The attitude of looking down on people because they are not as "developed" as we are comes from the period of Christendom when the West ruled the world. In the early church, the apostle Paul, who was definitely the top missionary, did not look down on people of other nationalities but saw them as new creatures in Christ and heirs to all God's promises (2 Cor. 5:17; Eph. 2:19). This allowed him to accept such people as co-workers.

Emmanuel Katongole from Uganda compares current mission proponents, likening them to either "tower-dwellers" or "travelers," making a distinction between those who operate from a position of "strength, power, and stability" versus those who see themselves as pilgrims (Crouch 2007c:36). With reference to missions in Africa, he sees three types of efforts being done: aid, partnership, and pilgrimage. He explains:

> There is the model of mission as aid, which arises out of the great need we see in the world—famine, AIDS, poverty—and also out of how much American Christians have … But the problem is that from this mission, Christians return to a tower. Their tower remains their world, and Africa's world remains Africa's world … Then there is the model of mission as partnership. It arises out of a sense of mutuality and solidarity between churches in the North and the South … This model also overlooks the difference in power between America and the rest of the world … We need to learn another model—mission as pilgrimage, which is based on a vision of the Christian life as a journey. This model grows out of being pilgrims together. (Crouch 2007c:38)

What Katongole advocates is nothing less than viewing one another as equals despite differing resources.

Is Harries dependent on local resources? [handwritten, left margin]

A variation on this model is for Western missionaries to live on a level closer to those they minister to. In an effort to move beyond colonial paradigms, a few Western missionaries have opted for "vulnerable mission." Jim Harries, who has lived and worked in rural Kenya for over fifteen years, launched vulnerable mission, based on his own mission practices:

> The Alliance for Vulnerable Mission proposes a bold strategy to counter neo-colonialism in mission; by advocating that some Western missionaries to the majority world follow two simple principles to "de-power" themselves:
> 1. Use the language of the people being reached in ministry. 2. Conduct ministry using only locally available resources. (Harries 2008)

Despite the natural simplicity of such an approach, few Western missionaries have actually adopted such a lifestyle. While quite a few learn local languages, not many are willing to minister with local resources only. — *Is this a* [handwritten]
do they live off local resources? [handwritten] *double standard?* [handwritten]

3. The rank and file of global Christians must be equipped to share the gospel.
The idea of professionals doing all the evangelism is also part of Christendom when ordinary people were excluded from certain ministries. The biblical role of professionals is to train the rest for ministry (Eph. 4:11-12). One of the top priorities for world missions today must be training and this is an area where Americans can certainly help. By far the top request I receive from Africans is training and I continue to travel there annually for that purpose, working with African leaders who also do the training. On the other hand, we may also invite non-Western missionaries to help us train our own people in evangelism.

4. High moral standards remain crucial for global Christians. Such standards help spread the gospel.
We Americans need help as standards for our church members have slipped dramatically. Church discipline has been thrown out in the current era of lawsuits and tolerance. Biblical standards call us back to holiness (1 Peter 1:15-16). On the other hand, we cannot be in the position of global policemen judging the morals of peoples of other cultures. Rather, missionaries can equip their converts with the basic tools so they can use Scripture to change their own cultures towards biblical standards.

5. Charitable acts must characterize global Christians.

Non-Christians should be able to see the love of God in concrete actions. Charity, however, should be characteristic of every Christian, not just those who are well off. During Christendom, rich Christians assumed the poor had nothing to give and patronized them. In the early church, even the poor were expected to give (Luke 21:1-4; 2 Cor. 8:2). Missionaries should teach their converts to give generously in order to take care of local physical needs. Even in American churches, it seems easier to raise funds to give to distant causes than to alleviate poverty next door.

6. Every church must put their members' bodies on the front line (Rom. 12:1).

It is not enough to send money; we must also send our best people into world missions. Committed people are much more important to God's mission than money, and local churches need to search and find who among their flocks to send, as the Antioch church did through prayer and fasting in Acts 13:1-3.

7. Western money must be used wisely in world missions in order not to create damaging dependency.

The common question whether Western Christians should continue to be generous is misdirected, since Scripture commands all Christians to give liberally. Assuming that the West alone is the banker for world missions comes from the Christendom period, when Western Christians became the paymasters for missions. This went along with a condescending attitude towards non-Western Christians, which spread the disease of dependency. Dependency caused non-Western Christians to assume wrongly that they had nothing worthwhile to contribute to world missions. The apostle Paul knew that money must be used carefully if it is to be a help and not a hindrance to God's mission (1 Cor. 9:14-16).

8. Mission methods must be cheaply reproducible for maximum effectiveness.

Americans have developed expensive methods that cannot be duplicated elsewhere. In fact, we have come to rely so heavily on borrowed money that many churches can no longer contribute as much to missions because of needing to repay loans for expensive buildings. Such luxuries did not characterize the early church, which had no buildings for the first couple of centuries. For Christianity to spread rapidly throughout the world, missions need to return to sustainable methods that do not require huge sums of money for success.

Oscar Muriu, pastor of Nairobi Chapel in Kenya, insists that Africans can create new models of mission that do not depend on money, but on traditional hospitality:

> The West has designed a model of missions that only works in the West. It depends on a monetary unit that is recognizable internationally; it depends on a strong economy that has a lot of disposable income, so that a lot of missionaries don't even go to the church for support. They go to the general community, to their networks of friends and family. In Kenya, you cannot support yourself that way as a missionary ... We can design new models that do not depend on money. We have our ways of getting into countries, our ways of surviving in those countries, of enabling one another. (Crouch 2007a:99)

9. Global Christians need to be teachable, humble enough to learn from each other (2 Tim. 2:2).
Christianity did not begin with us, nor will it end with us. God intends for every tribe, language, people, and nation to come to a knowledge of the truth (Rev. 7:9). As the gospel has entered different cultures, insiders in those cultures bring new insights to our understanding of God's will and purposes. We need not only to share what we know, but also to listen to what others have discovered in their reading of God's word.

Bishop David Zac Niringiye of Uganda warns North Americans, "One of the gravest threats to the North American church is the deception of power—the deception of being at the center" (Crouch 2006:32). This deception involves the assumption that the future of mission belongs to us Americans because of our current leadership and past performance. However, Niringiye counters, "If you really want to understand the future of Christianity, go and see what is happening in Asia, Africa, Latin America. It's the periphery—but that's where the action is" (Crouch 2006:34). We need to join those on the periphery and pray that they may learn from our mistakes rather than simply repeat them.

10. In our current time period, we can expect persecution.
This is an area where American Christians have much to learn from non-Western ones. We have been living through a long period of peace within our own borders, despite interminable wars going on outside them. This has made us forget that persecution is the norm for Christians (2 Tim. 3:12). In the early

church, persecution caused the spreading of the faith. This is still the case for many non-Western churches that have learned to use persecution to draw closer to God and his real purposes.

In 1998, I had the privilege of visiting a unique indigenous African church, L'Eglise Protestante Baptiste Oeuvres et Mission (EPBOM) in the West African country of Ivory Coast. This church grew from a handful of members in Abidjan in 1975 to 100,000 members spread out over the Ivory Coast and neighboring countries. Being indigenous and without direct Western connections, EPBOM developed a unique eschatology that predicted severe persecution in the impending end times. As a result of their self-theologizing, EPBOM divided up into thousands of cell groups, each with trained leaders. Church leaders anticipated a day arriving soon when their central leadership could no longer function openly because of persecution. Therefore, they decentralized all church functions into a myriad of cell groups, so that the church could go underground at short notice. Although persecution has yet to come in the form expected, the Ivory Coast entered a period of civil war in which the church was already prepared for violence and disruption (Reese 2007a:240-1).

We are not in exactly the same situation as early Christians, but there are enough similarities that we can learn much from their mission practices and understand the inspired examples of mission in the New Testament. We have some issues to face that they did not, such as the dependency syndrome. Overcoming dependency, which is the constant refrain of this book, is not an isolated issue. It is rather a means to an end. By overcoming dependency, we can put behind us colonial paradigms of mission and return to biblical practices. We can learn to operate from weakness using God's power as early Christians did. We can rediscover what the apostle Paul meant when he says, "That is why, for Christ's sake, I delight in weaknesses, in insults, in hardships, in persecutions, in difficulties. For when I am weak, then I am strong" (2 Cor. 12:10). The only dependency we need to cultivate is absolute dependency on God. Only then will we be in a position to draw on the whole body of Christ, leaving nobody sidelined because of unhealthy dependency, in order to complete the command contained in the Great Commission to make disciples of all nations.

Moving Forward

We cannot erase twenty centuries of Christian history and pretend we are back in New Testament times. In several ways, our situation is new and different. For example, the world is much more connected, making it easy to communicate with and travel to distant places. Globalization has made it easy to transfer funds anywhere with the click of a computer mouse. English is prominently used for international transactions. All of these present new opportunities as well as old temptations to continue the dependency syndrome, but this is precisely where New Testament mission practices can help us.

Christianity is now truly a global faith and yet there remain vast areas where the gospel has not been preached. Our basic task has not changed from the first century despite the many changes in our world. We will still use globalization in many ways, such as using the Internet to propagate Christianity, while realizing that such technology is expedient, but not essential to spreading the gospel. In many ways, the changes that have come about in our world in the past 2,000 years have allowed us to add some frills to world missions in much the same way that basketball players have added slam dunks to the basics of dribbling and passing. But as any coach knows, slam dunks are nothing without the basics. We can do without the frills of technology if we have to, but not without the basics of New Testament missions.

Bibliography

Ajayi, J. F. Ade.
　　1999　"From Mission to Church: The Heritage of the Church Mission Society."
　　　　　International Bulletin of Missionary Research 23(2):50-55.
Alexander, Archibald.
　　1971　*A History of Colonization on the Western Coast of Africa.* 2d ed. Philadel-
　　　　　phia: William S. Martien, 1849. Reprint, Freeport, NY: Books for Libraries
　　　　　Press.
Allen, Roland.
　　1923　*Voluntary Clergy.* London: SPCK.
　　1930　*The Case for Voluntary Clergy.* London: Eyre & Spottiswoode.
　　1962a　*Missionary Methods: St. Paul's or Ours?* Grand Rapids: Eerdmans.
　　1962b　*The Spontaneous Expansion of the Church.* Grand Rapids: Eerdmans.
Allen, Wayne.
　　1998　"When the Mission Pays the Pastor." *Evangelical Missions Quarterly*
　　　　　34(2):176-81.
Altman, Roger C.
　　2009　"The Great Crash, 2008: A Geopolitical Setback for the West." *Foreign Af-
　　　　　fairs* 88(1):2-14.
Anderson, Gerald H., ed.
　　1998　*Biographical Dictionary of Christian Missions.* Grand Rapids: Eerdmans.
Aryeetey, Solomon.
　　1997　"The Road to Self-Sufficiency in Africa's Missionary Development." *Evan-
　　　　　gelical Missions Quarterly* 33(1):34-8.
Augustine.
　　1984　*Concerning the City of God against the Pagans.* Translated by Henry Bet-
　　　　　tenson. London: Penguin.
Baden-Powell, R. S. S.
　　1901　*The Matabele Campaign.* London: Methuen.
Baur, John.
　　1994　*2000 Years of Christianity in Africa: An African Church History.* 2d ed. Nai-
　　　　　robi, Kenya: Paulines Publications.
Beaver, R. Pierce.
　　1967　*To Advance the Gospel: Selections from the Writings of Rufus Anderson.*
　　　　　Grand Rapids: Eerdmans.
　　1968　"Missionary Motivation through Three Centuries." In *Reinterpretation in
　　　　　American Church History.* Jerald C. Bauer, ed. Pp. 113-51. Chicago: Univer-
　　　　　sity of Chicago Press.
Bediako, Kwame.
　　1995　*Christianity in Africa: The Renewal of a Non-Western Religion.* Maryknoll,
　　　　　NY: Orbis.

Belz, Mindy.
 2006   "Daniels of the Year: Men of the Hard Cloth." *World* (December 16): 16-21.
Bergquist, James A., and P. Kambar Manickam.
 1974   *The Crisis of Dependency in Third World Ministries.* Madras, India: Christian Literature Society.
Berkhofer, Robert F., Jr.
 1965   *Salvation and the Savage: An Analysis of Protestant Missions and American Indian Responses, 1787-1862.* Lexington: University of Kentucky Press.
Beyerhaus, Peter.
 1979   "The Three Selves Formula—Is It Built on Biblical Foundations?" In *Readings in Dynamic Indigeneity.* Charles H. Kraft and Tom N. Wisley, eds. Pp. 15-30. Pasadena, CA: William Carey Library.
Beyerhaus, Peter, and Henry Lefever.
 1964   *The Responsible Church and the Foreign Mission.* Grand Rapids: Eerdmans.
Bhebe, Ngwabi.
 1979   *Christianity and Traditional Religion in Western Zimbabwe, 1859-1923.* London: Longman.
Bodo, John R.
 1954   *The Protestant Clergy and Public Issues, 1812-1848.* Princeton, NJ: Princeton University Press.
Bonk, Jonathan J.
 1991   *Missions and Money: Affluence as a Western Missionary Problem.* Maryknoll, NY: Orbis.
 2006   *Missions and Money.* Revised and expanded edition. Maryknoll, NY: Orbis.
Bosch, David J.
 1991   *Transforming Mission: Paradigm Shifts in Theology of Mission.* Maryknoll, NY: Orbis.
Boudinot, Elias.
 1970   *A Star in the West; or, A Humble Attempt to Discover the Long Lost Ten Tribes of Israel.* N.p., 1816. Reprint, Freeport, NY: Books for Libraries Press.
Bowen, Thomas J.
 1857   *Adventures and Missionary Labors in Several Countries in the Interior of Africa, from 1849 to 1856.* Charleston, SC: Southern Baptist Publication Society.
Brace, Charles Loring.
 1886   *Gesta Christi; or, A History of Humane Progress under Christianity.* London: Hodder & Stoughton.
Bridston, Keith R.
 1965   *Mission Myth and Reality.* New York: Friendship Press.
Brouwer, Steve, Paul Gifford, and Susan D. Rose.
 1996   *Exporting the American Gospel: Global Christian Fundamentalism.* New York: Routledge.
Burnett, David.
 2002   *Clash of Worlds: What Christians Can Do in a World of Cultures in Conflict.* Rev. ed. Mill Hill, London: Monarch Books.

Bush, Luis, and Lorry Lutz.

　1990　*Partnering in Ministry: The Direction of World Evangelism.* Downers Grove, IL: InterVarsity.

Campbell, Alexander.

　1830　"Prospectus." *Millennial Harbinger* 1(1):1-3.

　1863a　"Address on the Anglo-Saxon Language: Its Origin, Character, and Destiny." In *Popular Lectures and Addresses.* Pp. 17-46. Philadelphia: n.p.

　1863b　"An Oration in Honor of the Fourth of July, 1830." In *Popular Lectures and Addresses.* Pp. 367-78. Philadelphia: n.p.

Carden, Allen.

　1990　*Puritan Christianity in America: Religion and Life in Seventeenth-Century Massachusetts.* Grand Rapids: Baker.

Carver, William Owen.

　1932　*The Course of Christian Missions.* New York: Fleming H. Revell.

Chadwick, Henry.

　1993　*The Early Church.* Rev. ed. London: Penguin Books.

Cheyne, John Richard.

　1972　"Some Implications of the Social Structure of Bantu Society upon the Organization and Administration of Indigenous Churches in Central Africa." Ed.D. thesis, Southwestern Baptist Theological Seminary.

Coggins, Wade T.

　1974　"What's behind the Idea of a Missionary Moratorium?" *Christianity Today* 19(4): 7-9.

　1988　"The Risks of Sending Our Dollars Only." *Evangelical Missions Quarterly* 24(3):204-6.

Cogley, Richard W.

　1999　*John Eliot's Mission to the Indians before King Philip's War.* Cambridge, MA: Harvard University Press.

Collier, Jane, and Rafael Esteban.

　1998　*From Complicity to Encounter: The Church and the Culture of Economism.* Harrisburg, PA: Trinity Press International.

Collier, Paul.

　2007　*The Bottom Billion: Why the Poorest Countries Are Failing and What Can Be Done About It.* New York: Oxford University Press.

The Commission.

　1963　Vol. 26(8):31.

　1964　Vol. 27(8):31.

　1965　Vol. 28(11):14-5.

　1969　Vol. 32(2):1-2.

Conn, Harvie M.

　1978　"The Money Barrier between Sending and Receiving Churches." *Evangelical Missions Quarterly* 14(4):231-40.

Corwin, Gary.

　2000　"The Message of Short-Term Missions." *Evangelical Missions Quarterly* 36(4):422-3.

Costas, Orlando E.
    1974   *The Church and Its Mission: A Shattering Critique from the Third World.*
            Wheaton, IL: Tyndale.
Covey, Stephen R.
    1989   *The Seven Habits of Highly Effective People.* New York: Simon & Schuster.
Crawley, Winston.
    1985   *Global Mission: A Story to Tell; An Interpretation of Southern Baptist Foreign
            Missions.* Nashville: Broadman Press.
Crouch, Andy.
    2006   "Experiencing Life at the Margins." *Christianity Today* 50(7):32-5.
    2007a   "The African Planter." *Leadership* 28(2):96-101.
    2007b   "Powering Down." *Christianity Today* 51(9):38-42.
    2007c   "From Tower-Dwellers to Travelers." *Christianity Today* 51(7): 34-9.
Dayton, Edward R., and Samuel Wilson, eds.
    1983   *The Refugees among Us: Unreached Peoples '83.* Monrovia, CA: MARC.
De Soto, Hernando.
    2000   *The Mystery of Capital: Why Capitalism Triumphs in the West and Fails
            Everywhere Else.* New York: Basic Books.
Dew, Thomas R.
    1968   In *The Pro-Slavery Argument.* Pp. 287-490. n.p.: Walker, Richards and Com-
            pany, 1852. Reprint, New York: Negro Universities Press.
Dillon-Malone, Clive M.
    1978   *The Korsten Basketmakers: A Study of the Masowe Apostles, an Indigenous
            African Religious Movement.* Manchester, England: Manchester University
            Press.
Dodge, Ralph E.
    1986   *The Revolutionary Bishop Who Saw God at Work in Africa.* Pasadena, CA:
            William Carey Library.
Donovan, Vincent.
    1982   *Christianity Rediscovered: An Epistle from the Masai.* 2d ed. London: SCM
            Press.
Dotson, Clyde.
    n.d.   *The Power of God in My Life.* Bulawayo, Zimbabwe: Baptist Publishing
            House.
Easterly, William.
    2006   *The White Man's Burden: Why the West's Efforts to Aid the Rest Have Done
            so Much Ill and so Little Good.* New York: Penguin.
The Economist.
    2008   "Zimbabwe: Please Do Something—But What?" 389(8610):17-18.
Edwards, Jonathan.
    1965   *Jonathan Edwards on Revival.* Edinburgh: The Banner of Truth Trust.
    1974   *The Works of Jonathan Edwards.* 2 vols. n.p.: 1834. Reprint, Edinburgh: The
            Banner of Truth Trust.
Eitel, Keith E.
    2000   *Paradigm Wars: The Southern Baptist International Mission Board Faces the
            Third Millennium.* Oxford, England: Regnum.

Eldred, Ken.
    2005   *God Is at Work*. Ventura, CA: Regal.

Elliot, Elisabeth.
    1981   *Through Gates of Splendor*. Wheaton, IL: Tyndale.

Erickson, Millard J.
    1985   *Christian Theology*. Grand Rapids: Baker.

Ferguson, Everett.
    1993   *Backgrounds of Early Christianity*. 2d ed. Grand Rapids: Eerdmans.

Ferguson, Niall.
    2003   *Empire: The Rise and Demise of the British World Order and the Lessons for Global Power*. New York: Basic Books.

Fernando, Ajith.
    1999   "Some Thoughts on Missionary Burnout." *Evangelical Missions Quarterly* 35(4):440-3.

Foster, Lillian.
    1866   *Andrew Johnson, President of the United States: His Life and Speeches*. New York: Richardson & Co.

Fretz, Glenn.
    2002   "Toward Interdependent Ministry Partnerships: Fueling Ministry without Fostering Dependency." *Evangelical Missions Quarterly* 38(2):212-8.

Friedman, Thomas L.
    2000   *The Lexus and the Olive Tree*. New York: Anchor Books.
    2005   *The World Is Flat: A Brief History of the Twenty-First Century*. New York: Farrar, Straus & Giroux.

Garrison, Jim.
    2004   *America as Empire: Global Leader or Rogue Power?* San Francisco: Berrett-Koehler Publishers.

Garrison, William Lloyd.
    1968   *Selections from the Writings and Speeches of William Lloyd Garrison*. Boston: R. F. Wellcut, 1852. Reprint, New York: Negro Universities Press.

Gatu, John.
    1996   "Rationale for Self-Reliance." Lancaster, PA: World Mission Associates. http://www.wmausa.org/page.aspx?id=83845.

Gibbs, Eddie.
    2004   "Reinventing Evangelism." *Theology, News and Notes* 51(3):19-22.

Gilliland, Dean S.
    1983   *Pauline Theology and Mission Practice*. Grand Rapids: Baker.

Goffe, Leslie.
    2005   "God, Gospel and the Dollar." *BBC Focus on Africa* 16(3):10-13.

Goffin, Alvin M.
    1994   *The Rise of Protestant Evangelism in Ecuador, 1895-1990*. Gainesville, FL: University Press of Florida.

Gonzalez, Justo L.
    1999   *For the Healing of the Nations: The Book of Revelation in an Age of Cultural Conflict*. Maryknoll, NY: Orbis.

Goto, Nathan.
1994 "A Great Central Mission: The Legacy of the United Methodist Church in Zimbabwe." *Methodist History* 33(1):14-25.
Grant, Miriam R., and Andrew D. Palmiere.
2003 "When Tea Is a Luxury: The Economic Impact of HIV/AIDS in Bulawayo, Zimbabwe." *African Studies* 62(2):213-41.
Griffiths, Tudor.
2006 "Bishop Tucker—A Missionary before, of, or after His Time?" http://www. martynmission.cam.ac.uk/pages/hmc-seminar-papers/archive-seminar-papers.php
Grigg, Viv.
1984 *Companion to the Poor.* Sutherland, Australia: Albatross Books.
Gupta, Paul R., and Sherwood G. Lingenfelter.
2006 *Breaking Tradition to Accomplish Vision: Training Leaders for a Church-Planting Movement.* Winona Lake, IN: BMH Books.
Hanciles, Jehu.
2002 *Euthanasia of a Mission: African Church Autonomy in a Colonial Context.* Westport, CT: Praeger.
Handy, Robert T.
1971 *A Christian America: Protestant Hopes and Historical Realities.* New York: Oxford University Press.
Harries, Jim.
2008 "Vulnerable Mission—A 'Normalisation' of Christian Mission Practices in Anticipation of a Post-Colonial Situation." http://www.jim-mission.org.uk/ articles/normalisation-of-christian-mission-practices.pdf.
Hastings, Adrian.
1976 *African Christianity.* New York: Seabury Press.
1994 *The Church in Africa, 1450-1950.* Oxford, England: Clarendon Press.
Hatch, Nathan O.
1989 *The Democratization of American Christianity.* New Haven, CT: Yale University Press.
Hawkins, Mike.
1997 *Social Darwinism in European and American Thought, 1860-1945: Nature as Model and Nature as Threat.* Cambridge, England: Cambridge University Press.
Hedlund, Roger E.
1999 "Indian Instituted Churches: Indigenous Christianity Indian Style." *Mission Studies* 16(31):26-42.
Henry, Carl F. H.
2003 *The Uneasy Conscience of Modern Fundamentalism.* Grand Rapids: Eerdmans.
Hesselgrave, David J.
2005 *Paradigms in Conflict: 10 Key Questions in Christian Missions Today.* Grand Rapids: Kregel.

Hiebert, Paul G.
  1985   *Anthropological Insights for Missionaries.* Grand Rapids: Baker.
  2008   *Transforming Worldviews: An Anthropological Understanding of How People Change.* Grand Rapids: Baker Academic.
Hiebert, Paul G., R. Daniel Shaw, and Tite Tiénou.
  1999   *Understanding Folk Religion.* Grand Rapids: Baker.
Hobsbawn, Eric.
  1987   *The Age of Empire: 1875-1914.* New York: Vintage Books.
Hodges, Melvin L.
  1953   *The Indigenous Church.* Springfield, MO: Gospel Publishing House.
  1972   "Are Indigenous Church Principles Outdated?" *Evangelical Missions Quarterly* 9(1):43-6.
Holcombe, Hosea.
  1840   *A History of the Rise and Progress of the Baptists in Alabama.* Philadelphia: King & Baird.
Hopkins, Samuel.
  1972   *A Treatise on the Millennium.* Boston: Isaiah Thomas & Ebenezer T. Andrews, 1793. Reprint, New York: Arno Press.
Houghton, Graham.
  1983   *The Impoverishment of Dependency.* Madras, India: Christian Literature Society.
Howard, David.
  1997   "Incarnational Presence: Dependency and Interdependency in Overseas Partnerships." In *Supporting Indigenous Ministries.* Daniel Rickett and Dotsey Welliver, eds. Pp. 24-35. Wheaton, IL: Billy Graham Center.
Hudson, Winthrop S., and John Corrigan.
  1999   *Religion in America.* 6th ed. Upper Saddle River, NJ: Prentice-Hall.
Hunter, Archibald M.
  1959   *The Layman's Bible Commentary.* Vol. 22. Richmond, VA: John Knox Press.
Huntington, Samuel P.
  2003   *The Clash of Civilizations and the Remaking of World Order.* Paperback edition. New York: Simon & Schuster.
Idowu, E. Bolaji.
  1965   *Towards an Indigenous Church.* London: Oxford University Press.
Jenkins, Philip.
  2002   *The Next Christendom: The Coming Global Christianity.* New York: Oxford University Press.
Johnson, Rick.
  2000   "Going South of the Border for a Short-Term?" *Mission Frontiers* 22(3):40-4.
Johnstone, Patrick.
  1998   *The Church Is Bigger than You Think.* Fearn, Ross-shire, England: Christian Focus Publications.
Johnstone, Patrick, and Jason Mandryk.
  2001   *Operation World: 21st Century Edition.* Waynesboro, GA: Paternoster.
Kane, Joe.
  1996   *Savages.* New York: Vintage Books.

Kato, Byang H.
  1972 "Aid to the National Church—When It Helps, When It Hinders." *Evangelical Missions Quarterly* 8(4):193-201.
Kingsland, Rosemary.
  1980 *A Saint among Savages*. London: Collins.
Kividi, Kikama.
  1999 "Church Growth in an African City: CBCO Kinshasa." *American Baptist Quarterly* 18(3):217-42.
Köstenberger, Andreas J.
  1998 *The Missions of Jesus and the Disciples according to the Fourth Gospel: With Implications for the Fourth Gospel's Purpose and the Mission of the Contemporary Church*. Grand Rapids: Eerdmans.
Kraft, Charles H.
  1979 *Christianity in Culture*. Maryknoll, NY: Orbis.
Latourette, Kenneth Scott.
  1970a *A History of the Expansion of Christianity*. Vol. 4, *The Great Century in Europe and the United States of America, A.D. 1800-A.D. 1914*. Grand Rapids: Zondervan.
  1970b *A History of the Expansion of Christianity*. Vol. 5, *The Great Century in the Americas, Australasia, and Africa, A.D. 1800-A.D. 1914*. Grand Rapids: Zondervan.
Lingenfelter, Sherwood.
  1998 *Transforming Culture: A Challenge for Christian Mission*. 2d ed. Grand Rapids: Baker.
Little, Christopher R.
  2005 *Mission in the Way of Paul: Biblical Mission for the Church in the Twenty-First Century*. New York: Peter Lang.
Livermore, David A.
  2006 *Serving with Eyes Wide Open: Doing Short-Term Missions with Cultural Intelligence*. Grand Rapids: Baker.
Lupton, Robert D.
  2007 *Compassion, Justice and the Christian Life: Rethinking Ministry to the Poor*. Ventura, CA: Regal.
Mackenzie, Rob.
  1993 *David Livingstone: The Truth behind the Legend*. Chinhoyi, Zimbabwe: Fig Tree Publications.
MacMaster, Richard K., with Donald R. Jacobs.
  2006 *A Gentle Wind of God: The Influence of the East African Revival*. Scottdale, PA: Herald Press.
Maier, Paul L.
  1999 *Eusebius: The Church History: A New Translation with Commentary*. Grand Rapids: Kregel.
Marsden, George M.
  1980 *Fundamentalism and American Culture: The Shaping of Twentieth-Century Evangelicalism 1870-1925*. New York: Oxford University Press.
Masih, J. P.
  1986 "'People Movement' Problems." *Evangelical Missions Quarterly* 22(3):300-2.

Mather, Cotton.
    1979   *Magnalia Christi Americana*. 3d ed. 2 vols. London: n.p. 1702. Reprint, Edinburgh: The Banner of Truth Trust.

May, Stan.
    2000   "Short-Term Mission Trips Are Great, IF ... " *Evangelical Missions Quarterly* 36(4):444-9.

Mayers, Marvin K.
    1974   *Christianity Confronts Culture: A Strategy for Cross-Cultural Evangelism*. Grand Rapids: Zondervan.

McGavran, Donald A.
    1970   *Understanding Church Growth*. Grand Rapids: Eerdmans.

McKenna, George.
    2007   *The Puritan Origins of American Patriotism*. New Haven, CT: Yale University Press.

McQuilkin, Robertson.
    1999   "Stop Sending Money! Breaking the Cycle of Missions Dependency." *Christianity Today* 43(3):57-9.

Moffat, John S.
    1886   *The Lives of Robert and Mary Moffat*. London: T. Fisher Unwin.

Moll, Rob.
    2006   "Missions Incredible." *Christianity Today* 50(3):28-34.

Montgomery, Jim.
    1989   *DAWN 2000: 7 Million Churches To Go; The Personal Story of the DAWN Strategy for World Evangelization*. Pasadena, CA: William Carey Library.

Moreau, Scott A.
    2004   "Putting the Survey in Perspective." In *Mission Handbook: U. S. and Canadian Protestant Ministries Overseas 2004-2006*. 19th ed. Dotsey Welliver and Minnette Northcutt, eds. Pp. 11-64. Wheaton, IL: EMIS.

Morgan, Timothy C.
    2005   "Purpose Driven in Rwanda: Rick Warren's Sweeping Plan to Defeat Poverty." *Christianity Today* 49(10):32-6, 90-1.
    2008   "After the Aloha Shirts." *Christianity Today* 52(10):42-5.

Morse, Jedidiah.
    1970   *A Report to the Secretary of War of the United States on Indian Affairs*. New Haven, CT: S. Converse, 1822. Reprint, New York: Augustus M. Kelley.

Moss, Barbara.
    1999   "'And the Bones Come Together': Women's Religious Expectations in Southern Africa, c. 1900-1945." *The Journal of Religious History* 23(1):108-27.

Moyo, Dambisa.
    2009   *Dead Aid: Why Aid is not Working and How There Is a Better Way for Africa*. New York: Farrar, Straus, and Giroux.

Moyo, Levy.
    2006   *The Gloved Handshake*. London: Chosen Graphics.

Mpanya, Mutombo.
    1978   "Problems of the Churches in Central Africa." In *The Church in Africa 1977*. Charles R. Taber, ed. Pp. 117-35. Pasadena, CA: William Carey Library.

Mugabe, Henry.
    2004   Interview by author. 28 July, Gweru, Zimbabwe. Handwritten notes.
Mumper, Sharon E.
    1986   "An Indonesian Leader Speaks to the Church in the West." *Evangelical Missions Quarterly* 22(1):6-11.
Murphree, Marshall W.
    1969   *Christianity and the Shona.* London: Athlone Press.
Mwase, Isaac M. T.
    2005   "Shall They Till with Their Own Hoes?: Baptists in Zimbabwe and New Patterns of Interdependence, 1950-2000." In *The Changing Face of Christianity: Africa, the West, and the World.* Lamin Sanneh and Joel A. Carpenter, eds. Pp. 63-79. New York: Oxford University Press.
Myers, Bryant L.
    1999   *Walking with the Poor: Principles and Practices of Transformational Development.* Maryknoll, NY: Orbis.
Nacpil, Emerito P.
    1971   "Mission but not Missionaries." *International Review of Mission* 60(239):356-62.
Ndlovu, Stephen.
    1997   "Historical Brethren in Christ Missionary Attitudes in Zimbabwe." *The Conrad Grebel Review* 15(1-2):73-7.
Neill, Stephen.
    1964   *A History of Christian Missions.* Harmondsworth, England: Penguin.
    1966   *Colonialism and Christian Missions.* New York: McGraw-Hill.
Nevius, John L.
    1958   *The Planting and Development of Missionary Churches.* 4th ed. Philadelphia: Presbyterian & Reformed.
Newbigin, Lesslie.
    1989   *The Gospel in a Pluralist Society.* Grand Rapids: Eerdmans.
    1995   *The Open Secret: An Introduction to the Theology of Mission.* Rev. ed. Grand Rapids: Eerdmans.
Nickle, Keith F.
    1966   *The Collection: A Study in Paul's Strategy.* Naperville, IL: Alec R. Allenson.
Niebuhr, H. Richard.
    1937   *The Kingdom of God in America.* New York: Harper & Row.
Noll, Mark A.
    2009   *The New Shape of World Christianity: How American Experience Reflects Global Faith.* Downers Grove, IL: IVP Academic.
Noll, Mark A., Nathan O. Hatch, and George M. Marsden.
    1989   *The Search for Christian America.* Colorado Springs: Helmers & Howard.
Oliver, Roland.
    1991   *The African Experience.* New York: Harper Collins.
Orjiako, Humphrey.
    2001   *Killing Sub-Saharan Africa with Aid.* Huntington, NY: Nova Science Publishers.

O'Sullivan, John L.
 1839   "The Great Nation of Futurity." In *The United States Democratic Review.*
        6(23):426-30. New York: J. & H. G. Langley.
Parrott, Don.
 2004   "Managing the Short-Term Missions Explosion." *Evangelical Missions Quar-*
        terly 40(3):356-60.
Pate, Larry D.
 1989   *From Every People: A Handbook of Two-Thirds World Missions with Direc-*
        tory/Histories/Analysis. Monrovia, CA: MARC.
Peters, George W.
 1972   *A Biblical Theology of Missions.* Chicago: Moody.
Phillips, Kevin.
 2006   *American Theocracy: The Peril and Politics of Radical Religion, Oil, and Bor-*
        *rowed Money in the 21*ˢᵗ *Century.* New York: Viking Penguin.
Pickett, J. Waskom.
 1933   *Christian Mass Movements in India.* New York: Abingdon Press.
Priest, Robert J., and Joseph Paul Priest.
 2008   "'They See Everything, and Understand Nothing': Short-Term Mission and
        Service Learning." *Missiology: An International Review* 36(1):53-73.
Raboteau, Albert J.
 1978   *Slave Religion: The "Invisible Institution" in the Antebellum South.* New York:
        Oxford University Press.
Ramseyer, Robert L.
 1980   "Partnership and Interdependence." *International Review of Mission*
        69(273):32-9.
Ranger, Terence O.
 1967   *Revolt in Southern Rhodesia, 1896-7.* London: Heinemann.
 1999   "'Taking on the Missionary's Task': African Spirituality and the Mission
        Churches of Manicaland in the 1930s." *Journal of Religion in Africa* 29:175-
        205.
Read, William R., Victor M. Monterroso, and Harmon A. Johnson.
 1969   *Latin American Church Growth.* Grand Rapids: Eerdmans.
Reed, Colin.
 1997   *Pastors, Partners, and Paternalists.* Leiden, Netherlands: E. J. Brill.
Reese, John.
 2002   "Missions and Money (2)." *Action* 66(8):2.
Reese, Robert.
 2005   "Dependency and Its Impact on Churches Related to the Baptist Conven-
        tion of Zimbabwe and the Zimbabwe Christian Fellowship." Ph.D. diss.,
        Mid-America Baptist Theological Seminary.
 2006   "'You Have Been Stealing from God!'" *Christian Standard* (January 29):72-4.
 2007a "The Benefits of Chaos: Missionary Reflections on Zimbabwe's Decline."
        In *Missions in Contexts of Violence.* Keith E. Eitel, ed. Pp.231-43. Pasadena,
        CA: William Carey Library.
 2007b "The Surprising Relevance of the Three-Self Formula." *Mission Frontiers*
        29(4):25-7.

2008a "Globalization and Missions." *Missiology: An International Review* 36(3):307-15.

2008b "Short-Term Missions as a Spiritual Exercise." *Evangelical Missions Quarterly* 44(2):158-63.

Reichenbach, Bruce R.

1982 "The Captivity of Third World Churches." *Evangelical Missions Quarterly* 18(3):166-79.

Rickett, Daniel.

2000 *Building Strategic Relationships: A Practical Guide to Partnering with Non-Western Missions.* San Jose, CA: Partners International.

2002 "Fine-Tuning Financing: Principles of Giving and Receiving in Missions Partnerships." *Evangelical Missions Quarterly* 38(1):28-35.

Robert, Dana L.

2002 "The First Globalization: The Internationalization of the Protestant Missionary Movement between the World Wars." *International Bulletin of Missionary Research* 26(2):50-66.

Rowell, John.

2006 *To Give or Not To Give?: Rethinking Dependency, Restoring Generosity and Redefining Sustainability.* Tyrone, GA: Authentic.

Rundle, Steve, and Tom Steffen.

2003 *Great Commission Companies: The Emerging Role of Business in Missions.* Downers Grove, IL: InterVarsity.

Rutledge, Arthur B., and William G. Tanner.

1969 *Mission to America: A History of Southern Baptist Home Missions.* Nashville: Broadman Press.

Sachs, Jeffrey D.

2005 *The End of Poverty: Economic Possibilities for Our Time.* New York: Penguin.

Saint, Steve.

2001 *The Great Omission: Fulfilling Christ's Commission Completely.* Seattle: YWAM Publishing.

2005 *End of the Spear.* Carol Stream, IL: Tyndale/Salt River.

Sales, Jane M.

1971 *The Planting of the Churches in South Africa.* Grand Rapids: Eerdmans.

Sanneh, Lamin.

2003 *Whose Religion Is Christianity?: The Gospel beyond the West.* Grand Rapids: Eerdmans.

Saunders, Davis Lee.

1973 "A History of Baptists in East and Central Africa." Th.D. diss., Southern Baptist Theological Seminary.

Scherer, James A.

1964 *Missionary, Go Home! A Reappraisal of the Christian World Mission.* Englewood Cliffs, NJ: Prentice-Hall.

1993 "Church, Kingdom, and *Missio Dei*." In *The Good News of the Kingdom: Mission Theology for the Third Millennium.* Charles Van Engen, Dean S. Gilliland, and Paul Pierson, eds. Pp. 82-8. Maryknoll, NY: Orbis.

Schipper, Gary.
1988 "Non-Western Missionaries: Our Newest Challenge." *Evangelical Missions Quarterly* 24(3):198-202.
Schnabel, Eckhard J.
2008 *Paul the Missionary: Realities, Strategies and Methods.* Downers Grove, IL: InterVarsity.
Schwartz, Glenn J.
1989a "Church and Mission in Central Africa: A Missiological Study in Indigenization." Lancaster, PA: World Mission Associates. http://www.wmausa.org/page.aspx?id=83824.
1989b "A Review of Christian Conversion in an African Context." Lancaster, PA: World Mission Associates. http://www.wmausa.org/page.aspx?id=83837.
1993 "It's Time To Get Serious about the Cycle of Dependence in Africa." *Evangelical Missions Quarterly* 29(2):126-30.
2004 Interview by author. 23 October, Arlington, VA. Tape recording.
2007 *When Charity Destroys Dignity: Overcoming Unhealthy Dependency in the Christian Movement.* Bloomington, IN: AuthorHouse.
Shaw, Mark R.
1996 *The Kingdom of God in Africa: A Short History of African Christianity.* Grand Rapids: Baker.
Shearer, Roy E.
1966 *Wildfire: Church Growth in Korea.* Grand Rapids: Eerdmans.
Shelley, Bruce.
1982 *Church History in Plain Language.* Dallas: Word.
Shenk, David W., and Ervin R. Stutzman.
1988 *Creating Communities of the Kingdom: New Testament Models of Church Planting.* Scottdale, PA: Herald Press.
Shenk, Wilbert R.
1981 "Rufus Anderson and Henry Venn: A Special Relationship?" *International Bulletin of Missionary Research* 5(5):168-72.
1983 *Henry Venn—Missionary Statesman.* Maryknoll, NY: Orbis.
1990 "The Origins and Evolution of the Three-Self in Relation to China." *International Bulletin of Missionary Research* 14(1):28-35.
1999 *Changing Frontiers of Mission.* Maryknoll, NY: Orbis.
Sine, Tom W.
1999 *Mustard Seed versus McWorld: Reinventing Life and Faith for the Future.* Grand Rapids: Baker.
2003 "Globalization, Creation of Global Culture of Consumption and the Impact on the Church and Its Mission." *Evangelical Review of Theology* 27(4):353-70.
Slimbach, Richard.
2000 "First, Do No Harm: Short-Term Missions at the Dawn of the New Millennium." *Evangelical Missions Quarterly* 36(4):428-41.
Southern Baptist Convention Annual.
1961 St. Louis, MO: 23-26 May.
1963 Kansas City, MO: 7-10 May.
1966 Detroit, MI: 24-27 May.

Smalley, William A.
1979 "Cultural Implications of an Indigenous Church." In *Readings in Dynamic Indigeneity*. Charles H. Kraft and Tom N. Wisley, eds. Pp. 31-51. Pasadena, CA: William Carey Library.

Smith, David.
2003 *Mission after Christendom*. London: Darton, Longman and Todd.

Spain, Rufus B.
1961 *At Ease in Zion: Social History of Southern Baptists 1865-1900*. Nashville: Vanderbilt University Press.

Speer, Robert E.
1914 *Studies of Missionary Leadership*. Philadelphia: Westminster Press.

Stanley, Brian.
1990 *The Bible and the Flag: Protestant Missions and British Imperialism in the Nineteenth and Twentieth Centuries*. Leicester, England: Apollos.

Stark, Rodney.
1996 *The Rise of Christianity: A Sociologist Reconsiders History*. Princeton, NJ: Princeton University Press.

Steffen, Tom A.
1993 *Passing the Baton: Church Planting that Empowers*. La Habra, CA: Center for Organizational and Ministry Development.

Stiglitz, Joseph E., and Lyn Squire.
1998 "International Development: Is It Possible?" *Foreign Policy* 110:138-51.

Stoll, David.
1982 *Fishers of Men or Founders of Empire? The Wycliffe Bible Translators in Latin America*. London: Zed Press.

Stott, John R. W.
1975 *Christian Mission in the Modern World*. Downers Grove, IL: InterVarsity.
1996 *Making Christ Known: Historic Mission Documents from the Lausanne Movement 1974-1989*. Carlisle, England: Paternoster.

Stout, Harry S.
1986 *The New England Soul: Preaching and Religious Culture in Colonial New England*. New York: Oxford University Press.

Strong, Josiah.
1893 *The New Era; or, The Coming Kingdom*. New York: Baker & Taylor.

Sullivan, Mark.
1927 *Our Times: The United States 1900-1925*. Vol. 1, *The Turn of the Century*. New York: Scribners.

Taber, Charles R.
1979 "Contextualization: Indigenization and/or Transformation." In *The Gospel and Islam: A 1978 Compendium*. Don M. McCurry, ed. Pp. 143-54. Monrovia, CA: MARC.

Taylor, William.
1879 *Pauline Methods of Missionary Work*. Philadelphia: National Publishing Association for the Promotion of Holiness.
1882 *Ten Years of Self-Supporting Missions in India*. New York: Phillips & Hunt.

Terry, Douglas W.
  2004 "Assessing Missional Effectiveness of Midterm Missionaries." *Missiology: An International Review* 32(2):173-86.
Tippett, Alan R.
  1973 "The Suggested Moratorium on Missionary Funds and Personnel." *Missiology: An International Review* 1(3):275-9.
  1979 "Indigenous Principles in Mission Today." In *Readings in Dynamic Indigeneity*. Charles H. Kraft and Tom N. Wisley, eds. Pp. 52-70. Pasadena, CA: William Carey Library.
Tucker, John M.
  2001 Short-Term Missions: Building Sustainable Mission Relationships." *Evangelical Missions Quarterly* 37(4):436-9.
Tucker, Ruth A.
  1983 *From Jerusalem to Irian Jaya: A Biographical History of Christian Missions*. Grand Rapids: Zondervan.
Urban-Mead, Wendy.
  2002 "Girls of the Gate: Questions of Purity and Piety at the Mtshabezi Girls' Primary Boarding School in Colonial Zimbabwe, 1908-1940." *Brethren in Christ History & Life* 25(1):3-32.
Van Engen, Jo Ann.
  2000 "The Cost of Short-Term Missions." *The Other Side* 36(1):20-3.
Van Rheenen, Gailyn.
  1991 *Communicating Christ in Animistic Contexts*. Grand Rapids: Baker.
  1996 *Missions: Biblical Foundations and Contemporary Strategies*. Grand Rapids: Zondervan.
Vaughan, Alden T.
  1965 *New England Frontier: Puritans and Indians, 1620-1675*. Boston: Little, Brown, and Co.
Verstraelen, Frans J.
  1995 "Patterns of Missionary and Ecumenical Relationships in Zimbabwe." *Exchange* 24:189-221.
Vine, W. E.
  1940 *An Expository Dictionary of New Testament Words*. Westwood, NJ: Fleming H. Revell.
Wagner, C. Peter.
  1972 *Church/Mission Tensions Today*. Chicago: Moody.
  1975 "Colour the Moratorium Grey." *International Review of Mission* 64(254):165-76.
Wakatama, Pius.
  1976 *Independence for the Third World Church*. Downers Grove, IL: InterVarsity.
  1990 "The Role of Africans in the World Mission of the Church." *Evangelical Missions Quarterly* 26(2):126-30.
Wallace, Anthony F. C.
  1993 *The Long, Bitter Trail: Andrew Jackson and the Indians*. New York: Hill & Wang.
Wallis, Ethel Emily.
  1960 *The Dayuma Story: Life under Auca Spears*. New York: Harper & Brothers.

Walls, Andrew F.
   1992   "The Legacy of Samuel Ajayi Crowther." *International Bulletin of Missionary Research* 16(1):15-21.
   1996   *The Missionary Movement in Christian History: Studies in the Transmission of Faith.* Maryknoll, NY: Orbis.
Warren, Max.
   1956   *Partnership: The Study of an Idea.* Chicago: SCM Press.
Warren, Rick.
   1995   *The Purpose Driven Church: Growth without Compromising Your Message and Mission.* Grand Rapids: Zondervan.
Waruta, Douglas.
   1997   "A Gospel of Community, Compassion, and Continuity." In *Contemporary Gospel Accents: Doing Theology in Africa, Asia, Southeast Asia, and Latin America.* Daniel Carro and Richard F. Wilson, eds. Pp. 19-33. Macon, GA: Mercer University Press.
Wayland, Francis.
   1824   *The Moral Dignity of the Missionary Enterprise: A Sermon Delivered before the Boston Baptist Foreign Mission Society Oct. 26, 1823.* Boston: James Loring.
Weinberg, Albert K.
   1935   *Manifest Destiny: A Study of Nationalist Expansion in American History.* Baltimore: Johns Hopkins Press.
Wenger, Donna F.
   2000   "John and Emma Climenhaga: A Study in Commitment." *Brethren in Christ History & Life* 23(3):393-480.
Winter, Ralph D.
   1998   "Editorial Comment." *Mission Frontiers* 20(3-4):2-5.
Wood, Rick, ed.
   1997   "A Champion for Self-Reliance: An Interview with Glenn Schwartz, Founding Director of World Mission Associates." *Mission Frontiers* 19(1-2):15-7.
   1998a "Fighting Dependency among the 'Aucas': An Interview with Steve Saint." *Mission Frontiers* 20(5-6):8-15.
   1998b "Self-Reliance or Interdependence?" *Mission Frontiers* 20(9-12):36-7.
World Mission Associates.
   2006   "My Encounter with Self-Reliance Thinking: An Illustration from the Former Soviet Union." Lancaster, PA: World Mission Associates. http://www.wmausa.org/page.aspx?id=122398.
Worsley, Peter M.
   1959   "Cargo Cults." *Scientific American* 200:117-28.
Wright, Christopher J. H.
   2006   *The Mission of God: Unlocking the Bible's Grand Narrative.* Downers Grove, IL: IVP Academic.
Wuthnow, Robert.
   2009   *Boundless Faith: The Global Outreach of American Churches.* Berkeley, CA: University of California Press.

Yohannan, K. P.
  1986 *The Coming Revolution in World Missions.* Altamonte Springs, FL: Creation
      House.
Zvobgo, Chengetai J. M.
  1996 *A History of Christian Missions in Zimbabwe, 1890-1939.* Gweru, Zimba-
      bwe: Mambo Press.

Index

A

Africa, 6-8, 17, 24, 34, 37-42, 45, 49, 51-52, 56-64, 66-67, 70, 121-23, 129, 134, 143, 145-46, 165-66, 172, 178-79, 182, 189, 192

    independence in Africa, 2

    mission in Africa, 39

    sub-Saharan, 165

African Americans, 6, 8, 70

    Christians, 8

    evangelism, 6

    slaves, 39

African Independent Churches (AICs), 24, 48-49, 52

Ajayi, J. F. Ade, 24

Akinola, Peter, 178

Alexander, Archibald, 6-7, 25, 39

Allen, Roland, 1-2, 32-35, 37, 78, 127, 132, 136

Altman, Roger, 115

America (USA). *See* United States of America.

American Board of Commissioners for Foreign Missions (ABCFM), 9, 21, 25

American Colonization Society, 7, 39

American Methodist Episcopal Church (AME), 48

American Revolution, 11, 14, 40

Anderson, Rufus, 21, 25-27, 32, 35, 37, 51, 78, 93, 121, 158, 160

Anglo-Saxon Race, 15-19, 28, 39

Aryeetey, Solomon, 98

Asia, 134, 137, 178, 182, 192

    East Asia, 61

Augustine, Saint, 20

Australia, 168

    missionary, 169

Awakening, Great. *See* Great Awakening.

Awakening, Second Great. *See* Great Awakening.

Carver, William Owen, 118
Catholic Church. *See* Roman Catholic Church.
Chadwick, Henry, 183
Cheyne, John, 123-24
China, 30, 34, 126
    North China, 32
    rural, 172
Christendom, 12, 19-20, 91, 112-13, 157-59, 179, 181, 185-91
Christian, Jayakumar, 152
church buildings, 30, 66, 72, 87-88, 101, 126, 185
Church Missionary Society, 21-24, 37, 39
Climenhaga, John, 44, 46
clinics, 1, 58-59, 87, 172
Coggins, Wade, 54, 56, 97
Coke, Thomas, 29
Collier, Jane, 109
Collier, Paul, 90
colonialism, 2-3, 35, 43, 46, 50-53, 57, 64, 75, 91-92, 104, 109, 111-13, 117, 129, 154, 157, 159, 163-64, 176, 179, 186
The Commission, 67-68, 70, 127
Congregational Church, 48
Conn, Harvie, 94
Constantine, Emperor, 185-86
contextualization, 93-94, 134, 140-42, 158-59
Corwin, Gary, 99-100
Costas, Orlando, 50, 143
Covey, Stephen, 95
Crawford, T. P., 126
Crawley, Winston, 125-26, 150
Crowther, Samuel, 23-25

D
Darwin, Charles, 15-16
Dayuma, 83, 85-86
De Soto, Hernando, 107

Fort, Gordon, 74
Fourah Bay Institute, 23
Franklin, Benjamin, 10
Freetown, Sierra Leone, 23, 39
Friedman, Thomas, 106, 171-73
fundamentalist-modernist controversy, 174

G

Garrison, Jim, 10
Garrison, William Lloyd, 7
Gates, Bill, 112
Gatu, John, 54-56, 63, 139, 160, 167
Gerber, Virgil, 142
Gibbs, Eddie, 144
Gifford, Paul, 58-59, 62, 143
globalization, 2, 30, 88, 90, 106-10, 112-13, 115, 117, 157-58, 163-65, 168, 170-73, 175, 194
Goerner, H. Cornell, 68-69
Goffe, Leslie, 59
Goffin, Alvin, 84-86
Gonzalez, Justo, 109
Goto, Nathan, 49
Graham, Billy, 175
Grant, Miriam, 61
Great Britain, 19, 38, 69, 118, 188
Great Commission, 2, 58, 63, 90, 92, 95, 108, 114, 120, 137-38, 168, 175, 193
Great Awakening, 10, 13
    Second Great Awakening, 10-11, 13
Gregory the Great, 3
Grigg, Viv, 188-89
Gupta, Paul, 92, 161-62, 173

H

Hanciles, Jehu, 23-24
Handy, Robert, 16, 18
Harries, Jim, 190
Hastings, Adrian, 40-41, 51, 58

S